Time, Trees,
and Prehistory

Time, Trees, and Prehistory

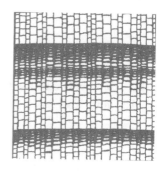

*Tree-Ring Dating
and the Development
of North American
Archaeology
1914–1950*

Stephen Edward Nash

The University of Utah Press
Salt Lake City

Typography by WolfPack

Library of Congress Cataloging-in-Publication Data

Nash, Stephen Edward, 1964–
    Time, trees, and prehistory : tree-ring dating and the development
of North American archaeology, 1914–1950 / Stephen Edward Nash.
        p.   cm.
    Includes bibliographical references (p.   ) and index.
    ISBN 0-87480-589-9 (alk. paper)
    1. Dendrochronology—United States—History—20th century.
    2. Dendrochronology—Southwest, New—History—20th century.
    3. Archaeology—United States—History—20th century.
    4. Archaeology—Southwest, New—History—20th century.
    5. Southwest, New—Antiquities.   6. Indians of North America—
Southwest, New—Antiquities.   I. Title.
CC78.3.N37   1999
930.1'028'5—dc21   98-56281

For Carmen

Contents

Figures

Tables

FIGURE 1. Andrew Ellicott Douglass (1867–1962) illustrates the use of a Swedish increment borer to take tree-ring cores from living trees, Forestdale Valley, east-central Arizona, 1929. Courtesy of the Laboratory of Tree-Ring Research, University of Arizona.

CHAPTER 1

Archaeological Tree-Ring Dating

Origins
and Principles

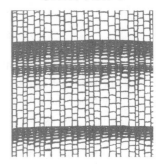

Time, we may comprehend.
SIR THOMAS BROWNE (1605–1682)

In the December 1929 issue of *National Geographic*, astronomer Andrew Ellicott Douglass (Figure 1) of the University of Arizona published common-era calendar dates for some 40 previously undated prehistoric sites in the American Southwest. He dated the sites using a revolutionary new technique he developed called *dendrochronology*, literally, the study of tree-time (Douglass 1929). Six years after this seminal publication, archaeologist Emil Haury (1935a:98) wrote, "It may be stated without equivocation that the tree-ring approach has been the single greatest contribution ever made to American archaeology." Five decades later, dendrochronologists Bryant Bannister and William Robinson (1986:51) stated, "The existence of a reliable chronological framework on which to chart the development of prehistoric cultures not only profoundly changed the structure of Southwestern investigations but also altered the thinking of all New World archaeologists." These are unequivocal endorsements. Haury, Bannister, and Robinson are recognized authorities in archaeological tree-ring dating, having between them well over a century of experience. Their published statements have never been critically evaluated, however, and archaeologists less versed in tree-ring dating may not concur with their assessments. This book, therefore, chronicles the development and application of archaeological tree-ring dating from 1914 to 1950 to test the assertions made by Haury, Bannister, and Robinson. It seeks to determine if, and if so how, the acquisition of precise and accurate dates for previously undated prehistoric sites changed the practice of North American archaeology and the interpretation of North American prehistory.

I

Chronology is the soul of archaeology.
FAY-COOPER COLE,
Dendrochronology in the Mississippi Valley

ARCHAEOLOGICAL THEORY AND CHRONOLOGY

The study of artifacts and temporal relationships distinguishes archaeology from the other subfields of anthropology. The analysis of material culture is older than the discipline of archaeology itself and traces back to the earliest recognition of prehistoric artifacts in Europe (Daniel 1963). The study of temporal relationships in the archaeological record has a much shorter pedigree, however, and critical examination of published and unpublished documents reveals a rather astonishing lack of interest in time by archaeologists (Chazan 1996; Dark 1995:64; Nash 1997a; Shanks and Tilley 1987:118). Indeed, archaeologists working before the second decade of the twentieth century believed temporal relationships were largely irrelevant to their research and were beginning to consider time only in the most general terms.

American archaeology before 1914 focused almost exclusively on artifact classification, description, and typology (Willey and Sabloff 1980). As archaeologists gained control over these realms, they began, slowly but surely, to examine temporal relationships in the archaeological record by experimenting with stratigraphic excavation techniques (Kidder 1924, 1958; Nelson 1916; see also Nelson 1918; Spier 1931) and serial analyses (Kroeber 1916; Spier 1917a, 1917b, 1931) developed by their European contemporaries and predecessors (see Browman and Givens 1996). North American archaeologists' stimulus to chronological research came not from within their own ranks but from their ethnological colleagues. Ethnologist Berthold Laufer offered his understanding of the task at hand in a review of archaeologist Roland Dixon's (1913) "Some Comments on North American Archaeology." Laufer wrote, "Chronology is at the root of the matter, being the nerve electrifying the dead body of history. It should be incumbent upon the American archaeologist to establish a chronological basis of the pre-Columbian cultures, and the American ethnologist should make it a point to bring chronology into the life and history of the pre-Columbian Indians" (1913:577).

Despite Laufer's admonition, nearly a decade later many North American archaeologists still did not share the interest in chronology already demonstrated by Alfred Kroeber, Nels Nelson, and Leslie Spier. Clark Wissler, of the American Museum of Natural History (Figure 2), explained the situation to his colleague Sylvanus Morley as he described

FIGURE 2. Clark Wissler (1870–1947) of the American Museum of Natural History and W. Sidney Stallings of the Laboratory of Anthropology examining tree-ring specimens from Aztec Ruin and Pueblo Bonito in 1932. Negative Number 280306, by Clyde Fisher, Courtesy Dept. of Library Services, American Museum of Natural History.

debate over the agenda for an archaeological conference to be held at Pueblo Bonito in Chaco Canyon, New Mexico:

> Strange to say, there was among anthropologists in general a considerable indifference and even hostility to the chronological idea. With the waning of [Frederick Ward] Putnam's influence [see Meltzer 1985] this reaction gathered strength until the whole subject [of chronology] was taboo. The time was, a few years ago, when no one dared mention the fact that there might be important differences in our dates [*sic*—no absolute dates were yet available to archaeologists]. Happily the development of anthropology in Europe has brought us to our senses again. We must establish a chronology for the New World and acknowledge our incompetence. Without a true time perspective the data of our subject will be a chaos of facts from which the general reader and even the student will flee as from a pestilence. (August 16, 1921)

Wissler exaggerated by alleging incompetence in his archaeological brethren, but it is clear that, with the sheer mass of archaeological data becoming available at that time, archaeologists desperately needed an organizing framework in order to avoid interpretive chaos. Alfred Vincent Kidder, of the Carnegie Institution, offered the first synthesis of southwestern archaeology several years later (Kidder 1924), but its organizational structure is geographic, not chronological.

Daniel Browman and Douglas Givens (1996:80) explain archaeologists' indifference to chronological matters as a result of the perception "of such [a] short time depth for habitation of the [North American] continent that attention was focused primarily upon the identification of archaeological areas as predecessor to the culture areas then being defined." That is, archaeologists assumed that "very little had changed since the first American Indians had arrived" in North America (Browman and Givens 1996:80), and therefore research centered on geographic and typological issues. Meltzer (1985:255) agrees, arguing that archaeologists of this period did not consider cultural change significant unless it was parallel in scope to that of the Paleolithic-Neolithic transition recently identified in Europe. This attitude may help explain why Richard Wetherill's discovery that the "Basketmaker" culture preceded the "Cliff Dweller" culture in the Four Corners region fell largely on deaf ears. Wetherill inferred this relationship in the 1890s after finding Cliff Dweller remains superimposed on Basketmaker remains in Cave 7 in Grand Gulch, Utah (Blackburn and Williamson 1997). Despite Wetherill's discovery and the obvious sequence in the deposits at this and other sites across the Southwest, however, archaeologists working as much as three decades later still did not acknowledge significant time depth to North American prehistory.

As academically trained southwestern archaeologists, especially Kidder (1924, 1932:2), began openly to consider chronological relationships in their research, their colleagues in geology and the as yet unnamed field of geoarchaeology were about to make a startling discovery that offered archaeologists indisputable evidence of time depth in the prehistoric record of North America. Archaeologists working at Folsom, New Mexico, in 1926 found projectile points in "undeniable association" with skeletons of extinct Pleistocene fauna (Haynes 1986:75). This discovery, as well as others at Whitewater Draw, Arizona, and later Clovis, New Mexico, provided conclusive evidence of long-term human occupation in the New World. Thus, although archaeologists still did not have an absolute chronology on which to hang their archaeological interpretations, the faunal, stratigraphic, and geological evidence demonstrated that humans had been present in the New World since at least the last Ice

Age, a surprisingly long time indeed. By the mid-1920s, then, the conventional wisdom was that the Basketmaker occupation of the San Juan drainage began "no later than 1000 B.C." (Kidder 1927a:206), that the Basketmakers were replaced by Puebloans "early in the first millennium of our era" (Kidder 1927a:207), and that the San Juan drainage had been completely abandoned by about A.D. 1000.

The increasing complexity evident in the archaeological record led Kidder to call the first Pecos Conference in late August 1927 (Kidder 1927a; Woodbury 1993). The goal was to allow archaeologists informally to present their 1927 fieldwork results and, more formally, to consider the lack of synthesis in southwestern archaeology and the interpretation of southwestern prehistory (Kidder 1927b, 1928). In contrast to the 1921 conference at Pueblo Bonito, where there was a "considerable indifference" to the study of time, chronology was definitely on the agenda of the first Pecos Conference (Kidder 1927a). On August 30, 1927, Douglass presented to the archaeological public, for the first time, a progress report on his decade-long effort to date archaeological sites by the analysis of growth rings in trees. Douglass was still two years away from publicly announcing reliable dates for southwestern sites, but there is evidence that at the time of the Pecos Conference he had a good idea of where many sites dated along the common-era calendar. Whether he baited his archaeological colleagues with his suspicions is not known, but there can be no doubt that interest in his research surged after the first Pecos Conference, especially among the 39 scientists, students, and spouses present. Despite the petulant departure of Edgar Lee Hewett (1930:33) from the meeting (Woodbury 1993) and his subsequent protestations that "the time factors in American [pre]history have received an amount of attention in excess of their importance" (Hewett 1930:156–157), southwestern archaeologists of the late 1920s were excited by the prospect of absolute chronology and time. The introduction of absolute dates, and the concomitant ability to make "empirically testable" assertions (Dunnell 1986:29), led to radical changes in the interpretation of North American prehistory. In so doing, tree-ring dating laid the empirical foundation on which a revolution in archaeological method and theory was built over the following decades.

ARCHAEOLOGICAL DATING THEORY AND DENDROCHRONOLOGY

Archaeologists' interest in temporal relationships has a surprisingly short pedigree in North American archaeology, but it is clear today that the construction of accurate and precise chronologies is crucial to the production of reliable interpretations of the archaeological record (Renfrew 1973). Chronology construction is only the beginning, however, for archaeologists interested in any aspect of prehistoric behavior must ensure that the scale of the chronology is manageable when applied to the known and often coarsely refined archaeological record. The level of resolution in any archaeological interpretation depends on the researcher's ability to resolve time intervals appropriate to the question being asked (Ahlstrom 1985). The degree of interpretive sophistication is therefore directly related to the degree of refinement of the available chronometric data. Put another way, it is impossible for archaeologists to consider prehistoric behavior at levels of resolution finer than that offered by the best dating technique applicable in a given situation. Despite the most intensive wishful thinking and even in the best of circumstances, archaeologists who have only radiocarbon dates, for instance, cannot infer behavior more resolved than one or two human generations.

It is not surprising, then, that before the advent of absolute dating techniques, archaeologists employed rather simplistic notions of unilineal evolution, culture trait diffusion, and population migration to explain variability in the archaeological record: none of these interpretive constructs requires chronologic data more resolved than those that can be provided by relative dating techniques such as stratigraphy and seriation. One cannot begin to discuss sophisticated economic, environmental, social, or political relationships between prehistoric sites, and therefore prehistoric populations, unless the relevant archaeological data are demonstrably contemporaneous.[1] It therefore behooves the archaeologist to understand the limitations of any absolute dating and to make considered use of the resulting data in any interpretation of prehistory (Ahlstrom 1985; Mellars, Aitken, and Stringer 1993).

Tree-ring dates are the most accurate, precise, and therefore reliable chronometric data available to archaeologists (Dean 1978a). Tree-ring

---

1. Contemporaneity, however, is a necessary but insufficient condition for sound archaeological interpretation, for there are intrinsic limitations to absolute dates and dating techniques as well. Contemporaneity established on the basis of radiocarbon dating is qualitatively different from that established on the basis of tree-ring or obsidian-hydration dating. In addition, the demonstration of contemporaneity does not allow one to consider rates of culture change and other diachronic processes; a suite of reliable dates, no matter how derived, is required before such questions may be addressed.

dating is vastly more complicated than ring-counting, however, and successful tree-ring dating requires that a large number of environmental, dendrochronological, and archaeological conditions be satisfied in any given research area (Ahlstrom 1985; Baillie 1982, 1995; Dean 1978a; Stokes and Smiley 1968). These stringent conditions are often met in the American Southwest, and archaeologists working in that part of the world are blessed to have tree-ring dates available to guide their analyses. It is nevertheless the case that, through no lack of effort, tree-ring dating simply does not work in many areas and time periods.

Archaeologists working in areas or time periods in which dendrochronology cannot be applied have since World War II adopted a host of dating techniques developed in the physical and chemical sciences (Mellars, Aitken, and Stringer 1993; Michels 1973; Smiley 1955). Foremost among these is radiocarbon dating, which came to archaeology shortly after World War II as a result of the Manhattan Project (Libby 1955). Despite its own set of limitations, radiocarbon dating can be performed on organic matter younger than about 75,000 years from anywhere in the world. It therefore has become the most widely used absolute dating technique in archaeology (Taylor 1985, 1987). Many other absolute dating techniques have since been added to the archaeological repertoire. Most notable in North America are obsidian-hydration dating (Friedman and Smith 1960), archaeomagnetic dating (Eighmy and Sternberg 1990), and luminescence dating (Feathers 1997). Each of these techniques has its own set of limitations, and none can match the level of resolution offered by tree-ring data. Indeed, tree-ring dates and chronologies are used to calibrate the data offered by many other absolute dating techniques (see Renfrew 1973). As such, and despite its limited applicability, dendrochronology still offers the chronometric grail to which all archaeological dating, and therefore archaeological interpretation, must aspire. It is therefore imperative that we understand the development, application, and impact of dendrochronology in North American archaeology before we attempt to assess the impact of dating techniques whose results are evaluated against tree-ring dates.

HISTORY OF ARCHAEOLOGICAL DENDROCHRONOLOGY

Histories of archaeology typically do not consider the development of archaeological tree-ring dating in any detail. Willey and Sabloff (1980:112) devote one paragraph to the subject, as does Steibing (1993:261). Brew (1968:76) allots one sentence. Trigger (1989:305) considers dendrochronology (in the sense of the Douglass method) only in light of radiocarbon dating. Textbooks and regional histories of archaeology do a little better, though discussions typically focus on the interpretation of tree-ring dates and not on the history of the technique. The classic treatment of tree-ring dating contains no discussion of the history of the science (Stokes and Smiley 1968). Scott (1966:9) argues that "the story of the discovery of archaeological tree-ring dating by A. E. Douglass and others has been told and retold and is now familiar to scientists and laymen alike." Michael (1971:49) concurs. I beg to differ.

Conventional discussions of the history of archaeological tree-ring dating are often hagiographic. Douglass was indeed a remarkable scientist, but there were many others involved in the development of archaeological tree-ring dating for whom these treatments to not do justice. George Webb, Douglass's biographer (Webb 1983), provides a typical précis (Webb 1978:105):

> The National Geographic Society financed three "Beam Expeditions" (1923, 1928, and 1929) in an attempt to obtain material to establish a usable calendar. From the first two expeditions Douglass collected a large number of tree-ring specimens which enabled him to construct a growth record extending several centuries. This "Relative Dating" sequence, however, could not be tied to the known chronology from living trees. The Third Beam Expedition provided the missing evidence. Douglass selected the Whipple Ruin in Show Low, Arizona, for excavation during the summer of 1929, because it contained burned beams (charcoal endured better than wood specimens) and a transitional form of pottery believed to date from the absent part of the tree-ring chronology. On July [sic—June] 22, his assistants uncovered a seven-by-ten-inch charcoal beam which displayed a ring record bridging the known and relative sequences. From this 1200-year record, Douglass concluded that Pueblo Bonito and other ruins in Chaco Canyon had been inhabited in the eleventh and twelfth centuries. He spent the next six years correlating various floating sequences, eventually completing a record extending back to 11 A.D.

Douglass in fact supervised or conducted seven field trips between 1923 and 1929 that qualify as "Beam Expeditions." He did not actually "select" Whipple Ruin for excavation; the decision was made by him and a team of senior archaeologists who were guided by the relative ceramic and architectural chronologies of Lyndon Lane Hargrave as well as Douglass's tree-ring analysis. Although Douglass had by 1935 extended the tree-ring chronology back to A.D. 11, archaeological tree-ring dating was never a high priority for him: he was already at retirement age, and he spent less and less time in dendroarchaeological pursuits over the next four decades.

In addition to the dendrochronological hagiography of Douglass, the discovery of specimen HH-39 is often presented as nothing less than legend. In these semihistorical accounts, Douglass, on June 22, 1929, performs a candlelight minuet with HH-39, *the* specimen that bridged the gap and allowed calendar dating of southwestern sites (Haury 1962, 1985). In fact, several other tree-ring specimens had bridged the gap as early as 1927, but Douglass's own scientific strictures required that he obtain additional confirming evidence before he could feel confident enough in his chronology to announce publicly (or, for that matter, privately) any dates. The discovery of HH-39 was indeed a dramatic moment in southwestern archaeology, and the "Legend of HH-39" is a fabulous heuristic device. Nevertheless, to reduce the development of archaeological tree-ring dating to such a "eureka" event (Restivo 1994) does not do justice to the brilliant and cumulative dendrochronological research behind that event or to the many contributions of Douglass's archaeologist collaborators in that research. In short, such treatments do not supply the social or the intellectual context of this highly specialized development in the history of science. This book supplies that context and demonstrates that, to continue the metaphor, the history of archaeological tree-ring dating should be characterized as a concerto, not a minuet. As we shall see, Douglass conducted his dendrochronological research while orchestrating the contributions of a number of archaeological soloists through six decades of symphonic cooperation. The discovery of HH-39 is merely the crescendo in this "intense intellectual drama" (Gould 1989:24).

The history of archaeological tree-ring dating before 1950 can be considered in three periods. Archaeological dendrochronology developed, with varying degrees of intensity, between 1914 and 1929, a period of unparalleled prosperity and popular interest in the archaeology of the Southwest. The National Geographic Society's generous sponsorship of Douglass's work and the popular reaction to its publication stand as testimony to the middle-class interest in scholarly research that tends to characterize periods of economic prosperity.

The second phase is marked by the explosion of archaeological tree-ring research that occurred between 1930 and 1942, a period roughly coincident with the Great Depression. The collapse of many economic markets and systems had important ramifications for North American archaeology, affecting the availability of funding, labor, and materials.

Most of the archaeological tree-ring research conducted in the Southwest between 1930 and 1941 was funded by three private institutions (Gila Pueblo Archaeological Foundation, Museum of Northern Arizona, and Laboratory of Anthropology) whose financial portfolios survived the market collapse more or less intact. Tree-ring dating in the American Midwest was funded for a time by the Tennessee Valley Authority, though even there private funding was obtained toward the end of the decade. Additional tree-ring projects were funded by federal agencies such as the National Park Service, and labor was occasionally supplied by the Federal Emergency Relief Administration, but these projects, in the Southwest at least, tended to be smaller in scale and narrower in scope than the monumental projects in the East (see Fagette 1996). The economic situation thus did not determine in any strict sense the nature and scope of archaeological tree-ring dating research, but it may be that students and young scholars sought dendrochronological training in order to differentiate themselves in the tight labor market of the time.

The third phase in the development of archaeological tree-ring dating, from 1942 to 1950, is marked by a near cessation of archaeological tree-ring research, primarily brought on by U.S. involvement in World War II. If the 1930s have been described as the "halcyon days" (Bannister and Robinson 1976:52) of archaeological tree-ring dating, the 1940s can only be described as a period of disintegration, emphatically ended by the publication of the first radiocarbon dates for North American archaeology (Libby 1955). After 1950, then, absolute dates became the luxury of archaeologists the world over. The complicated history of archaeological tree-ring dating since 1950 has yet to be written. Suffice it to say that, after a number of trials and tribulations, archaeological tree-ring dating has over the last five decades matured into a healthy and vibrant discipline.

PRINCIPLES OF DENDROCHRONOLOGY

Dendrochronology, the study of tree-time, is the highly specialized science of assigning common-era calendar dates to the growth rings of trees (Stokes and Smiley 1968). It currently enjoys a broad array of applications in climatology, forest ecology, geomorphology, art history, and archaeology across the globe (see Baillie 1995; Cook and Kairiukstis 1990; Dean, Meko, and Swetnam 1996; Hughes et al. 1980; Schweingruber 1988). Tree-ring dating is a straightforward procedure, at least in principle. In practice, it can be astonishingly difficult.

FIGURE 3. The principle of crossdating as presented by Stokes and Smiley (1968:6).

Tree-ring dating is not ring counting, despite what many recent text-books and popular treatments of archaeology state. To determine accurate common-era calendar dates for tree rings, the dendrochronologist must have intimate knowledge of the vagaries of ring growth found in trees in a given region. To gain this knowledge, she or he must visually compare and match the patterns of ring growth in large numbers of specimens from a single species. This fundamental practice, which has since been elevated to a principle of tree-ring dating, is *crossdating* (Douglass 1941d).

Crossdating is classically defined as "the procedure of matching ring width variations . . . among trees that have grown in nearby areas, allowing the identification of the exact year in which each ring formed" (Figure 3; Fritts 1976:534). Note the emphasis on ring-width pattern matching, the absence of any suggestion of "ring counting," and the implication that accurate tree-ring dating begins with the analysis of specimens from living trees. As Douglass noted as early as 1911 (Douglass 1914), crossdating must be conclusively demonstrated in living trees of a given region before dendrochronological analysis may be used in any research situation, whether archaeological, ecological, or climatological.

More recently, Fritts and Swetnam (1989:121) have argued that crossdating is a procedure that "utilizes the presence and absence of

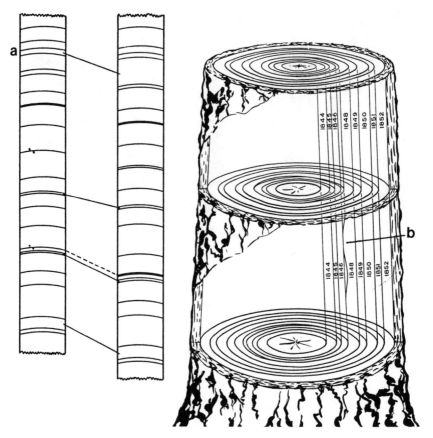

FIGURE 4. Problem rings: (a) missing ring; (b) locally absent ring (A.D. 1847)
(Stokes and Smiley 1968:15).

[ring] synchrony from different cores and trees to identify the growth
rings that may be misinterpreted." This definition alludes to the problematic nature of some tree rings, including missing rings and double rings.
Implicit here also is a working assumption of dendrochronology—that
datable tree-ring species produce only one growth ring per year. To make
a long story short, in the absence of accurate crossdating by the dendrochronologist, tree-ring specimens and chronologies cannot be considered correctly dated, and any interpretations that are predicated on those
specimens or chronologies must be considered invalid (Baillie 1995).

There are four conditions that must be fulfilled before tree-ring dating may be seriously considered in any given area (Stokes and Smiley
1968). The first requires that the examined tree species add only one

DOUBLE

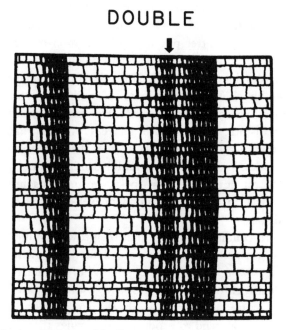

FIGURE 5. Double ring (Stokes and Smiley 1968:17).

growth ring per calendar year. In a particularly stressful year, however, such tree species may fail to produce a growth ring, in which case the dendrochronologist notes a *missing ring* (Figure 4). In stressful years, trees may also produce rings that are apparent only at certain points along the stem, in which case the dendrochronologist notes a *locally absent ring* (Figure 4). In either of these cases, if the problem rings are not identified, the rest of the sequence will be assigned dates that are too early by one or more years. If the ring for 1847 is locally absent or missing, for example, and has not been recognized as such, the ring grown in 1848 will be incorrectly assigned the date of 1847, the ring for 1912 will be dated 1911, and so on. Additional difficulties are presented by *double rings* (Figure 5), which are created when climatic conditions prompt a tree to begin shutting down growth, only to have growth resume when favorable conditions return. If not properly identified, a double ring will lead to crossdating that is off by one year, and subsequent rings will be dated one year too late. The potential for missing and double rings varies by tree species and location; it is therefore imperative that the dendrochronologist identify such problems by properly crossdating the specimens.

The second condition that must be satisfied requires that tree growth be limited by the relative availability of one environmental factor. Extensive research in tree physiology has demonstrated that many factors affect tree growth, including environmental, genetic, and idiosyncratic variables, but for tree-ring dating to work, a single environmental, and preferably climatic, factor must be dominant. In semiarid areas of the American Southwest, for instance, tree growth varies in response to available moisture, whereas in Alaska trees respond primarily to temperature fluctuations. In the Southwest, trees that are stressed, *sensitive* in their ring series, and therefore useful for dendrochronology are typically found at forest borders and on rocky, steep, and south-facing slopes. Insensitive trees are typically found in well-watered areas with well-developed soils.

The third condition requires that the growth-limiting factor exhibit annualized variability that is recorded in the growth rings in trees. Circular reasoning belabors the point, but it remains nevertheless: Because dendrochronology requires ring-width pattern matching, there has to be a pattern in the ring widths to match. Trees that enjoy beneficial growth factors tend to produce annual rings that are relatively uniform in their width and, in a sense, have no pattern. (In a strict sense, they have a uniform pattern.) Such insensitive ring series are labeled *complacent*.

The fourth condition of dendrochronology requires that the *climate signal* recorded in the ring series be in an area geographically extensive enough that the same ring-width sequence can be identified in trees found in localities far removed from one another.

The principle of crossdating and the prerequisite conditions for tree-ring dating are invariable. Accurately dated tree-ring chronologies cannot be developed if any of the conditions are breached, and all specimens must be accurately crossdated before a reliable tree-ring chronology can be developed (Baillie 1995). Only then can the dendrochronologist attempt to date archaeological specimens. As we shall see, the former task is the more difficult of the two—it took Douglass 15 years to develop a tree-ring chronology for archaeological sites in the American Southwest.

The actual process of dating a tree-ring specimen in the Douglass method requires, first and foremost, creation of a smooth surface on which the rings are clearly visible. Once such a surface is prepared, the dendrochronologist creates a graphic representation of the ring-width variability known as a *skeleton plot*, in which long lines are written on

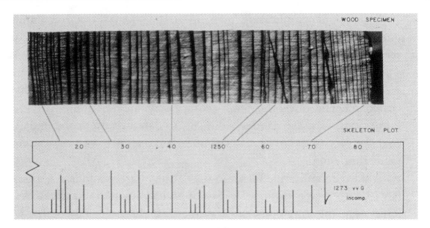

FIGURE 6. The skeleton plot, a schematic representation of ring-width variability developed by Douglass. Courtesy of the Laboratory of Tree-Ring Research.

graph paper to indicate relatively narrow rings, a "B" indicates a relatively large ring, and other unique attributes that may assist in the dating are noted (Figure 6; see Stokes and Smiley 1968). The skeleton plot is then compared to the master chronology. When the pattern indicated in the plot matches the pattern on the chronology, and all missing, double, or locally absent rings have been identified, an accurate and precise date can be assigned to all rings on the given specimen. Archaeologists are primarily interested in the date assigned to the outer ring, but the archaeologist's task with regard to tree-ring dating has just begun when the date is determined by the dendrochronologist. The interpretation of archaeological tree-ring dates is complicated by the vagaries of prehistoric behavior and archaeological sampling and preservation.

The first factor complicating the task of archaeological tree-ring dating is behavioral: the prehistoric inhabitants of the site of interest must have made use of species that satisfy the requirements mentioned above. If inhabitants of the prehistoric American Southwest had built their dwellings with cottonwood trees and cooked their food exclusively with cottonwood logs, we would not have tree-ring dates in that region, because that species violates one or more of the required conditions. A good example of such a situation can be found in the Phoenix and Tucson basins of Arizona, where preservation in the dry environment is often exquisite but few tree-ring dates are available because datable species were not locally available (for an exception, see Dean, Slaughter, and Bowden 1996).

The second complicating factor for archaeological tree-ring dating is one of preservation. Datable wood and charcoal specimens must be preserved in the archaeological record for recovery by archaeologists. Thirteenth-century cliff dwellings in the American Southwest tend to be well dated because wood beams have been preserved in dry rockshelter environments. Conversely, tenth-century open-air sites and pit structures in the Southwest are relatively difficult to date because wood and charcoal samples are poorly preserved in even moderately wet environments (Ahlstrom 1997).

A third complicating factor in the dating of archaeological specimens has to with the professional biases of archaeologists themselves. As we have seen, the development of a tree-ring chronology is perhaps the quintessential cumulative and iterative procedure. Archaeologists since the late nineteenth century have devoted far more attention to glamorous and romantic sites than to poorly preserved or apparently mundane ones. In spite of archaeologists' aesthetic bias, tree-ring chronologies are more democratic and require that all time periods be equally well represented. This situation often demands that archaeologists make specific, targeted searches for appropriate tree-ring material in sites that they might not otherwise investigate. The specimens that allowed Douglass to announce that he had "bridged the gap" in his southwestern tree-ring chronology in 1929 came not from Mesa Verde or Chaco Canyon, or even a long-occupied Hopi village, but from a disturbed open-air site in east-central Arizona.

Even to consider the use of tree-ring analysis for archaeological dating, however, one must find specimens that meet the four conditions identified by Stokes and Smiley (1968) as well as determine (1) whether crossdating exists between archaeological specimens, (2) whether the climate signal that produces crossdating in living-tree specimens is the same as that in archaeological specimens, and (3) whether archaeological and living-tree specimens crossdate.

From a dendrochronological perspective, all properly crossdated tree-ring dates are equal. There is no statistical uncertainty associated with properly crossdated tree-ring dates; a corollary is that tree-ring specimens either date or do not. Responsible dendrochronologists do not succumb when archaeologists ask for a "likely date" (Baillie 1995). Once a tree-ring date is determined, however, its interpretation becomes the archaeologist's responsibility. From the archaeologist's standpoint, all tree-ring dates are not created equal, and a body of theory has been developed over the last seven decades for the proper interpretation of

TABLE 1. Symbols Used to Qualify Tree-Ring Dates by the Laboratory of Tree-Ring Research.

Symbols used with the inside date

year	No pith ring is present.
p	Pith ring is present.
fp	The curvature of the inside ring indicates that it is far from pith.
+p	Pith ring is present, but because of the difficult nature of the ring series near the center of the specimen, an exact date cannot be assigned to it. The date is obtained by counting back from the earliest date ring.

Symbols used with the outside date

B	Bark is present.
G	Beetle galleries are present on the surface of specimen.
L	A characteristic surface patination and smoothness, which develops on beams stripped of bark, is present.
c	The outermost ring is continuous around the full circumference of the specimen.
r	Less than a full section is present, but the outermost ring is continuous around the available circumference.
v	A subjective assessment that, although there is no direct evidence of the true outside of the specimen, the date is within a very few years of being a cutting date.
vv	There is no way of estimating how far the last ring is from the true outside.
+	One or more rings may be missing from the end of the ring series, whose presence or absence cannot be determined because the specimen does not extend far enough to provide an adequate check.
++	A ring count is necessary because beyond a certain point the specimen could not be dated.

Note: The symbols B, G, L, c, and r indicate cutting dates in order of decreasing confidence. The + and ++ symbols are mutually exclusive but may be used in combination with all other symbols.

archaeological tree-ring dates (Haury 1935a; Bannister 1962; Dean 1978a; Ahlstrom 1985; 1997; Nash 1997b). Most contributions to archaeological dating theory occurred after the period of interest in this book, but several key concepts should be noted here.

The Laboratory of Tree-Ring Research at the University of Arizona assigns codes (Table 1) to archaeological tree-ring dates to describe certain attributes of the specimens and indicate the qualities of the assigned tree-ring date. At the most general level, dendrochronologists distinguish between "cutting" and "noncutting" dates. Cutting dates are assigned to specimens that have evidence that the last ring present on the specimen was the last ring grown by the tree before it died. Noncutting dates represent the opposite situation—there is no evidence that the last ring present on the specimen was the last one grown by the tree before it died, and indeed there is no way of knowing exactly how many rings are missing from the outside of the specimen.

From an interpretive standpoint, cutting dates are of far greater utility to the archaeologist than noncutting dates (Dean 1978a; Nash 1997b). Cutting dates do not necessarily indicate the year of construction of a given site or date the occupation or abandonment of a site, but they indicate the year a tree died and therefore are far closer to the behavior of interest to the archaeologist. There are many more potentially mitigating circumstances that must be accounted for when archaeologists interpret noncutting dates, however. In the absence of additional data, noncutting dates can provide only a *terminus post quem*, a date after which a given event must have occurred. Despite recent efforts to alleviate the interpretive difficulties associated with noncutting dates (Nash 1997b), they remain the most recalcitrant of tree-ring dates.

A final concept useful to archaeologists is that of *date clustering* (Ahlstrom 1985). If a number of tree-ring dates from a given site cluster in one or more, but usually less than three (Ahlstrom 1985), calendar years, one can infer that some construction event in prehistory has been well dated.

These principles, terms, and conditions of successful dendrochronology have been developed and refined throughout the course of the twentieth century, but the principle of crossdating remains basic to all applications of the technique. Archaeologists have made significant contributions to dendrochronological method and theory, and with a common vocabulary in hand, we may turn to a detailed treatment of the development of archaeological tree-ring dating.

CHAPTER 2

Lord
of the Rings

*A. E. Douglass and the
Development of Archaeological
Tree-Ring Dating, 1914–1929*

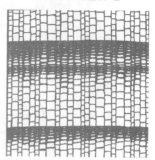

Before the publication of the December 1929 issue of *National Geographic* (Douglass 1929), archaeologists working in the American Southwest had no idea how old the prehistoric ruins they studied actually were (Haury 1995; Zeuner 1951). Educated guesses suggested that ruins such as those of Pecos Pueblo might be 1,000 or 1,500 years old (Kidder 1927b, 1936) and that Basketmaker occupations in the San Juan region might be between 3,000 and 4,000 years old (see Baldwin 1938; Cornelius 1938; Kidder 1924; Renaud 1928; Roberts 1935, 1937). The goal of *some* southwestern archaeologists by the late 1920s was to establish a firm, if undated, chronology on which to place southwestern archaeological sites.

An astronomer by training, A. E. Douglass first became interested in the study of tree rings in 1901 while working at the Lowell Observatory in Flagstaff, Arizona (Bannister 1963; Douglass 1937; Glock 1933; Webb 1983). He realized that his research on sunspots would be greatly enhanced if he could find a terrestrial, long-term, proxy record of their activity, and he began looking for possible record sources. Since tree growth was known to be partially dependent on rates of photosynthesis and therefore sunlight intensity, Douglass began examining stumps of long-lived coniferous trees left by loggers in the Flagstaff area. It was during this period of exploratory analysis that he formulated the basic principles of dendrochronology, but archaeological applications for his research had not yet been considered.[1]

---

1. For detailed treatments of Douglass's research before 1914, see Douglass 1909, 1914, 1919, 1921, 1928 and Webb 1983.

FIGURE 7. Inveterate digger and tree-ring sample collecter Earl Halstead Morris in Broken Flute Cave in northeastern Arizona, 1931.

Since the publication of tree-ring dates for southwestern sites (Douglass 1929), archaeologists have marveled at Douglass's contribution to their discipline (e.g., Haury 1935a, 1962). It is important to recognize, however, that there existed a critically important reciprocal relationship between archaeologists and Douglass during the period leading to the bridging of the gap in 1929. Although it is probable that Douglass would not have examined archaeological tree-ring samples had he not been approached by Clark Wissler in 1914, it is now clear that in the absence of professional archaeological expertise, particularly that provided by Lyndon Lane Hargrave of the University of Arizona and Earl Halstead Morris (Figure 7) of the American Museum of Natural History, Douglass would not have developed the prehistoric tree-ring chronology as quickly as he did. As we shall see, Hargrave and Morris are the "invisible technicians" (Shapin 1989) in the history of archaeological tree-ring dating. The key events in this narrative are listed in Table 2.

TABLE 2. Timeline of Archaeological Tree-Ring Research through 1929

1909	Clark Wissler begins Archer M. Huntington Survey for American Museum of Natural History.
1914	May: Wissler contacts Douglass regarding possible collaboration.
1915	Summer: First archaeological tree-ring samples collected, in Gobernador region, New Mexico.
1916	January: First archaeological tree-ring samples submitted.
1918	Summer: Earl Morris collects samples at Aztec Ruin and Pueblo Bonito, New Mexico.
1919	Douglass demonstrates crossdating in Aztec and Pueblo Bonito samples.
	Douglass and Morris develop tubular drill to gather archaeological samples.
	Douglass conducts first dendroarchaeological fieldwork.
1920	American Museum support for Douglass's research ceases.
1921	Douglass publishes "Dating Our Prehistoric Ruins: How Growth Rings in Timbers Aid in Establishing the Relative Ages of the Ruined Pueblos of the Southwest."
	Neil Judd of the United States National Museum contacts Douglass, at Wissler's behest, regarding future collaboration.
1922	Judd suggests the possibility of National Geographic Society funding.
	Douglass places five Chaco Canyon sites: Hungo Pavi, Chetro Ketl, Pueblo Bonito, Pueblo del Arroyo, and Penasco Blanco, in a relatively dated sequence.
	September 1–4: Douglass visits Chaco Canyon.
	National Geographic Society awards Douglass $2,500 per year for three years.
1923	June 3: First Beam Expedition leaves Phoenix.
1924–1926	No significant progress made.
1926	Douglass and nephew Malcolm undertake first unofficial "Beam Expedition" to Oraibi, Chinle, Gallup, the Zuni Reservation, Albuquerque, and Santa Fe.

(continued)

Table 2. Timeline of Archaeological Tree-Ring Research through 1929 (CONTINUED)

	Douglass adopts "bridge-the-gap" strategy for dating archaeological sites.
1927	Douglass identifies Gap A, between Chaco Canyon and Wupatki specimens, and Gap B, between the Wupatki sequence and the dated chronology.
	Douglass and nephew undertake second unofficial "Beam Expedition" to Betatakin and Kiet Siel.
1928	April: Lyndon Hargrave at Old Oraibi as the third unofficial "Beam Expedition."
	Specimen BE-269 extends dated sequence to A.D. 1260.
	June: Hargrave and J. W. Hamilton embark on official Second Beam Expedition (actually the fifth such expedition).
	Hargrave begins analysis of ceramic sequences, recommends collection and analysis of charcoal specimens.
	August: Douglass demonstrates that the prehistoric site of Kawaiku dates to A.D. 1329–1410.
	Douglass bridges Gap A, between the earlier Chaco Canyon ring-width series and the later Wupatki series.
1929	February 20: National Geographic Society awards Douglass unsolicited $5000.
	March: Douglass and Hargrave conduct fourth unofficial "Beam Expedition."
	March 25–29: Douglass, Colton, Hargrave, and Judd confer in Flagstaff.
	May: Douglass examines tree-ring specimens at the Gila Pueblo Archaeological Foundation, Globe, Arizona.
	June 11: Third Beam Expedition departs Flagstaff.
	June 22: Specimen HH-39 recovered.
	June 29: Douglass uses the term "Great Drought" to describe problematic ring sequence that comprised a portion of Gap B.
	December: Douglass publishes dates for prehistoric archaeological sites in "The Secret of the Southwest Solved by Talkative Tree-Rings."
1930	Nelson takes Judd to task for failing to acknowledge American Museum's role in development of archaeological tree-ring dating.

Clark Wissler and the American Museum of Natural History, 1914–1920

Shortly after Douglass formulated his crossdating principle, archaeologists working in the American Southwest began to consider more seriously the question of chronology. In 1909, Wissler organized and began leading the Archer M. Huntington Survey of the Southwest for the American Museum of Natural History (AMNH) (Wissler 1919). An explicit goal of the Huntington Survey was to discover the chronological relationships of the prehistoric ruins of the Southwest, and it was Wissler who first recognized the archaeological implications of Douglass's research (Wissler 1921). The first documented contact between the two is a letter from Wissler to Douglass dated May 22, 1914. Wissler had become interested in Douglass's work after reading "A Method for Estimating Rainfall by the Growth of Trees" (Douglass 1914).[2] The 15-year effort to apply the Douglass method of tree-ring analysis to archaeological specimens began tentatively, if not in earnest, when Wissler wrote that day, "Your work suggests to me a possible help in the archaeological investigation of the Southwest." He expanded on this thought: "We do not know how old these ruins are, but I should be glad to have an opinion from you as to whether it might be possible to connect up with your modern and dated series of tree specimens [with wood specimens] from these [prehistoric] ruins by correlating the curves of growth. . . . I shall be glad to hear from you as to whether you think it is possible for us to secure any chronological data from the examination of this material."

Pliny Earle Goddard, curator of ethnology at AMNH, remarked in a subsequent letter to Douglass (June 19, 1914) that Wissler had informed him of Douglass's research and that scholars at the American Museum wanted the examination of archaeological wood samples to begin as soon as possible. Unfortunately, Goddard noted that all the wood specimens in the American Museum collections either lacked adequate provenience information or were so badly decayed that the AMNH staff members considered them useless for dendrochronological analysis. Whether or not Douglass would have agreed with this assessment is now a moot point. Nevertheless, Goddard assured Douglass that "as soon as

2. Published accounts of the development of archaeological tree-ring dating suggest that Wissler may have approached Douglass after hearing him lecture at the Carnegie Institution of Washington in 1914 (Robinson 1976:10; Stallings 1932:90). I have found no original documentary evidence that such a lecture "came to the attention of Wissler" (Robinson 1976:10), however.

Mr. Nelson, one of our field men, reaches the Southwest he will be able to secure [for] you carefully identified material."

Goddard referred to Nels Christian Nelson, who at the time was applying and refining stratigraphic excavation techniques in the Galisteo Basin of north-central New Mexico (Nelson 1914, 1916). Despite Goddard's assurances, there is only circumstantial evidence that Nelson ever submitted wood samples to Douglass for dating. A letter (November 6, 1934) from Douglass to H. F. Osborn of the American Museum suggests that Wissler and Nelson submitted tree-ring samples from Grand Gulch, Utah, but that the samples were complacent in their ring series and therefore useless for dating purposes. Nevertheless, it is curious that Nelson, who worked closely with Morris (whom Nelson knew to be an ardent tree-ring specimen collector; Nelson 1917), and whose own research and publications document a significant interest in chronology and chronological analysis (Nelson 1914, 1916), did not participate more fully in archaeological tree-ring research.

At the same time that Nelson was pioneering stratigraphic techniques, Jesse Walter Fewkes of the Smithsonian Institution's Bureau of American Ethnology counted 360 rings in a cedar (juniper) tree growing in the middle of Sun Temple at Mesa Verde National Park (Fewkes 1915). On that basis he argued that the structure was at least 360 years old. This ring-counting effort cannot be considered "dendrochronology," however, because it did not acknowledge the possibility that missing, locally absent, or double rings were present on the specimen in question. In addition, even if Fewkes had addressed these dendrochronological issues, a date from a tree growing on a site merely provides a date before which the site must have been occupied (a *terminus ante quem)* and is therefore of extremely limited analytic utility.

The first archaeological tree-ring samples analyzed by Douglass were collected in 1915 by a joint expedition of the AMNH and the University of Colorado in the Gobernador area of northwestern New Mexico. The specimens were apparently submitted to Douglass on March 21, 1916, but no record of the samples currently exists at the Laboratory of Tree-Ring Research at the University of Arizona. It is likely that Douglass did not have a curatorial system in place at the time, and the specimens may have been lost or destroyed. Catalog cards at the Laboratory of Tree-Ring Research indicate that the first archaeological specimens examined and saved by Douglass were submitted by Morris from four unnamed sites he excavated in Gobernador Canyon, New Mexico, and Johnson Canyon, Colorado, in the summer of 1916.

Between the fall of 1916 and 1919 no samples were submitted to Douglass. The correspondence between Douglass, Wissler, and others during this period reveals that, though not actively collecting tree-ring specimens, some archaeologists were beginning to think about dendro-archaeological sampling issues. One issue was theoretical: How many beams should be sampled? Which beams should be sampled? What constitutes a promising specimen? What defines an adequate sample? These questions should be considered on a case-by-case basis, but over the last eight decades a substantial body of tree-ring dating theory has been developed to guide archaeologists in their efforts (Haury 1935a; Bannister 1962; Dean 1978a; Ahlstrom 1985).

The second sampling issue was purely methodological: How are tree-ring samples best collected? The collection of tree-ring samples from living trees was already an established practice by the early 1900s: the Swedish increment borer was designed to remove 5-mm-wide cores from living trees and had received extensive use in forestry studies in Europe and to a lesser degree North America. The removal of samples from archaeological beams is a more difficult matter because Swedish increment borers cannot easily penetrate dry wood. Cross-sections can obviously be cut from archaeological beams, but these often prove unsightly and can be dangerous if they compromise the structural integrity of a dwelling.

Despite the passage in 1906 of federal legislation protecting archaeological resources, many archaeologists did not consider archaeological beams to be of much significance and did not attempt to protect them. Archaeologists of some renown are known to have used beams for firewood (see Cummings 1952; Douglass 1929; Judd 1930b) and construction and restoration activities (see Kidder 1957). Prohibition-era "moonshiners" apparently used beams from Wupatki Pueblo as fuel for their stills (H. S. Colton to J. Nusbaum, June 12, 1934). Nevertheless, Douglass, in conjunction with Earl Morris, had by 1919 devised a hollow-bit drill (Figure 8) of sufficient size to remove cores from archaeological wood beams safely, if not arduously. Today archaeologists use a similar though electronically powered device to remove specimens from archaeological beams.

On March 23, 1916, Wissler wrote to Douglass and asked for specific advice on how to collect archaeological beam sections. Douglass's handwritten notes list his recommendations, though his thoughts went beyond sample collection and into the process of dating. Douglass suggested that Wissler (1) get samples of pine from only one ruin; (2) determine the relative ages of building of the ruins (on the basis of

FIGURE 8. Manually operated tubular borer designed by Douglass and Morris in 1919 to remove cores from archaeological beams. Cores obtained with this device often took two hours to remove. Courtesy of the Laboratory of Tree-Ring Research, University of Arizona.

archaeological evidence); (3) determine the site's proximity to an extant pine forest; and (4) determine that forest's elevation, exposure, and rainfall. On April 19, 1916, Douglass made additional recommendations in a letter to an otherwise unknown "Mr. Goldsmith" of Santa Fe, New Mexico: "For samples from prehistoric ruins, get *Pines (Pinus ponderosa)* containing 100 rings (cedars [junipers] probably of little or no value for this purpose)—five different ones from one ruin preferred, or from [sites] near together and of same date of building. Also, at least five sections of living pine trees from nearby places, and approximately of same size" (emphasis in original). Many of these recommendations formed the basis for current tenets of archaeological tree-ring dating. Whereas dendrochronologists now collect specimens from all beams in a ruin wherever possible, archaeologists still must consider relative dating when interpreting tree-ring dates, and archaeological specimens must have come from climatically sensitive trees to be datable.

In late April 1918, Wissler suggested to Douglass the intriguing possibility of using tree rings to date sites relatively even if they could not yet be absolutely dated: "The point that appeals to me now is the possibility of comparing the timbers from the ruins in the Chaco Valley with those in the vicinity of Aztec. . . . I infer from your past work [that] it would be possible to determine whether those were contemporaneous or not. In any case, we shall try to furnish you with sections from timbers in both ruins together with parallel cuttings from living trees in the vicinity." Douglass replied that such an analysis would be possible as long as the tree-ring sequence in specimens from each site had at least one 50-year segment in common, 50 rings being the minimum number Douglass felt was sufficient to establish good crossdating. Today dendrochronologists prefer 100 or more rings at a minimum, though the actual number needed depends on the sensitivity of the climate signal recorded in any given specimen.

There is no correspondence between Wissler and Douglass from April 1918 to May 1919, but during that time Morris, as directed by Wissler, collected specimens from Aztec Ruin near Farmington, New Mexico, and Pueblo Bonito in Chaco Canyon, New Mexico. Morris dutifully submitted six samples from the former and three from the latter (Douglass 1921). On May 22, 1919, five years to the day after Wissler first approached Douglass, the latter reported to Wissler that he could prove, through crossdating, that the six samples from Aztec Ruin were cut within a period of two years. The specimens from Pueblo Bonito seemed not so satisfactory, but Douglass recognized, with no small degree of caution, a "fair possibility that this ruin ([Pueblo] Bonito) might have been built about 25 years before the Aztec Ruin, but I would not like to be quoted as saying that the two were co-existent to that extent." Wissler's reply came by airmail less than one week later: "I have read this with a great deal of interest and congratulate you upon the progress made. I am now sure that you will be able to make a very important contribution to the archaeology of the Southwest" (May 28, 1919). In retrospect, Wissler's measured tone belies what must have been unbridled enthusiasm for Douglass's seminal accomplishment, especially given the published goals of the Huntington Expedition. Douglass had, for the first time, calibrated the temporal relationship of two prehistoric sites against an annual, if not yet common-era, calendar.

The importance of this feat from a dendrochronological perspective cannot be overstated, for Douglass had established crossdating in archaeological specimens, thus satisfying one of the conditions for successful dating. From an archaeological perspective, it is good to remember that two years later, at the Pueblo Bonito conference of 1921, there was "among anthropologists in general a considerable indifference and even hostility to" the proposal for detailed considerations of chronology (Wissler to Sylvanus Morley, August 16, 1921). If this indifference was characteristic of archaeologists in general, then Wissler's perspective was clearly ahead of its time.

Dendrochronologically, 1919 is recounted as a watershed year for several reasons (Douglass 1928). Archived correspondence bears witness to the increasing pace of archaeological tree-ring research and a number of other important developments. First, Douglass and Morris designed and manufactured the aforementioned tubular borer for collecting archaeological cores instead of cross-sections (Douglass 1928; see Elliott 1995:66). Second, Douglass conducted his first dendroarchaeological fieldwork at Aztec Ruin in late August (Robinson 1976). This firsthand experience verified his theory that contextualizing architectural and archaeological data are relevant to the evaluation of tree-ring dates. Finally, Douglass in 1919 decided to undertake a more focused attempt to understand how microclimatic variability affects crossdating. That is, he turned to the second task identified for the development of archaeological tree-ring dating—establishing the congruent nature of the prehistoric and historic climate signals.

By the end of January 1920, Douglass had become more confident in the crossdating found in the nine specimens from Aztec and Pueblo Bonito: "A convincing cross-identification between Aztec and Puebla [*sic*] Bonito shows that the latter was built some 40 to 45 years before the former. . . . The relative dating of these ruins is now an accomplished fact and similar relative dating can probably be extended to many other ruins. At the same time a long yellow pine record will be secured which will give a valuable climatic comparison with the sequoia" (January 29, 1920). The last sentence refers to Douglass's dendrochronological work on sequoia specimens from California. At the time, his primary strategy for dating the prehistoric pueblos was to compare their ring series with his 3,200-year sequoia chronology from northern California, for he noticed similarities in the climate signal recorded in trees from both regions. Even as late as 1928, Douglass still attempted to date southwestern ruins by comparing their ring-width patterns with the sequoia chronology. Ultimately, however, the dating of southwestern ruins was achieved by bridging the modern and archaeological ring series rather than crossdating with the sequoia series, but Douglass's preference for the sequoia chronology was understandable. First, archaeologists at the time had no idea how old southwestern sites were (Haury 1995), but estimates often ran into thousands, not hundreds, of years. Thus the 3,000-year sequoia chronology might have seemed the only viable alternative for dating prehistoric sites. Second, Douglass's interest in tree rings was primarily astronomical and climatological, not archaeological, and his research centered on the sequoia series. This emphasis is revealed in a list of research priorities he wrote on May 6, 1919, regarding the future course of his tree-ring studies:

1. Study of short period cycles
2. Temperature factor
3. 10 best sequoias for best record
4. 1580a[3]
5. Trees giving pure ss [sunspot] cycle
6. [Illegible] Districts—Altitude effects
7. Multiple red winter rings and rain distribution
8. Fossils [perhaps petrified wood specimens?]
9. Age of Indian Ruins
10. Periodograph development

Entry 9, "Age of Indian Ruins," had been in the tenth position, but at some point after the list was compiled Douglass moved it up one notch. Obviously, archaeological tree-ring dating was not high on his list of priorities in 1919 and indeed would continue to be of secondary importance to him throughout his career (Nash 1997a; see Webb 1983).

The successes of 1919 led to a year of stocktaking, analysis, and the preparation of publications. Wissler continued to advocate sample collection by archaeologists in the field, though only one of the six major excavations of 1920 cooperated. Kidder was at Pecos for the Phillips Academy of Andover, Massachusetts; Frederick Hodge was at Hawikuh for the Museum of the American Indian; Samuel Guernsey was in Tsegi Canyon for the Peabody Museum; Hewett was at Chetro Ketl for the School of American Research; and Fewkes was at Mesa Verde National Park for the Smithsonian Institution. None of these archaeologists submitted tree-ring samples to Douglass. Only Byron Cummings, working in Tsegi Canyon for the University of Arizona, submitted samples, and these may well have been collected by John Wetherill, not Cummings after all (Dean 1969:103). It is not clear why the others did not submit tree-ring specimens, though ignorance of Douglass's work is certainly possible, for publication of this early archaeological tree-ring research did not occur

---

3. This refers to a problematic (double) ring in Douglass's sequoia chronology (Brown et al. 1992).

until the following year (Douglass 1921; Wissler 1921). On the other hand, this small cohort of established professionals certainly knew one another, and Wissler probably spoke with at least some of them about Douglass's research. Chronology was simply not a focus of their work.[4]

Despite his own low priority for archaeological tree-ring research and the apparent lack of cooperation from eminent southwestern archaeologists, Douglass did not stop thinking about archaeological problems. By 1920, he had outlined a program of research that included the plans for a "Beam Expedition" of the sort that actually occurred later in the decade. In a letter to Wissler (May 27, 1920), Douglass argued for "a young archaeologist from some large institution with summer's time and . . . a Ford who will visit all possible ruins and take samples from all possible beams, especially those that are in place[,] with sketches and other data showing location of beam and other general facts regarding the ruin." The letter from which this passage was taken was, for reasons that remain unclear, never sent; the original remains on file at the University of Arizona Main Library Special Collections. The American Museum of Natural History's support of Douglass's tree-ring work through the Huntington Expedition ended in 1920. The results of Douglass's and Wissler's research were subsequently published in *Natural History* in 1921 (Douglass 1921; Wissler 1921). Douglass's article was based on a paper he gave anthropologists at the American Association for the Advancement of Science meetings in Chicago in late 1920 which presented, for the first time, his dendrochronological evidence for the relative dating of Aztec Ruin and Pueblo Bonito. The article by Wissler summarized the work of the Huntington Survey as a whole, and he wrote triumphantly that tree-ring dating "is another improvement in our methods for dating ruins in the Southwest, and was first applied . . . by the Archer M. Huntington Survey" (Wissler 1921:23).

In an effort to continue Douglass's archaeological tree-ring research, Wissler suggested that Neil Merton Judd (Figure 9), of the United States National Museum, who at the time was planning long-term excavations at Pueblo Bonito for the National Geographic Society, contact Douglass

---

4. Kidder began collecting beams for Douglass in 1922. Douglass first solicited material from Hodge on August 1, 1922. Guernsey never submitted samples despite nearly two decades of work in the Kayenta district of Arizona. Fewkes had considered sending samples to Douglass in 1917 but apparently never did. Hewett was in written contact with Douglass as early as 1916 but never submitted samples either, though in the early 1930s he supported tree-ring dating by employing Florence Hawley as dendrochronologist at Chetro Ketl.

FIGURE 9. Neil Merton Judd (1887–1976) at Alkali Ridge in southeastern Utah in 1908. Courtesy of the Peabody Museum, Harvard University.

to inquire about supporting long-term tree-ring research. Wissler emphasized to Judd that "I regard this work as of very great importance since, by it, it is possible to determine the approximate time taken for the construction of the building and the relative ages of the different parts. It will also be possible, from chance finds of logs in the sediment nearby, to determine the time relation of the pueblo to these deposits" (March 26, 1921). Note that Wissler, and therefore Douglass, understood that cross-dated tree-ring series could be used to establish prehistoric construction sequences as well as to date sites relatively, even if absolute dates could not yet be determined. Judd immediately replied that he would contact Douglass and learn the appropriate methods of sample recovery (March 26, 1921). On April 1, 1921, Judd wrote to Douglass and invited him to visit the Pueblo Bonito camp at Chaco Canyon. Douglass, however, knew nothing about young Judd and lamented to Hewett on May 20, 1921, "I have had a letter of invitation from Mr. Judd. I have no idea how he happened to send it."

It is clear that Clark Wissler and the American Museum of Natural History were the archaeological forces that initiated the development of archaeological tree-ring dating. Wissler initially contacted Douglass in 1914, Morris collected the first archaeological tree-ring samples while he was employed by AMNH, and the American Museum funded Douglass's analyses through 1920. It is worth emphasizing that Douglass's and Wissler's 1921 articles established in print the American Museum's priority in tree-ring dating. This reiteration is important because, in later publications, Judd failed to credit the museum properly for its support of early archaeological tree-ring dating (Judd 1930a, 1962, 1964, 1968).

The practice of science requires integrity in the crediting of one's predecessors in research, though the field is not always rational or devoid of personal or institutional conflicts. In 1930, Nelson, then curator of prehistoric archaeology at AMNH, took Judd to task for failing to acknowledge (see Judd 1930a) the American Museum's contributions to the early development of archaeological tree-ring dating. The ensuing dispute between Nelson and Judd illustrates some of the conflicts that can arise when scientists inappropriately claim priority over others' research. It also has a direct bearing on who still may ultimately receive credit, through selective examination of the literature, for the development of archaeological tree-ring dating.

Nelson, after reading Judd's (1930a) account of the development of archaeological tree-ring dating, was angered by Judd's failure to acknowledge the American Museum in general and Wissler in particular. He sought to correct Judd's oversight, and a flurry of letters was exchanged between the two in May 1930 to resolve the crisis. The opening salvo was fired by Nelson on May 6:

> Concerning the study of tree rings, insofar as it relates to archaeology, you [Judd] are perhaps a shade less generous than Douglass himself in the matter of its initiation and early development. Personally I have done very little to help him with actual material, though I have furnished some from various localities, including Grand Gulch. So has

Morris. But aside from such details, to the best of my recollection, if it was not Wissler's original idea (and I think it was), it was Wissler who got him started and who nursed him along for several years. . . . Everybody, I suppose, has to blow his own horn. At the same time, if anybody shares credit with Douglass, there are others besides the National Geographic Society.

Judd was less than apologetic in his reply of May 8:

I must take exception to this implication that I have been unjust in failing at this time to credit others. . . . Morris has been more than helpful . . . [but] neither the December number of the [National] Geographic Magazine nor the recent Smithsonian Explorations volume was the proper place to acknowledge such cooperation. . . . I am fully aware that Dr. Wissler forwarded to Douglass several beam sections from both Aztec and Pueblo Bonito. But these sections were sent to, and received by, Douglass for whatever they might contribute toward his study of rainfall variations and sunspot influences, evidenced by growth rings. . . . If Douglass, prior to the December 8, 1920, meeting here in Washington, had even thought of the possibility actually of dating our southwestern ruins by means of tree rings I am entirely confident that he did not give the subject serious consideration. The idea was at least novel when I proposed it on the occasion of that meeting.

Judd continued to argue that the idea to date southwestern archaeological sites was his, not Wissler's:

While I do not wish to sound boastful or ungenerous, I am nevertheless convinced that a tree-ring chronology would not so soon have been erected had I not enlisted the aid of the NGS following Dr. Douglass's expressed willingness to assume this independent investigation. . . . If you or anyone else can show me that the idea of dating our southwestern ruins by means of tree rings had been proposed prior to the [December 8, 1920] conference [in Washington] above mentioned I shall be the first to admit my error. . . . Truly, I think you quite wrong. (Judd to Nelson, May 8, 1930)

Nelson replied to Judd on May 12, 1930, that he was "not personally sufficiently interested in the history of tree ring chronology to go to any trouble about it," but his actions suggest otherwise. In a letter the next day, Nelson revealed that he had enlisted the assistance of Wissler's personal secretary, who found a considerable volume of correspondence "which would indicate that Wissler wrote his first letter to Prof. Douglass on May 22, 1914, inquiring as to the possibility of dating the Pueblo

ruins by means of additional tree ring studies on timbers from the ruins."
Nelson added that he felt Wissler would be "surprised to learn that he
was interesting himself in Douglass's work merely to supply data on climate" (May 13, 1930). Nelson's protestations apparently caused Judd
some concern, for he soon wrote Douglass: "Our good friend, Nelson, of
the American Museum of Natural History, took exception to my statement in the current number of Smithsonian Explorations volume that
completion of your tree-ring chronology is owing solely to the NGS and
that I was primarily of interest in starting you off on the dating of the
ruins by means of tree-rings" (May 13, 1930).

One week later, Wissler wrote to Judd in an attempt to clarify the situation, explaining from memory that the American Museum provided
initial support for Douglass's research and that support was subsequently assumed by the Carnegie Institution[5] and finally by the National
Geographic Society. Wissler stated that he thought the American
Museum should receive some acknowledgment, as should Morris and
Nelson, but that he felt no need for any personal credit.

Judd formally addressed Nelson's admonition and recognized the
American Museum's contribution to the development of archaeological
tree-ring dating in the foreword to Douglass's 1935 paper "The Dating
of Pueblo Bonito" (Judd 1935). He explained to Douglass, "I have gone
to some pains to do justice to Wissler and the American Museum since I
was gently taken to task [by Nelson] for not giving the credit in my 1930
paper [Judd 1930a]." He admitted that his failure to recognize the
American Museum was "an unintended omission due solely to my un-
acquaintance with what had gone on before."

It appears that Judd merely paid lip service to the AMNH contributions, for in the 1960s he reverted to his contention that Douglass's effort
to bridge the gap was exclusively a National Geographic Society–funded
effort to date Pueblo Bonito and that the idea for using tree rings to date
archaeological sites was his (Judd 1962, 1964, 1968). Judd (1962) wrote
that Douglass had been working with the American Museum in the late
1910s, but after Douglass traveled to the East Coast and met with
Wissler in the fall of 1920, the American Museum declined "to pursue
Douglass's climatic researches further and relinquished whatever claim it

5. I have found no explicit evidence that the Carnegie Institution funded
Douglass's efforts at archaeological tree-ring research per se, though Carnegie
did fund much of Douglass's dendrochronological and climatological research
during the course of his career.

had on his cooperation" (Judd 1962:88). Later Judd wrote that "it was [Douglass's work on tree-rings] that brought our paths together, for I reasoned that if growth rings could tell the age of a forest tree, they could also tell the age of timbers used in Spanish colonial buildings, and from there back into pre-Spanish times" (Judd 1968:129). It is clear from an analysis of archived documents that Wissler, the Huntington Expedition, and the American Museum were interested in and provided funding for Douglass's early attempts to date archaeological sites. They were not expressly interested in "Douglass's climatic researches," as Judd maintained. Also, given Wissler's prior commitment to and professional interest in Douglass's research, it is unlikely that he would have "relinquished whatever claim" he or the American Museum had on Douglass's research unless he was forced to by a lack of funds or some other mitigating circumstance. Aside from the cessation of American Museum funding, the professional relationship between Wissler and Douglass did not change after 1920, nor did it change after Judd began his collaboration with Douglass. Wissler had been, and continued to be, a facilitator of Douglass's research.

The foregoing episode might be only an interesting anecdote in the history of archaeological tree-ring dating were it not for the fact that Judd's (1964, 1968) accounts of this history contain misinformation that cannot reasonably be explained as typographic errors or ignorance.[6] It is clear that Judd ignored his own correspondence files and that, even after being taken to task by Nelson and the American Museum, he continued to discount the contributions of other archaeologists and institutions, except in his foreword to Douglass's (1935a) paper. To be fair, Judd and the National Geographic Society did finance the majority of Douglass's archaeological tree-ring research in the 1920s, and the success achieved in 1929 certainly would not have been attained more rapidly in the absence of their support. A detailed analysis of the archived records relating to this research, however, clearly indicates that there is much more to the story than simply the fabled National Geographic Society "Beam Expeditions" of 1923, 1928, and 1929 (Douglass 1929, 1935a; Haury 1962; Nash 1997a).

6. Nelson contributed to the confusion many years later when he wrote, in Wissler's obituary, "At my own suggestions, [Wissler] supplied A. E. Douglass with his first tree-ring material from ruins in the Chaco Canyon, New Mexico, which, supplemented by others, ultimately led to an absolute chronology" (Nelson 1948:246). There is no archival evidence to substantiate Nelson's claim.

NEIL JUDD AND THE NATIONAL GEOGRAPHIC SOCIETY, 1921–1929

The National Geographic Society sponsored three so-called Beam Expeditions, one each in 1923, 1928, and 1929. Results of the Third Beam Expedition have often been published, with original accounts written by Douglass (1929, 1935a), Haury and Hargrave (1931), and Haury (1935a, 1962). All these accounts (except Douglass 1935a) tend to ignore significant fieldwork and analytical developments that did not occur under the rubric of a "Beam Expedition," though some of Douglass's other publications provide more detail in this regard (Douglass 1928, 1937). This non–beam expedition research requires examination.

When Judd first contacted Douglass about tree-ring dating in 1921, he was reluctant to collect tree-ring samples himself because he did not know the appropriate technique. Although Douglass was unable to go to Pueblo Bonito that year, he mailed coring devices to Judd and suggested that Karl Ruppert, then a staff member at Pueblo Bonito and a graduate student of Cummings's at the University of Arizona, be assigned to collect the samples. The equipment arrived too late in the season for Ruppert to collect more than three samples, but that fall Douglass hired Ruppert to "put in some time in my research room going over my methods of tree study [so that] . . . perhaps [he] will be able to help out by his knowledge next summer."

On January 14, 1922, Judd mentioned to Douglass for the first time the possibility of National Geographic Society support for Douglass's research. By Valentine's Day, Judd's enthusiasm in the project was palpable as he wrote to Douglass that they were "working together in a spirit of kindly cooperation." Judd's goal in this research was clearly limited to the dating of Pueblo Bonito, but Douglass had much grander visions, for he was interested in developing a tree-ring chronology appropriate for sites across the Southwest. Douglass wrote Judd:

> I may come [to Washington] armed with a proposal in regard to a more direct and determined effort to gather such material in the immediate future as may bear upon getting some real results in the dating of Chaco Canyon within two or three years. . . . I took such a plan up with Dr. Wissler and Dr. Goddard [of the AMNH], but the financial conditions during the past year prevented it from being carried out. It may be that you can consider it as a part of the work of your expedition. At least I am submitting the proposal to you and would be glad to talk it over with you when I come east. (March 10, 1922)

Because of his broader interest in tree-ring chronology rather than the dating of Pueblo Bonito per se, Douglass did not restrict his 1922 sample-collection efforts to that site. He wrote to Fewkes and requested samples from Mesa Verde. Fewkes instructed Douglass to write to Jesse Nusbaum, superintendent of Mesa Verde National Park, and Douglass wisely chose to emphasize the public relations advantage if they succeeded in dating the Mesa Verde ruins: "The actual dating of the Mesa Verde ruins in relation to Aztec and Pueblo Bonito would be a very interesting matter and would help very greatly in getting the interest of many workers in the Southwest, which I am trying to do on this trip, in order to effect a combination in procuring material for a more general chronology of the ruins of the Southwest" (March 15, 1922). Nusbaum replied on April 2, 1922, that he would be more than happy to oblige Douglass's requests. A 25-year cooperative relationship was thus initiated (see Chapter 6), though samples were not immediately submitted.

The stage for National Geographic Society–funded Beam Expeditions was set by the end of May 1922, when Frederick V. Coville, chair of the Research Council of the society, received an endorsement of Douglass's proposal from Wissler, who suggested that John Wetherill conduct the First Beam Expedition. Douglass and Judd both favored Ruppert, apparently because of his formal academic training. Judd also recommended Jean Jeançon of the State Historical and Natural History Society of Colorado. The plans for intensive field collecting were only in the formative stages, but a letter from Douglass to Judd on June 14, 1922, reveals how much of an understanding Douglass had of "the gap" as early as 1922:

> I have been asking questions of everyone in regard to beams and I get the impression that there are a number of localities where suitable beams are very abundant. These would include your own Chaco Canyon, Aztec, Mesa Verde, and Pecos. Then there are other places such as Hawikuh near Zuni which Hodge told me about, where there are one or two beams which seem very promising and valuable. He has promised to have sections cut for me. From his data it seemed as if they would carry my tree sequence back to 1300. This modern tree sequence now goes back only to 1400. One or two small beams have been found at Flagstaff in the Cliff Dwellings. Dean Cummings and Ruppert saw some in Northeastern Arizona.

As it turned out, the gap between the prehistoric and modern sequences of Douglass's chronologies occurred in the late A.D. 1200s, but it would be another six years before Douglass had specimens that bridged that gap, and seven years before he was confident enough in the gap period ring sequence to publish his results.

No dendroarchaeological fieldwork was conducted in 1922 because plans were being made for the following summer, but Douglass continued working on his undated prehistoric chronology and was able to provide Judd with the following progress report on August 1, 1922:

> In order to make it plain I will recall to your mind that I adopted a hypothetical date for certain large rings in the Aztec beams. That date I called R.D. [Relative Date] 500. Most of the beams from Aztec were cut between 523 in this chronology and 531. The beams brought from Pueblo Bonito from the Hyde Expedition 20 years ago gave dates of cutting from 478–484 and I think one pole at 486. The set of sections which I have received from you and which I have called the J.P.B. [Judd Pueblo Bonito] series show that construction work was going on where you are excavating from 491 to 495. The special group numbers 9 to 13 which you marked very important came out 495. Number 6 in your series and in mine came out about 506, which you see is later than the other Pueblo Bonito beams and about 8 years later than Penasco [Blanco], and only 20 years earlier than Aztec.

In his reply four days later, it is obvious that Judd, the archaeologist, considered stratigraphic and seriation analyses critical to the solution of their problem. He wrote, "[Tree-ring] sections 9, 11, 12, 13 were obtained from a pit house one mile east of Pueblo Bonito. The ruin was exposed by caving of the bank and its floor is 12 feet below the present surface. From the pottery and other artifacts found within it, I should judge it to represent a culture much older than that of Pueblo Bonito" (August 5, 1922). As we shall see, the successful development of tree-ring dating included many more such negotiations between archaeologist and dendrochronologist.

In October 1922, the knowledge Douglass had of the ring sequences at Aztec and Pueblo Bonito allowed him to begin to interpret the tree-ring sequences with regard to the periods of construction, and therefore occupation, implied by the relative dates.

> I have reviewed all of the material from there including the material I collected, the samples you have sent me, and the old pieces from the Hyde Expedition and three from Mr. E. H. Morris of the American Museum. I am pretty confident that I now have good tree records from two distinct periods of building, one of 250 years, coinciding in part with Aztec, and one of 160 years, whether before or after the other [I am] not yet sure. It will probably be easy to place it both from the material itself and from your report on the locations where these logs were found. There are indications of a third period but they may not

prove to be sufficient as yet. These periods of construction are separate from the period of the pit house. (October 22, 1922)

Douglass's simplistic one-to-one equation of the length of ring-width sequences and "periods of building" is unacceptable in light of modern dendrochronological dating theory. Archaeologists today rely on date clustering rather than sequence length to infer construction sequence and occupational histories (Ahlstrom 1985; Bannister 1962; Dean 1978a). Although we cannot expect Douglass to see into the future and be cognizant of a sophisticated body of dendrochronological dating theory that developed in the decades after he derived the first absolute dates, it is interesting that the astronomer-dendrochronologist appears to have considered these issues before his archaeologist colleagues did.

In a personal memorandum dated October 22, 1922, Douglass outlined the relative dates of the Chaco sites in greater detail. He had assigned an arbitrary relative date "RD 500" to an especially large ring that he found in many tree-ring samples from Chaco Canyon. On the basis of that "date," he assigned, by crossdating ring sequences, relative dates for specimens from the Chaco Canyon ruins. Specimens from Hungo Pavi dated to RD 477; Chetro Ketl dated to RD 484; Pueblo Bonito to RD 484–491, 496; Pueblo del Arroyo to RD 493; and Penasco Blanco to RD 497. In the same memorandum, a series of notes indicates that he was becoming more interested in the demographic and logistical implications of his work, something that archaeologists had not even begun to consider:

> The outstanding result of the writer's trip to Chaco Canyon, September 1–4, 1922, is the conclusion that construction was nearly simultaneous in the five large ruins. Twenty years would cover almost every date so far obtained. . . . The above is the result of the first superficial examination of the material from Chaco Canyon. . . . The fact that similar dates are found in the various ruins suggests that a large number of people came at about the same time to this region and began building. . . . The problem of where the builders obtained these hundreds and even thousands of large logs is most interesting. (October 20, 1922)

In a letter to Judd the next day, Douglass again stressed the demographic, logistic, and climatic implications of his preliminary results: "The fact that similar dates are found in the various ruins suggests that a large number of people came at about the same time to this region and began building. . . . To suppose that they obtained wood from 25 miles away . . . recognizes the enormous labor [required]. To suggest that trees grew nearby would suggest climate change" (October 21, 1922).

By October 1922, plans for the First Beam Expedition were finalized, and on December 15, 1922, Dr. Gilbert Grosvenor, president of the National Geographic Society, awarded Douglass a grant of $2,500 (roughly $22,000 in 1995 dollars) per year for three years. Although the personnel roster of the First Beam Expedition was not settled until the following spring, public interest in Douglass's research began to grow after an announcement was published in the *Tucson Star* on January 10, 1923. Well-meaning organizations, including the Yavapai County (Arizona) Chamber of Commerce, offered their assistance, and individuals from all walks of life contacted Douglass in an effort to obtain employment. Notable among the latter is an unsolicited letter of recommendation from Mr. Cyril Sanders of Los Angeles for Mr. A. L. Heister of Magdalena, New Mexico. Sanders wrote: "[Mr. Heister might be valuable] with the research expedition you are proposing to make into New Mexico and Arizona. . . . I think I am correct in stating that he has himself unearthed more prehistoric relics than any man now living. He personally knows the location of all the principal ruins in New Mexico and it seems to me he should be very reliable to you in the capacity of guide and otherwise" (January 23, 1923). In other words, Heister was a pothunter. Three weeks later, the 74-year-old Heister wrote to Douglass, stating that he had been a collector for more than 31 years, had the recommendation of ex-governors and senators from New Mexico, and could lead Douglass to wonderful cliff dwellings and "the Sphinx of North America" (February 7, 1923).

Candidates seriously considered by the First Beam Expedition include John Wetherill, Ruppert, and Noel Baer, a graduate student in wood technology at the University of Arizona. For reasons that remain unknown, none of them was hired. Two individuals who are not usually associated with tree-ring research staffed the expedition: Oliver Ricketson of Harvard University was hired in February 1923, and Jeançon was engaged by April 1923. After acquiring the relevant permits, discussing appropriate collection techniques, and making contact with relevant parties, Jeançon, Ricketson, and Dr. E. S. Miller, whose presence remains unexplained, left Phoenix on June 3, 1923, to begin collecting archaeological wood specimens (Figure 10; *El Palacio* 1923a, 1923b).

Their search for beams was not structured in any formal way, though Douglass outlined a general fieldwork plan. In the first year the task was to "get quantity from the best places," in the second year the task was to "get exhaustive material from outlying places," and in the third year the task was simply to "get everything omitted in previous years." Jeançon

FIGURE 10. Oliver Ricketson (in automobile) and Jean Jeançon preparing to leave on the First Beam Expedition, 1923. Courtesy of the Laboratory of Tree-Ring Research, University of Arizona.

and Ricketson understood that, at a minimum, they had to collect samples from sites in Chaco Canyon, on Mesa Verde, and at Pecos, Aztec, Hawikuh, and other locations in Arizona, New Mexico, and Colorado. They received a blanket permit to obtain both living-tree and archaeological cores from sites on Forest Service land and in national monuments. Although they collected only about 100 specimens in the first year, the list of sites they visited is impressive, especially in light of the fact that their travel velocity was limited to eight to ten miles per hour by the poor road and climatic conditions. In addition, each core took about two hours to gather with the manually operated tubular borer. Among other sites, the First Beam Expedition collected samples from Oraibi and Walpi on the Hopi Mesas; Antelope Cave, Mummy Cave, and White House Ruin in Canyon de Chelly; Hawikuh on the Zuni Reservation; Cliff Palace, Square Tower House, and Spruce Tree House in Mesa Verde National Park; and Nambe, San Ildefonso, and Acoma pueblos in New Mexico (Figure 11).

Although the First Beam Expedition was considered a success, it was not without its share of tribulations. First, Jeançon became seriously ill with appendicitis and was forced to leave the project on August 22. Then

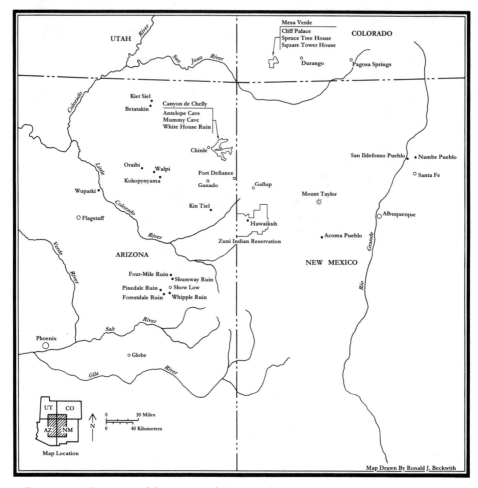

FIGURE 11. Sites visited by National Geographic Society Beam Expeditions and mentioned in the text.

the McKinley County Bank in Gallup, New Mexico, failed, and the Beam Expedition lost the $1,174.87 it had remaining on deposit. Ricketson was placed in the embarrassing situation of having to borrow almost $400 from the Pueblo Bonito Expedition to make ends meet. Finally, Jeançon, Ricketson, and, by extension, Douglass and Judd found themselves in difficulty with National Park Service authorities because Jeançon and Ricketson apparently ignored Jesse Nusbaum's prohibition and abandoned the tubular borers in favor of more destructive but easier to use hand saws to gather samples in Mesa Verde National Park (see Chapter 6).

In 1924, Judd was loath to ask the Research Council of the National Geographic Society for more money before positive results could be shown, so he suggested that Douglass continue analyzing the materials already in hand. The attempt to date prehistoric sites still hinged on a comparison of Douglass's archaeological ring sequences with his well-dated and established California sequoia chronology, not on the "bridge" method that ultimately proved successful. In a letter to Judd dated June 4, 1924, Douglass wrote that seven of the Chaco samples crossdated at RD 508–515, and he explained his research strategy: "I am also thinking very seriously of a secondary line of attack on this dating matter involving use of very old trees from the Northwest. . . . What I want to investigate is whether these [archaeological] trees will assist in the correlation between the yellow pines of northwestern New Mexico and the sequoias of northern California."

Douglass worked on the archaeological specimens from time to time, but the period from 1924 to 1926 is characterized by nothing if not a lack of tangible results. Judd's impatience, as well as that of the NGS Research Council, became palpable in the late spring and early summer of 1926: "I shall do all within my power to aid in these researches in as much as I am anxious to have such data as you may find in the beam sections sent you available for publication by the year end" (May 12, 1926). These sentiments are clear again one month later when Judd wrote: "Just before I left Washington both Dr. [Frederick] Coville and Dr. [Gilbert] Grosvenor [of the National Geographic Society] expressed the hope that your beam studies in connection with our Pueblo Bonito explorations may be concluded this summer. We have emphasized the possibility of being able to date the ruins from the tree rings" (June 9, 1926).

Douglass wrote to Judd on June 28, 1926, that he was "canceling all engagements" to focus on the beam study. In August, and with NGS funding, Douglass and his nephew Malcolm undertook what should be called a "Beam Expedition." From Flagstaff, the Douglass team went to Oraibi, Ganado, Chinle, Fort Defiance, Gallup, Mount Taylor, the Zuni Reservation, Albuquerque, Santa Fe, two unidentified forests west of the Rio Grande, and possibly Pagosa Springs and Aztec. Although this effort did not bridge the gap, the progress made as a result of the trip was sufficient to win Judd's confidence. He wrote, "I am reporting within two weeks to the Research Committee and I am confident that the members will be both interested and pleased with the result of your study."

Douglass now had a series of relative dates for the Chaco Canyon specimens from RD 332 to 567, a span of 235 years. Previously, he had specimens covering the range RD 446 to 567, to which Judd protested that "one hundred twenty years is altogether too short a period within which the Pueblo Bonito timbers were cut" (November 11, 1926). This comment reveals a bias in the perspective of most southwestern archaeologists. In addition to believing that the classic Chaco and Mesa Verde sites were very old (see Kidder 1927a), they assumed that the sites were built and occupied over long periods of time, perhaps because of ethnocentric biases similar to those that led to the Myth of the Moundbuilders and other speculative theories regarding prehistoric Native Americans (see Steibing 1993:170–180).

Douglass's success in 1926 also restored his own confidence in the likely achievement of an archaeological chronology. For the first time, he seriously considered dating archaeological sites by "bridging the gap" between the modern, dated series and the undated archaeological series, rather than comparison with the sequoia chronology: "I am more and more interested in the possibility of eventually bridging back to Pueblo Bonito by this range extension in Pueblo Bonito and say Oraibi and perhaps other ruins" (November 13, 1926).

Meanwhile, Judd, Morley, and Morris were in Washington working on a way to find money to provide Douglass with an assistant. Judd wrote: "[Morley and Morris] agree with me that you should have a young man whom you can train in this particular branch of research; both agree the Carnegie Institution is probably the logical one to provide such an assistant. You need not be surprised, therefore, if you receive intimation during the winter that developments are being made in this direction." Douglass was intrigued by this proposal, but his reply to Judd emphasized his climate and cycle studies, not archaeology, and it is interesting that none of the three individuals ("Mr. Tremaine," "Mr. Messier," and "Mr. Clements") suggested by Douglass as candidates were archaeologists.

In a letter to Judd on March 24, 1927, Douglass summarized his progress to date and used the opportunity to bring up again the subject of an assistant. He emphasized the "bridge" method and requested the evaluation of archaeological contexts in the comparison of specimens from White House Ruin and Wupatki Pueblo:

> To the 325 years of ring records from Pueblo Bonito, I have recently added 180 years from Wupatki, 35 miles northeast of here (Flagstaff), making over 500 years. Then the material from Morris at White House ruin in Canyon de Chelly will give probably another 150 years or so; possibly some fine [Pecos Pueblo] beams sent by Kidder

will add some time; and we have the makings of a long part of the great ring record needed for dating the ruins by the "bridge" method. And I have great hope that material from Oraibi will give the rest or most of it. I suppose that we can consider that both Wupatki (I have 25 sections from these and a good set of rings) and White House come in the gap between Pueblo Bonito and 1300 when my modern trees begin; which of the two do you think came first, White House? I hope that every influence will be used to get all excavation . . . put in on ruins that have beams which will aide [sic] in this search for the true dating of these ruins. . . . If only I had a good assistant. (March 24, 1927)

The spring of 1927 marks a critical period in the development of archaeological tree-ring dating for several reasons. First, as indicated, Douglass was adding more and more specimens and sites to his relatively dated sequence, and the relative chronology of those sites could now be examined more closely. Second, Judd was again becoming impatient and desirous of positive results, especially since the last excavation season at Pueblo Bonito would occur that year. By late April, Douglass had prepared a report for Judd, but it was not submitted because Douglass's wife read it and told him that no literate person would understand his treatment of the research at hand! In spite of this editorial delay, Douglass offered Judd a tantalizing and confidential piece of information: he suggested that RD 500 dated to A.D. 1006 on the common-era calendar (letter of April 29, 1927). If correct, the Pueblo Bonito ring sequence dated from A.D. 838 to 1073. Douglass equated this date range with a period of occupation for the site and inquired whether Judd felt these dates were unreasonable based on the archaeological evidence. Although the common-era calendar date for RD 500 was later revised, the letters between Judd and Douglass over the course of the next week indicate the excitement with which this preliminary result was received. Douglass first considered the implications of this dating for the potential length of the gap between the modern and undated series: "Many more points support that [RD 500 at A.D. 1006] dating. I haven't time to give them now, but if it is right then the gap between the Chaco beams and modern trees is only 250 years and it ought not to be difficult to find beams to cover the gap, for example at Old Oraibi—is there any way of doing that this summer? Please express very frank opinion about this: I am treating it as confidential" (April 29, 1927).

Four days later, Judd considered the implications of that dating and guaranteed his silence on the matter: "I am delighted with your RD 500 dating. This would seem not at all unlikely or impossible for we have always believed from the archaeological information that Pueblo Bonito was abandoned approximately 1000 years ago. . . . This is such an extremely important matter that you will, of course, check the results from every possible angle, in the meantime I will keep the secret. Please accept sincere congratulations and I know that the individual members of the Research Committee will be equally delighted; this latter when it becomes desirable to inform the Committee" (May 3, 1927).

Despite these encouraging developments, Douglass still did not seem to consider the dating effort to be very important in the big picture, so to speak. In a memorandum entitled the "Present Status of Tree Ring Studies" (probably written to the administration of the University of Arizona), Douglass wrote that "the main purpose of these studies is the determination of the history of solar and climatic changes with a view to climate prediction" (May 7, 1927). Archaeological tree-ring research is mentioned in the memorandum only in a section entitled "Material in Hand," in which Douglass noted that he had a dated chronology back to A.D. 1300 and had 175 specimens from Chaco Canyon, 75 from Aztec Ruin, and another 100 early historic specimens from across the Southwest. There is no explicit mention of his effort to date archaeological sites via tree-ring analysis.

By the summer of 1927, Douglass's analysis of the archaeological specimens was so refined that he could identify not one but two gaps in the tree-ring chronology. The first, "Gap A," occurred between ring sequences in specimens from Chaco Canyon and those in specimens collected at the Citadel in Wupatki National Monument. The second, "Gap B," occurred between the Citadel sequence and the modern, early historic, and dated chronology. In an attempt to close Gap B, Douglass again took to the field with his nephew and J. C. Clark and engaged in what should rightfully be referred to as the "Third Beam Expedition." They gathered additional specimens at Wupatki and then motored north to supplement previous collections from Betatakin and Kiet Siel in Navajo National Monument, both of which were known, on the basis of archaeological and dendrochronological evidence, to date within Douglass's Wupatki sequence (i.e., between Gaps A and B).

It is remarkable how close Douglass was to bridging the gap at this time. He already knew, for instance, that "the second gap [Gap B] is only some 50 years [long], between 1250 and 1300" (August 20, 1927). He could not have provided the beginning date of A.D. 1250 for Gap B if he had not already had some idea of how, or more literally, where, the relative sequences crossdated with the dated chronology. Some as yet unidentified specimen must therefore have, as of August 1927, bridged Gap B and suggested the beginning date of A.D. 1250. Douglass apparently did not feel comfortable with the data and thus sought additional and confirming evidence. He had always believed that long-occupied sites, especially Oraibi on the Hopi Mesas, would contain the specimens necessary to bridge the gap, and he argued for a focused return trip to search for gap specimens.

By December 1927, Douglass had formulated his plans for the next summer's fieldwork, initially singling out the Chinle area, Mesa Verde, and Wupatki as well as Old Oraibi as foci for the beam collection research. Progress in the laboratory was also being made, as Morris's specimens from Sliding Ruin in Canyon de Chelly had been crossdated with the RD sequence. Douglass wrote Judd: "[The Sliding Ruin samples] add a good 75 years to the RD record and fill Gap A by that amount. . . . So it looks as if Gap A were larger than I had thought. . . . Gap B seems to me probably not very long but yet I am anxious to fill it with good ring records and I think it can be done by collecting in Old Oraibi. This can be done by placing someone there for a few weeks to secure samples from all 'stone ax' [cut] logs and all other large logs" (December 3, 1927). Douglass knew the stone ax–cut logs were likely to be prehistoric because metal axes did not appear in the American Southwest until the Spanish arrived in the late 1500s.

In a letter to Judd on February 3, 1928, Douglass requested funds to make a collecting trip to Old Oraibi with Lorenzo Hubbell. In a telegram on February 12, he specifically asked for $800 to fund a graduate student of Cummings and two "Indian helpers." In another letter on February 13, 1928, Douglass further outlined his reasons for targeting Old Oraibi and again asked Judd to obtain $800, for Cummings seemed to have just the man for the job. In this letter Douglass revised his tentative dating of RD 500 and in so doing baited Judd with the following possibility: that Gap A (between the Chaco Canyon and the Wupatki specimens) was either 135 or 275 years long, depending on whether RD 500 fit at A.D. 965 or A.D. 825. Two weeks later, Judd wrote Douglass that an $800 check had been sent by the NGS Research Council, and he made explicit his desire that Douglass obtain results as soon as possible and focus exclusively on dating Pueblo Bonito: "I am desirous of aiding you in every way possible but am hopeful you can conclude the Society's Beam studies with this recent allotment of funds. . . . There will be related problems and many lines of research suggested by your current studies . . . all temptations that should be put aside while we follow the major theme of the Pueblo Bonito Chronology" (February 25, 1928).

The aforementioned "graduate student of Dean Byron Cummings" for whom Douglass sought funding was probably Lyndon Lane Hargrave (Figure 12),[7] a student of Cummings but not yet a graduate student. Hargrave cut his teeth in the Southwest while serving as a hydrographer for Roosevelt Dam from 1919 to 1926, and it was during this time that he became interested in southwestern archaeology (Taylor and Euler 1980:478). By early April 1928, he was in the field collecting tree-ring samples for Douglass at the Hopi village of Old Oraibi, though he was immediately faced with a moral dilemma, for the samples Douglass wanted him to collect were often in private homes and sacred structures. Hargrave had to ask individual owners for permission to collect samples in their homes, but even when permission was granted, he was burdened by his conscience: "Everywhere I work I have a guilty feeling" (April 7, 1928). Nevertheless, three days later he informed Douglass that he had in hand 114 samples, 68 of which were cores, but noted also that he was often refused permission to collect. Hargrave collected the quantity of samples that Douglass needed, and it is interesting that he single-handedly collected nearly 200 specimens in April, one-third of which were cores, whereas the First Beam Expedition collected only 100 cores during the entire field season of 1923. This may have to do with the less intensive sampling strategy of the First Beam Expedition, but there is some reason to believe that the expedition personnel were less than enthusiastic about the arduous task of drilling cores with the manual boring device.

Hargrave spent the better part of April at Oraibi, and by the end of the month Douglass reported his success to Judd, including the discovery of a single specimen, BE-269, whose ring sequence extended back to A.D. 1260. This sample thus bridged Douglass's Gap B, but he was again unwilling to release the results until he could obtain additional verification. He suggested to Judd that they keep Hargrave in the field to collect additional specimens from June through August at a salary of $110 per month. Though Judd again expressed his reluctance to ask the Research Council for funds in the absence of concrete results, he did so anyway.

7. The irony inherent in Figure 12 is that, for all the contributions Hargrave made to the development of archaeological tree-ring dating, he was not a dendrochronologist and there is no evidence that he was interested in studying tree rings professionally.

FIGURE 12. Lyndon Lane Hargrave of the University of Arizona. Courtesy of the Museum of Northern Arizona.

Hargrave's month-long collecting expedition at Old Oraibi was not considered part of the National Geographic Society's Second Beam Expedition in 1928 and indeed represents the "Fourth" Beam Expedition. The official Second Beam Expedition, which was also conducted by Hargrave, entered the field in mid-June of 1928 after Judd had acquired additional funding from the Research Council. In a 1928 report to Douglass, Hargrave did not mention the effort at Old Oraibi as part of the Second Beam Expedition. Though this may seem a minor point, it illustrates the fact that the effort to bridge the gap consisted of a great deal more fieldwork and analysis than the prominently mentioned National Geographic Society Beam Expeditions of 1923, 1928, and 1929.

On June 23, 1928, Hargrave and his assistant, J. W. Hamilton, left Flagstaff for the White Mountains of east-central Arizona in a car purchased for the Second Beam Expedition by NGS. The first sites examined were the Pinedale and Forestdale ruins, but Hargrave was disappointed with these sites because of the poor preservation exhibited in the wood specimens. He informed Douglass that "conditions that are favorable to the growth of pines seem to be equally favorable for rotting of logs" (June 25, 1928).

In another letter to Douglass three days later, there is evidence that Hargrave used his knowledge of the local pottery sequences to evaluate the possibility that a given site might contain timbers that were capable of bridging the gap:

> [The] pottery sequence [at Four Mile Ruin] is interesting in that the chronology is unbroken from the Black-on-white and corrugated [wares] through to and including the early Hopi Ware. . . . My impression is that the Four Mile Ruin, while having the wares sought and undoubtedly beams in the Gap Period, the probability of finding pine specimens [there] is poor since the ruins are so low [and wood preservation therefore would not be good]. . . . The Whipple ruin at Show Low is even less promising than the above mentioned site. . . . One of the most important ruins yet visited is Shumway, which was referred to by [Walter] Hough as having Hopi Pottery. (June 28, 1929)

Hargrave was not always correct in his assessments—the Whipple Ruin would later yield the specimen (HH-39) that bridged the gap in Douglass's chronology. The significance of Hargrave's ceramic analysis with respect to the development of archaeological tree-ring dating should not be underestimated, however, and it is unfortunate that his brilliant inductive analysis goes unrecognized in print. Neither Douglass (1929) nor Judd (1935) mentioned it in his summary of the development of archaeological tree-ring dating. Hargrave thus remains the "invisible technician" (Shapin 1989) of the beam expeditions.

On July 3, 1928, Hargrave informed Douglass that Zuni was the most promising site the Second Beam Expedition had yet examined. Because of a sensitive diplomatic situation regarding the collection of samples at the pueblo, however, he and Hamilton were forced to move on to Hawikuh, then to sites on the Navajo Reservation including Kin Tiel and sites in Keams Canyon and the Jeddito Valley. By July 16, Hargrave was able to lay out in detail for Douglass the ceramic sequence he used to find gap-period sites. He inferred that the best places to look for such sites were at Awatovi and Kokopnyama. The relatively dated ceramic chronology Hargrave identified was as follows:

PERIOD	CERAMICS
Revival	Modern
Early History	Recent Hopi
Prehistoric/Historic	Transition
Late Prehistoric	Cream (Awatovi)
Late Gap	Sikyatki
Middle Gap	Jeddito yellow

Early Gap	Orange-yellow ware
Early Gap	Red-orange ware

This sequence was based on the examination of sherds from some two dozen ruins in east-central Arizona, the Hopi Mesas, and west-central New Mexico, including Four-Mile Ruin, Whipple Ruin, Pinedale Ruin, Forestdale Ruin, Pottery Hill Ruin, Awatovi, and Hawikuh.

The unassuming Hargrave later transmitted his results to University of Arizona classmate and future dendrochronologist John C. McGregor:

> I have covered over 3,000 miles in a survey of ruins preliminary to [the] search for Gap material. Dr. Douglass was impressed with my Pottery Chronology for the Southwest, it is an outgrowth of my Roosevelt work, and is based upon the development of the red ware. Using the theory that the red ware came into use as the Black-on-White ware declined, and that since all polychromes were further developments of this ware, thus Zuni, Hopi, and all cultures that existed on to Historic times were evolutionary developments from my red ware developed at [sites near Lake] Roosevelt. Then assuming that every ruin is as recent as the latest type of pottery found in it, I could visit a ruin, make a collection or notes of sherds and definitely place that ruin in a relative time sequence.
>
> Dr. Douglass tested my theory by checking my order of ruins: such as, Pueblo Bonito, Mesa Verde, Kiet Siel, Betatakin, etc. and found that my order agreed perfectly with his dating of these sites. Finding that my sequence was right, he authorized me to make a survey to locate and determine all ruins that are contemporaneous with the development of the Hopi sequence which all comes in the Gap. I visited the Zuni area and found that the tradition . . . [of the] seven cities of Cibola was either all wrong or misinterpreted since six of the reported pueblos are several hundred years too early: All but Hawikuh were early B/W sites. I also proved [Leslie] Spier wrong when he said that the Modern Village of Zuni was inhabited through the prehistoric period. When the Zuni moved from Hawikuh about 1685 they built on a prehistoric site, now the present town of Zuni. . . . My chronology proves that the so-called Proto-Kayenta ruins are really later than the true Kayenta sites. . . . In addition to this I collected over a hundred specimens for Dr. Douglass. (August 22, 1928)

The results of Hargrave's analysis were, to say the least, impressive. Unfortunately, his study was never published.

Despite Hargrave's success in 1928, in the intensive sampling of Oraibi, the productive (official) Second Beam Expedition, and the development of the ceramic chronology with which to target gap-period sites, Douglass still had no (or was unwilling to announce) absolute dates for Judd and the NGS. In spite of Judd's admonition to refrain from non–Pueblo Bonito–related research, Douglass kept in close contact with other archaeologists, especially Morris and to a lesser degree Kidder and Frank H. H. Roberts of the Bureau of American Ethnology. Roberts was a respected member of the archaeological community and had offered Douglass his own perspective on the latter's task in 1928 (Figure 13). Harold Sellers Colton, of Flagstaff, Arizona, was also consulted in the hope that he might supply timbers or expertise that would help bridge the gap. Judd was pessimistic. He declined Douglass's suggestion of continued excavation at Wupatki and lamented that "we seem to have reached our limit of available timbers . . . the Research Committee will be disinclined to extend this search" (August 15, 1928). All was not lost, however.

In his research summary for 1928, Hargrave provided Douglass with a relative chronology of sites based on wall preservation. This architectural chronology, when considered in conjunction with his ceramic chronology and Douglass's relatively dated tree-ring chronology, gave Judd the additional data necessary to present a strong case for further funding to the Research Council. In late August, Douglass provided Judd with an even better attraction for the Research Council. Douglass triumphantly reported that he had dated, through the analysis of tree rings, a prehistoric southwestern site. On the basis of the progress of 1928, Douglass was able to demonstrate that the ring sequence from Kawaiku (Kawaikuh) dated from A.D. 1329 to 1410. In a handwritten note on the letter in which Douglass reported these results to Judd, he suggested that "good sense says [to] hold these dates till I get longer sequences" (August 31, 1928). Again, Douglass was on the verge of significant results, but his scientific conservatism required him to seek additional tree-ring data to verify his conclusions.

The official and unofficial beam expeditions of 1928 could thus count a number of achievements. They allowed Douglass to extend his modern chronology with confidence back to A.D. 1400 and with reasonable confidence back to A.D. 1300. The official Second Beam Expedition usually gets credited with the recovery of BE-269, which extended the chronology with some confidence back to A.D. 1260 (Robinson 1976; see also Field Trip 1929), but this specimen was gathered by Hargrave in April 1928 on what was, unofficially, the "Fourth Beam Expedition." Taken together, these developments allowed Douglass to date Kawaiku

Bridging the Gap at Kokop 1929.

FIGURE 13. Frank H. H. Roberts's cartoon of Douglass "bridging of the gap." "Kokop" is short for Kokopynama, one of the four sites excavated by the Third Beam Expedition. Courtesy of the Laboratory of Tree-Ring Research, University of Arizona.

and 33 other protohistoric and historic sites. With regard to the earlier and undated segments of the chronology, Douglass in 1928 bridged Gap A, the gap between ring sequences from Chaco Canyon and those in the Wupatki/Navajo National Monument specimens. This brought the entire undated prehistoric sequence into one 590-year-long undated sequence. Only one gap (Gap B) now existed, and it appears that it, too, had been tentatively bridged, if only by one specimen.

In late 1928, Douglass was beginning to think about the implications of Gap B and the dating of southwestern sites in anthropological as well as dendrochronological terms. He wrote: "There is evidence in all of this that the gap [Gap B] represents some great crisis in the history of the Pueblo people. . . . Beams which shall bridge this gap probably will be found in the form of charcoal" (December 5, 1928). Charcoal had not been collected before 1928, but Hargrave had pointed out on the basis of his ceramic chronology that specimens needed to bridge the gap were going to be found not in protected cliff dwellings but rather in open-air sites where wood does not preserve well but charcoal does. Indeed, Kawaiku had been dated using charcoal specimens (Robinson 1976).

As the East Coast "establishment" archaeologists (Kidder, Morris, Roberts, and Judd) digested the results of Douglass's and Hargrave's 1928 research, they established their own prioritized list of sites that they felt should contain gap-period beams based on their analysis of ceramic assemblages at the United States National Museum in Washington, D.C. In so doing, they appeared to ignore the bulk of Hargrave's suggestions and argued instead that the best sites for the search were Homolovi, Chevelon Ruin, Four Mile Ruin, Chaves Pass Ruin, and to a lesser degree Jensen Ruin in Shumway, Arizona.

While archaeologists mulled over the ceramic assemblages in Washington, the administrative wheels were turning in that city as well. Despite Judd's pessimism about the Research Council's intentions, Douglass was, to say the least, pleasantly surprised by a February 20, 1929, letter from the National Geographic Society that awarded him an unanticipated $5,000, equivalent to about $45,000 in 1995. In addition to this outright award, Douglass was reimbursed for $769.57 worth of Second Beam Expedition expenses that he had paid out of his own pocket.

Five days later, Judd suggested they focus their efforts on the prioritized list of ruins but added to that list the Whipple Ruin near Show Low, Arizona, and the Forestdale Ruin, near its namesake town. Judd further related his interest in having Morris, Roberts, and Kidder assist Douglass and him in a field reconnaissance before the Third Beam Expedition. Although this survey never materialized because of their disparate research schedules, Judd was once again optimistic: "Based on what we learned from your work last summer, we ought this year to bridge the gap remaining in your chronology if it is bridgeable. . . . The desirability and the possibility of closing the gap this season suggests that all possible cooperation should be enlisted" (February 25, 1929).

With adequate funding, a prioritized list of sites, and evidence that they were tantalizingly close to bridging the gap, it would seem to be a relatively straightforward procedure to return to the field and collect appropriate specimens. But as late as March 1929, the personnel roster for the Third Beam Expedition remained unresolved. Hargrave wrote to Douglass *asking* for a job on the expedition, apparently finding it necessary, after his many contributions in 1928, to use Morris as a reference. Hargrave informed Douglass that Morris had written him as follows: "The prospects seem pretty good for a beam campaign this summer under Dr. Douglass's direction. I hope you [Hargrave] will have a hand in this for I still believe that the material to close the gap needs only a persistent search for its recovery and you know better than anyone else where to look for it" (Hargrave to Douglass, March 2, 1929).

Hargrave's discomfort may have been well founded. In a letter to Judd after the Research Council grant was awarded, Douglass wrote: "I rejoice in the grant and reimbursement. Let's engage Morris at once" (March 8, 1929). It appears then that Hargrave was not Douglass's and Judd's first choice for the expedition, or that Hargrave's participation was taken so much for granted that no one bothered to notify him of that fact. Later in March 1929, Douglass again failed to mention Hargrave as a potential member of the Third Beam Expedition, writing Grosvenor of the National Geographic Society that Judd would be in overall charge of the archaeological work and that he hoped Judd and Morris would be able to review their plans with Douglass and "Mr. Houry [*sic*] of this University, if I can get him this summer."

The oversight of Hargrave begs explanation. Perhaps it was because of his lack of formal academic credentials. Perhaps it was a reprimand from Douglass: Hargrave had apologized to him for "leaving you in the lurch at the archaeology meeting" (Hargrave to Douglass, March 2, 1929), but this scenario seems unlikely. Perhaps it was because Hargrave was then employed at the Museum of Northern Arizona (MNA) and was therefore somehow "out of the loop." MNA was not yet formally involved in the development of archaeological tree-ring dating, though Colton and Douglass had exchanged 16-mm films of the Second Beam Expedition in late 1928. It is possible that Judd and Douglass simply assumed Hargrave would be available and would be interested in leading the Third Beam Expedition. Though Douglass did not mention Hargrave as a candidate for the expedition, the two were in active collaboration, for they conducted a beam-collecting trip in March 1929. Their excursion is not recorded as an official beam expedition, but it qualifies as the "Sixth" Beam Expedition nonetheless.

Douglass apprised Judd of their trip (March 31, 1929): "Hargrave and I visited the private Whipple-Huning ruin at Showlow, Jensen and 4-mile at Taylor, Stone Axe and 'Black Axe' at the Petrified Forest, Rim Ruin and Little Black Butte Ruin and Water Trough Ruin (Hough's First Ruin) in the Biddahoochee Valley and Chevelon Ruin at Winslow and collected sherds. . . . Whipple-Huning Ruin has too many houses on it. To this list should be added M14 (see Mindeleff's Ruin 14 miles north of Oraibi) and Giant's chair, and 3 Jeddito ruins" (see Field Trip 1929).

There is evidence also that a "Third Beam Expedition Conference" including Douglass, Colton, Hargrave, and Judd occurred at the Museum of Northern Arizona on March 25–27, 1929. Hargrave's presence indicates that he was "in the loop" at that time; given his March field trip with Douglass and his participation in the conference, the oversight of Hargrave must be more apparent than real.

Personnel issues had not yet been resolved for the Third Beam Expedition, however, and the assumed availability of Hargrave was beginning to pose a problem, for he had contractual obligations as assistant director of the Museum of Northern Arizona. Shortly after their collecting trip in March, Douglass recognized the problem of Hargrave's availability and hoped to secure Morris, Kidder, and Judd as lobbyists to ensure his participation. Haury's name was then raised by Douglass for the second time, not only for Haury's merits but for the advantages in interdepartmental university relations as well. Douglass wrote Judd: "I am therefore talking with Houry [*sic*] tomorrow who wants something to use his time from June first to late in the year. He is an excellent man and as he is here [in Tucson] I could begin at once in training him in ring-reading. He has had a good deal of field experience and would be a first class man. Such a plan would also bring this Department into the work in a way that I think would help" (March 31, 1929). This last sentence refers to Dean Byron Cummings and the Department of Archaeology at the University of Arizona, which had not, up to this point, been actively assisting Douglass's research, except that Ricketson and Hargrave had been students there when hired by the First and Second Beam Expeditions, and Emil Haury was then an instructor there.

In a flurry of telegrams, letters, meetings, and probably a few phone calls spanning the month of April 1929, negotiations for Hargrave's participation in the Third Beam Expedition were completed. Douglass had wanted senior archaeologists such as Morris, Kidder, and Colton to participate in the fieldwork, but it was Judd who felt that Hargrave was critical for successful completion of the Third Beam Expedition. Judd's attempt to sign Hargrave included no small amount of pressure on Colton, Hargrave's supervisor.

In a telegram of April 10, 1929, to Judd, Douglass mentioned that Hargrave might be available for the month of May, but possibly for only one week each in June, July, and August. Douglass therefore suggested that Haury be the permanent field man and assistant to Hargrave, who would return periodically to direct Haury's work. Douglass's suggestion seems to have been interpreted by Judd to mean that Hargrave might not be available at all. This only served to galvanize Judd's resolve to obtain Hargrave's services at all costs. On April 12, 1929, he wrote to Colton:

> I am truly discouraged by [Douglass's] report for I had counted so strongly upon Hargrave's assistance. His experience with Douglass during the past two summers [*sic*—Hargrave worked with Douglass in 1928 and the spring of 1929] has well equipped him for this third and,

we trust, concluding expedition. . . . The importance and possible significance of the current expedition cannot, therefore, be overestimated.
Hence my lingering hope that, even at some temporary sacrifice to the
work of your institution, you may find means of loaning Hargrave to
us to carry on a search of such vast moment to all interested in southwestern archaeology.

Judd's impassioned lobbying seems to have worked, for Colton wired
Douglass that "on urgent appeal of Dr. Judd I will arrange to let you
have Hargrave May 15 to July 30" (April 17, 1929). That same day
Colton explained his reasoning and reluctance in a letter to Judd: "I
believe that the work of Dr. Douglass is the most important archaeological work being undertaken in the Southwest. If Hargrave is indispens-
able to the work, we will make every sacrifice to contribute to it. . . .
Hargrave has just learned his job [as assistant director of MNA] and
relieves me of a mass of detail. You can understand my reluctance to
release this very able crutch." Colton, however, included a series of stipulations regarding Hargrave's participation: the Museum of Northern
Arizona must be mentioned in publications regarding the Third Beam
Expedition, a ceramic type collection from all sites visited must be
deposited at MNA, and Hargrave must be allowed to use whatever
archaeological data he collected for his own research. Judd agreed to
Colton's stipulations in his reply of April 23:

> We are all justified, I am sure, in putting aside so much of our
> planned work as may be temporarily neglected the more completely to
> cooperate in this endeavor to complete the Douglass chronology. . . .
> You are generous with Hargrave. My hopes of closing the "gap" this
> summer rose measurably upon learning that you would find some
> means of sparing Hargrave. . . . Since the sole purpose of the current
> expedition is the search for beam material, Mr. Hargrave would be
> entirely free to use as his own any related archaeological information
> disclosed. He would not be free, however, to use or to release any
> information pertaining to Doctor Douglass's tree-ring chronology
> without specific authority from Doctor Douglass or myself.

Emil Walter Haury (Figure 14), a recent recipient of a master's
degree from the University of Arizona, was hired by the beam expedition sometime in the late spring of 1929, though the exact date is
unknown. It is clear from the correspondence that Haury was considered the junior member of the expedition: "Hargrave by all means is
necessary in this work because of his familiarity with the pottery and
your beam studies. . . . Houry's [sic] lack of experience in this particular

FIGURE 14. Emil W. Haury (1904–1992) at Pinedale Ruin in east-central Arizona for the Third Beam Expedition, 1929. Courtesy of the Laboratory of Tree-Ring Research, University of Arizona.

work before us does not warrant our paying him the salary he would expect. Hargrave is the man we must have if at all possible" (April 10, 1929). Haury was paid $150.00 per month for his efforts; Hargrave was paid $175.00 per month.

Early in May 1929, Douglass went to the Gila Pueblo Archaeological Foundation in Globe, Arizona, to examine charcoal specimens that had been acquired from the Whipple Ruin by Harold S. Gladwin, Gila Pueblo's director. Whipple Ruin's owner, Ed Whipple, had placed his ceramic vessel collection on the market for $1,000; Gila Pueblo purchased the collection and in the process acquired a number of tree-ring specimens. There is evidence also that Douglass and Hargrave collected samples at the archaeological site of Gila Pueblo during their reconnaissance in March 1929 (see samples SHO-13 and SHO-14b collected March 23, 1929, on file at the Laboratory of Tree-Ring Research, University of Arizona, Tucson).[8]

Douglass heard that Whipple was planning to level the site in his backyard, so he sent him a self-addressed envelope in which charcoal

8. I would like to thank Jeffrey S. Dean for bringing this to my attention.

specimens might be mailed to Tucson collect. For some reason, Douglass did not trust Whipple, however, so he also wrote to a teacher at Show Low Junior High School (whose name is not recorded because Douglass had apparently forgotten it) and asked him or her to secure specimens from Whipple before the ruin was leveled. Douglass's examination of the Whipple Ruin specimens suggested that they filled the gap, and in separate letters to Gladwin, Hargrave, and Judd, Douglass outlined his suspicions in a way that not only suggests he had verified the bridging of Gap B but also elucidates his reasons for hesitancy in basing a segment of his chronology on only one tree-ring specimen:

> I have been over the Showlow ring sequence as found in its complete form last Sunday and have been unable to locate it either in historic or prehistoric chronology. That looks very much as if it were in the gap. I shall not feel sure until I find other trees giving the same ring record. A single tree might have defects which would injure the accuracy of its records. (Douglass to Gladwin, May 8, 1929)

> [I] carefully examined the complete group of charcoal pieces from the Whipple-Huning ruin at Showlow. . . . There are marked peculiarities in this series which would seem to make it distinctive and which I am as yet unable to find in either modern or prehistoric series . . . at present moment I am seriously considering it as being in the gap. If that is so then the gap is longer than I thought and at present we are justified in thinking out any conclusions that might come from an idea of the gap as covering 150 years or more. . . . With very slight encouragement I am ready to make another trip to Showlow to see if further material can be obtained. (Douglass to Hargrave, May 8, 1929)

> I have some very fine pieces of charcoal from the Whipple-Huning Ruin at Showlow which I have at last found through the courtesy of Mr. H. S. Gladwin, Gila Pueblo, Globe. This gives a complete sequence including 140 rings with nearly 100 of them in good condition . . . I am unable to locate them either in prehistoric or historic periods, and the suggestion is that they are in the gap. If that is the case the gap is longer than I supposed but I cannot take them seriously until there is corroborating evidence in other specimens which cross date with these. (Douglass to Judd, May 8, 1929)

The official National Geographic Society Third Beam Expedition began fieldwork on June 11, 1929, at Whipple Ruin. Judd and Douglass remained at Beam Expedition headquarters at MNA, though they joined

Hargrave and Haury in the field from time to time. Haury offered some idea of the working conditions at the first site: "Old man Whipple informed us before we started that he laid claim to all relics and for half a day watched us like a hawk, but left yesterday for an extended stay in Albuquerque" (June 13, 1929). By June 19, Hargrave was optimistic about the prospects of finding suitable specimens at Whipple Ruin, though he was less hopeful about their next site, Pinedale Ruin. He requested Douglass's help in determining which specimens at Pinedale looked promising. Judd and Douglass thus motored from Flagstaff to Show Low in the early morning hours of Saturday, June 22, 1929.

THE DISCOVERY AND IMPLICATIONS OF SPECIMEN HH-39

The events at Whipple Ruin of June 22, 1929, are now famous in southwestern archaeology (Douglass 1929, 1935a; Haury 1962; Robinson 1976), and accounts of the discovery of specimen HH-39 (Figure 15) have attained nearly legendary status. Unfortunately, as with all legends, the "Legend of HH-39" contains a number of inaccuracies. The conventional wisdom has it that "HH" stands for "Haury-Hargrave," which is incorrect, for Haury was the junior partner on the team. This misunderstanding probably stems from the fact that the publication of the Third Beam Expedition results lists Haury as senior author (Haury and Hargrave 1931). Haury was conscientious throughout his career to note that "HH" stood for "Hargrave-Haury" and not the reverse (e.g., Haury 1962).

The second discrepancy between the "Legend of HH-39" and the actual course of events is somewhat more opaque but should nevertheless be considered. Published accounts suggest that Haury or Hargrave excavated, or at least discovered, the specimen, which in a strict sense may be incorrect. Douglass's handwritten notes state, however, that HH-39 was "recovered by Judd." It is difficult and, in the grand scheme of things, probably irrelevant to determine who actually pulled HH-39 from the ground, especially because photographs archived at the Laboratory of Tree-Ring Research suggest that in addition to Hargrave, Haury, Judd, and Douglass, other individuals were present at Whipple Ruin on June 22, 1929, and published photographs of the specimen (see Douglass 1929) include an unidentified individual, probably Reed Whipple. Nevertheless, published reports have it that Haury, or at least Hargrave, excavated HH-39 (Elliott 1995:128, 141; Taylor and Euler 1980:478; Thompson 1995:646). In a strict sense, neither may have excavated the specimen.

Finally, the "Legend of HH-39" suggests that it was the first specimen to bridge the gap between Douglass's undated prehistoric chronology

FIGURE 15. Reed Whipple and tree-ring specimen HH-39 in situ, at Whipple Ruin in east-central Arizona, June 22, 1929. Courtesy of the Laboratory of Tree-Ring Research, University of Arizona.

and the dated modern and historic chronology. Unpublished documents indicate that (1) Douglass suspected in 1927 that Gap B fell between A.D. 1250 and 1300, (2) Douglass knew in 1928 that specimen BE-269 bridged the gap, and (3) Douglass found in the spring of 1929 specimens at Gila Pueblo that may have bridged Gap B. Douglass's patient conservatism and strict adherence to rigorous scientific principles required that he gather additional specimens to replicate the gap-period ring sequence and reinforce his understanding of its crossdating. Specimen HH-39 is nevertheless critically important because it provided him with the corroborative evidence he needed before he could announce and publish his results (Douglass 1929).

On June 23, 1929, Douglass and Judd took Hargrave and his assistant, Mr. Green, to Kin Tiel to continue the search for beams. It may have been on this journey that Judd and Hargrave visited Cummings's field school at Turkey Hill Pueblo near Flagstaff, at which time they informed the fledgling archaeologists that the gap had been bridged (Wedel 1978:401). Hargrave and Green later continued the search at Kokopnyama; Haury remained at Whipple Ruin for some days and then moved to Pinedale Ruin a short distance away. After the teams split, tree-ring specimens collected by the Third Beam Expedition are labeled "EH-##" or "LH-##," depending on which team recovered them.

One week after the discovery of HH-39, Douglass wrote triumphantly to Gilbert Grosvenor of the National Geographic Society that the "Gap" had been bridged. In this letter Douglass first used the term "Great Drought" to refer to the difficult ring sequence between A.D. 1276 and 1299.

> I am very glad to say that the "Gap" was actually crossed a week ago today by the aid of material obtained at Showlow (50 miles S of Holbrook), using the "skeleton plot" method, which is my simple general method of cross-dating different tree-records. The gap period was due to a great drought in the late twelve-hundreds and therefore we have not yet let up in the attempt to get good tree records passing through this period in which the large majority of trees were defective. We should have, I think, not only trees that give a reliable count but tree specimens that will serve satisfactorily for photographs and measurements. . . . In any case you can see that I feel relieved that the help given by you and the NGS, is not in vain, and that my belief that these dates could be derived from tree rings, is justified. (June 29, 1929)

Grosvenor conveyed his congratulations via telegram on July 3, 1929, emphasizing the official National Geographic Society position that no announcement be made except through NGS channels and that the NGS would remain silent on the issue until Douglass's article was complete and an official press release could be prepared. The official silence on the bridging of the gap kept a number of archaeologists, including many who had contributed to Douglass's research, ignorant of his results until they were announced to the public six months later.

The Judd-Douglass correspondence for the last five months of 1929 sheds light on the decision-making process with regard to the official announcement of the Beam Expedition results. Characteristically, Douglass tried to ensure that the dating was correct, while Judd reiterated that the privilege of announcement was the National Geographic Society's; as the funding agency, the society was entitled to enjoy the prestige of announcement. Judd also advised Douglass to be restrained and cautious in his presentation of their results for reasons that have nothing to do with NGS. He reminded Douglass that "disbelief is certain to arise from the biologists, the astronomers, and perhaps other groups. The odor of Huntington still permeates scientific halls wherever tree-rings are concerned" (November 26, 1929). Ellsworth Huntington of the Carnegie Institution had conducted simplistic tree-ring research that had been criticized on methodological and theoretical grounds in the early part of this century (Huntington 1912, 1925; Huntington and Visher 1922). His research had obviously not been forgotten and indeed made it difficult for Douglass to convince already skeptical foresters, biologists, and other scientists that his results had any validity.

The results of Douglass's research were published in the December issue of *National Geographic* (Douglass 1929), and there is some indication that the society actually delayed publication of the issue in order to include Douglass's contribution, a decidedly rare event in that journal's history (see Lutz and Collins 1993).

The following accolades, just a sample of the correspondence Douglass received from archaeologists, convey the tone of their reaction:

I am greatly impressed by the remarkable results you have reached by your unexcelled method of dating. (Ernst Antevs, January 23, 1930)

I have just read your most interesting article in the last *Geographic*, which I believe is the most valuable contribution ever made to American archaeology. (J. Charles Kelly, November 28, 1929)

Completion of your chronology is by all odds the most important thing that has happened thus far in American prehistory. (Neil M. Judd, October 24, 1929)

With most sincere congratulations on the splendid results which I understand you have achieved and which I am looking forward with the greatest interest to hearing about at the proper time. (A. V. Kidder, November 4, 1929)

I have just finished reading your report of your tree ring study. . . . It not only amazes me, but convinces me that your study is the greatest thing in American archaeology that has ever been done. I feel just as excited over your finds as if I had made them myself! . . . I am grateful as an archaeologist that you happened into this subject, for it puts that much of our study of the Southwest on a sound basis. . . . I am so excited about the whole thing that I tell everyone around here about you and your discoveries. (Paul Martin, December 5, 1929)

When one stops to recall the guesses—including those of noted anthropologists—as to the age of the various Pueblos, the historical value of Dr. Douglass's positive dates as ascertained from tree rings becomes overwhelmingly apparent. And one cannot but admire Douglass's great patience and endless enthusiasm in pushing to the end this monumental investigation. (C. Hart Merriam to Gilbert Grosvenor, July 29, 1935)

The more I think about it the more wonderful your achievement seems. (Earl Morris, November 22, 1929)

Sincerest congratulations on successful closing of [the gap]. Your contribution to archaeological progress in Southwest [is] singularly outstanding. (Jesse Nusbaum, November 19, 1929)

I congratulate you for reaching a happy conclusion in this extremely important task. I consider your discovery one of the most significant in many years and a very remarkable contribution to the archaeology of the SW in particular and also to archaeology in general as it can be applied to other fields as well. (E. B. Renaud, January 23, 1930)

I wish to congratulate you upon your great achievement in completing the tree ring series for Southwest archaeology. This is to me one of the great scientific achievements of the time and I am sure will always be so regarded. (Clark Wissler, December 10, 1929)

These statements foreshadow what Haury (1935a:98) would later put into print: "It may be stated without equivocation that the tree-ring approach has been the single greatest contribution ever made to American archaeology."

One archaeologist was not so congratulatory, however. On June 15, 1935, Warren K. Moorehead sent Douglass, via Colton, a reprint of his article in *Science* entitled "A Forgotten Tree-Ring Record" (Moorehead 1934). In it he argued that he performed the first tree-ring dating of an archaeological site in North America when he counted rings on a walnut stump in the Midwest (see Moorehead 1890). Not only is ring counting not dendrochronology, but Moorehead did not set the precedent for ring counting in archaeology: he ignored the work of Thomas Jefferson and E. D. Cope, among others (Studhalter 1955). Nevertheless, Moorehead (1934) exhorted Douglass to begin making reference to his contribution. Douglass ignored this admonition.

Douglass received many accolades from business people, scientists, craftsmen, religious fanatics, and eugenicists as well. Although some of these solicitations are less than amusing, it is clear that lay people were interested in Douglass's research (see Carew 1930 for a popular account of Douglass's studies).

Arizona businessmen were politely restrained in their comments: "You have certainly added a most valuable service . . . in being able to place the dates of the old Pueblos and you have presented the subject in a most interesting way" (P. G. Spilsbury, president, Arizona Industrial Congress, November 29, 1929). "[Your article] has aroused more interest and elicited more comment than anything else of the kind in a long time" (C. C. Tillotson, United Verde Copper Company, December 14, 1929).

Foreign businessmen seemed less than concerned with federal and state antiquities laws. M. R. Shelly, for example, a "Flower, Seed and Plant Expert" from Sydney, Australia, sought to establish a connection for the export of Hopi pottery, which he was convinced would fetch a higher price on the market if accurately dated. Well-meaning but un-informed professionals and craftsmen ignored antiquities laws as well. Max Giesecke, chairman of the Local Arrangements Committee, American Dental Association, Denver, noted that his organization had made an honorary gavel out of a beam section members had collected in Mesa Verde National Park and wanted to know how old it was before they presented it to their president at their annual convention in July. Walter T. Laras, a woodworker from Denver, asked Douglass to date the Medusa-like, serpent-shaped lamps he made from dead juniper snags (Figure 16). H. H. Clayton, of the Clayton Weather Service, Canton, Massachusetts, wrote to Douglass regarding the prospects for dating "antiquarian furniture" in New England. A. W. Groves, a violin maker from Temple, Texas, argued that the only difference between his violins and Stradivarius violins was that Stradivarius had access to 1,000-year-old wood in Europe. Groves suggested that in collaboration with Douglass he could "practically insure the perpetuity of the wood and hand your name and mine down to posterity" (September 15, 1935). One year later another violin maker, Frances Kerns of Copperhill, Tennessee, approached Douglass with the same idea.

Pseudoscientists and religious fanatics were interested in Douglass's research as well, perhaps because his publication in *National Geographic* revealed him to be intelligent and insightful. Washington G. Endicott of Chicago wanted Douglass to apply tree-ring dating to support his theory that the event that created Meteor Crater could explain the geology of Utah, Arizona, Colorado, and New Mexico. Endicott argued that Native American folklore proves a human presence in the Southwest before the existence of the Grand Canyon, which, incidentally, was created in six

FIGURE 16. Artisan Walter T. Laras and his juniper snag lamps, January 1934. Courtesy of the University of Arizona Library Special Collections.

weeks or less as a result of the Meteor Crater impact. L. E. Wethey of Montreal wanted Douglass to apply tree-ring dating to his biblical studies, which somehow combined dinosaur eggs, totem poles, Easter Island, Macchu Picchu, Egypt, and other cultural and natural phenomena in a survey of the current plight of humankind. Walter R. Cuthbert, of National Address Investigators, inquired as to whether Douglass had found relationships between tree rings and the "prosperity of the world," noting that economic depressions typically occur before presidential elections and after periods of low rainfall. Cuthbert wanted Douglass to use tree rings to predict rainfall, and therefore economic depressions, not to mention—and by extreme extension—presidential elections!

Eugenicists came into the fold as well. E. S. Gosney, president of the Human Betterment Association in Pasadena, asked Douglass to review that organization's pamphlet entitled "Human Sterilization," which included commentary on racial degeneration, eugenics, and other sinister topics. A subsequent letter stated that the Human Betterment Association was taking steps "in the direction of a protection against what would seem to be a threat of degeneracy in the civilized world"

(April 10, 1931). Douglass politely explained the possibilities and limitations of tree-ring dating to most of these correspondents.

This review illustrates just how widespread the general public's interest in Douglass's work was. The announcement of his dendrochronological breakthrough came on the heels of the stock market crash of October 1929, when many people were in dire straits both economically and psychologically (see McElvaine 1993). Many sought positive news; others were interested in Douglass's work because of their romanticism regarding the prehistoric and historic cultures of the Southwest. Whatever their reasons, the announcement of the "bridging of the gap" and the dating of the southwestern pueblos had a pronounced and profound effect on archaeology and popular culture in North America.

CONCLUSION

It is clear that the development of archaeological tree-ring dating from 1914 to 1929 entailed a much larger research endeavor than simply the work of the National Geographic Society Beam Expeditions of 1923, 1928, and 1929. First, Clark Wissler and the American Museum of Natural History played the critical role in the early development of archaeological tree-ring dating. Wissler made initial contact with Douglass in 1914 to suggest applying his research to archaeological sites, he induced archaeologists to submit samples from their excavations, and he instigated a number of professional collaborations between archaeologists and Douglass, including the one involving Neil Judd, the National Geographic Society, and Douglass. Second, critically important beam-collecting trips, which rightfully should be designated "Beam Expeditions," occurred in 1926, 1927, 1928, and 1929 and set the stage for the successes achieved by the last two official Beam Expeditions of 1928 and 1929. Third, Lyndon Hargrave should be regarded as the unsung archaeologist-hero and "invisible technician" in the development of archaeological tree-ring dating. He perhaps also is a victim of the "Matthew Effect" (Restivo 1994:7), in which "greater increments of recognition . . . accrue to scientists with established reputations," who in this case were Douglass and Judd. Fourth, the Museum of Northern Arizona was not a participant in the effort to bridge the gap until 1929, when Colton loaned Hargrave's services and provided the Third Beam Expedition with logistical and administrative support. Fifth, though the discovery of HH-39 at Whipple Ruin on June 22, 1929, is a vastly important event in the history of North American archaeology, the specimen was not recovered, in a strict sense, by Hargrave or Haury and may have been excavated by Judd. Finally, it is clear that the "Legend of HH-39," which simplifies the development of archaeological tree-ring dating to a "eureka" event, obscures a much more interesting research dynamic that was obtained between archaeologists and Douglass over 15 years. Indeed, the ebb and flow of this research, the accomplishments and set-backs, and the personalities involved make a strong case that the process of developing archaeological tree-ring dating may be as interesting as the product.

Clark Wissler remained at the American Museum of Natural History for the remainder of his career, serving as president of that institution from 1937 to 1943 (see Mandelbaum 1948; Murdock 1948; Nelson 1948). He did not materially contribute to the development of archaeo-logical tree-ring dating after enlisting Judd's assistance in the project, though he continued his correspondence with Douglass and other den-drochronologists well into the 1940s. He died in 1947.

Neil Judd became a recognized leader in southwestern archaeology and over the years published many books and articles, including a sur-prising number of obituaries. His desire for perfection in printed matter apparently kept his bibliography shorter than his colleagues had hoped, however (Wedel 1978). Judd maintained an extensive correspondence with Douglass, Haury, Gladwin, Kidder, and others until his death fol-lowing surgery in 1976 (Brew 1978; Wedel 1978).

Tree-Ring Dating
at the University
of Arizona,
1929–1945

The eloquence of passing time.
POI DOG PONDERING, 1992

Archaeological tree-ring research at the University of Arizona after 1929 was no longer focused on establishing the veracity of archaeological tree-ring dating as a technique (Figure 17). Instead, it blossomed into a multifaceted if somewhat oblique effort to extend the dated chronology back in time; to train promising students in archaeological tree-ring dating; to test the crossdating qualities of additional tree species, especially pinyon and juniper; and to apply tree-ring dating to archaeological problems in other parts of North America and, to a lesser extent, the rest of the world. In the fall of 1929, Douglass, who was fast approaching retirement age, was grooming Haury to be his successor in the archaeological aspect of tree-ring dating. Haury's 1930 departure from the University of Arizona to become assistant director of the Gila Pueblo Archaeological Foundation in Globe, Arizona, left Douglass with a significant void in his archaeological research program and essentially stifled archaeological tree-ring research out of Tucson for a couple of years until another student could be trained to Haury's level of expertise. Table 3 provides a chronology.

The Departure of Emil Haury

The professional relationship between Harold Sterling Gladwin, founder and director of the Gila Pueblo Archaeological Foundation, and Douglass began in April 1926, when Gladwin was honorary curator of archaeology at the Southwest Museum in Highland Park, California. Gladwin had planned to conduct an archaeological survey of Sycamore and Beaver Creeks along the Verde River in north-central Arizona, and he wrote

69

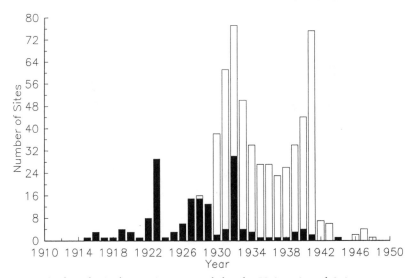

FIGURE 17. Archaeological tree-ring research by the University of Arizona 1915–
1944. Clear bars indicate the sum of sites sampled (prior to 1929) and dated
(after 1929) by all institutions active in southwestern archaeological tree-ring
research; shaded bars indicate activity by the University of Arizona. Note the
shaded-bar peaks of 1923, 1928, and 1929, resulting from the sampling activity of the Beam Expeditions, as well as peaks in 1927, resulting from sampling
conducted by Douglass and his nephew, and 1932, resulting from Harry T.
Getty's work for the National Park Service at Mesa Verde. The clear bars illus-
trate the burst of sampling activity after Douglass bridged the gap in 1929 and
the precipitous decline in sampling activity after 1940.

Douglass to ask if he could be "of any assistance to you in procuring old
trees or beams from ruins in order to further your work in dating the
ruins of the Southwest" (April 28, 1926). In a handwritten note on
Gladwin's letter, Douglass indicates that he would be pleased to have
such samples, and he suggests that Gladwin submit cores as well as cross-
sections, because all samples were potentially valuable in the analysis. It
is not clear whether Douglass ever formally replied to Gladwin, however,
for Gladwin did not submit any specimens as a result of this fieldwork.
There is no subsequent recorded contact between the two men until
preparations were being made for the Third Beam Expedition in 1929.
After that, the next recorded contact came in the spring of 1930 when
Douglass taught his first formal course on tree-ring dating.

    Douglass had planned to employ Haury as his assistant for archaeo-
logical dating, a task that "would keep a good assistant busy for ten
years." In late August 1929, Douglass reported to the National

TABLE 3. Timeline: Archaeological Tree-Ring Research at the University of Arizona after 1929.

1927	Summer: Earl Morris collects many samples from Basketmaker III–Pueblo I sites in Canyon de Chelly and Canyon del Muerto, New Mexico.
1929	Fall: Haury verifies Douglass's tree-ring chronology.
1929	October 24: Morris excavates specimen M200 at Site 33 in Mancos/La Plata area of Southwestern Colorado.
1930	May: Douglass and Morris begin intensive effort to extend tree-ring chronology before A.D. 643.
	May 29: Haury accepts Gladwin's offer and soon leaves the University of Arizona to become assistant director of Gila Pueblo Archaeological Foundation in Globe, Arizona.
1931	Douglass examines Morris's specimen M200.
	Haury and Hargrave publish results of the Third Beam Expedition in *Recently Dated Pueblo Ruins in Arizona*.
	Morris submits samples from Site 33, Obelisk, Broken Flute Cave, Mummy Cave, and other sites.
1932, 1933	Harry T. Getty gathers myriad samples from Mesa Verde National Park.
1935	Douglass and Morris succeed in extending the Central Pueblo Chronology to A.D. 11.
	Douglass publishes dendrochronological results of the Third Beam Expedition in *Dating Pueblo Bonito and Other Ruins of the Southwest*.
1936	Douglass and Morris publish results of their effort to extend the Central Pueblo Chronology in "The Central Pueblo Chronology" and "Archaeological Background of Dates in Early Arizona Chronology," respectively.
1937	Laboratory of Tree-Ring Research is formally incorporated at the University of Arizona.

Geographic Society that Haury was working on the several thousand charcoal specimens collected by the Third Beam Expedition and that his efforts were directed at resolving basic theoretical and methodological issues associated with archaeological tree-ring dating. Specifically, Haury considered the analytically variant nature of cutting versus noncutting dates; he explored the troubling problems of sample depth and sample replication in an effort to determine exactly how many specimens are necessary for a chronology to be considered reliable; he developed new techniques to aid in ring measurement and photography; and he conducted the first systematic analysis of the crossdating qualities in pinyon pine specimens, at which he ultimately was successful (Haury 1930).

During this highly productive period in the fall of 1929, and before publication of Douglass's contribution in *National Geographic*, Douglass also verified the crossdating in his prehistoric chronology surreptitiously: without letting Haury know of his intent, Douglass assigned him a series of specimens that, if crossdated correctly, would reconstruct the very chronology that Douglass had spent the previous 15 years establishing. Haury correctly crossdated the specimens and reconstructed the chronology in short order. Douglass thereby obtained the independent test and verification of the tree-ring chronology that he needed in order to feel comfortable before publishing his results (Douglass 1935a:39–401; Thompson 1995:646).

Although the bulk of the correspondence between Judd and Douglass in the fall of 1929 concerned the publication of their Beam Expedition results, Judd also expressed concern over the future of archaeological tree-ring studies and in so doing offered Douglass his endorsement of Haury. He inquired whether Douglass had money to retain Haury past the termination date of his current NGS-funded appointment, set to expire in December 1929. Just as Judd presupposed with Hargrave, he assumed Haury's continued interest in archaeological tree-ring research: "I'm assuming that his interest will grow rather than decrease; [and] that you have no better prospect in sight" (September 22, 1929). On Judd's advice, Douglass wrote directly to Grosvenor for funds to keep Haury on the project, arguing that to do so would allow Haury to verify Douglass's results and therefore provide complete assurance that their site dating was correct. Douglass stressed the importance of consistency and experience in tree-ring dating. Haury, he told Grosvenor, "is trained as the only other person aside myself who can do the dating" (October 28, 1929). This was no small endorsement from a man who was not long in praise.

In late October, Douglass wrote Morris on a variety of topics, including his desire to return to climatic tree-ring studies. He noted that he was going to offer a class on tree-ring dating the following semester, hoping to attract three to six students. The actual number of students officially enrolled in Astronomy 211, "Tree-Ring Interpretation," was 15, including one student who audited the class from off-campus. The opening-day class attendance sheet includes the signatures of fourteen students, four of whom (marked by asterisks) would spend much of the next decade engaged in archaeological tree-ring dating:

Cornelius Dierking	Oliver Knutson
Florence Hawley*	Loyde Knutson
Marie Gunst	Donald Blackmon
Charles Wisdom	Waldo Wedel
Murel Hanna	Clara Lee Fraps
E. W. Haury*	J. C. McGregor*
Della Russell	William Stallings*

The auditing student, noticeably absent from the list, was Gladwin, who made the 3.5-hour automobile journey from Globe to Tucson every Tuesday to audit the course with his wife, Winifred, and their secretary, Edith Sangster. Their names do not appear on the opening-day roster because they were in California on business.

As we shall see, Gladwin and Douglass had their professional differences over the next two decades, due, at least in part, to Gladwin's inability to crossdate tree-rings using the Douglass method (Gladwin 1940a:1). His inability led to a categorical rejection of, and lack of faith in, tree-ring dates produced by the Douglass school. Though there are many reasons for Gladwin's dendrochronological contentiousness, part of the problem certainly stems from the fact that he missed at least the first two classes of the semester and then never successfully completed the course (Thompson 1995:646). It appears, then, that Gladwin may never have seriously attempted to learn the Douglass method of tree-ring dating and that his attacks constitute a somewhat less-than-informed critique. Instead of taking responsibility for his own poor attendance record, he attacked Douglass's mode of analysis and its practitioners. Nevertheless, Gladwin and Gila Pueblo supported a great deal of archaeological tree-ring research over the years, and their contributions in this regard should not be overlooked.

In mid-November 1929, Gladwin, on behalf of Gila Pueblo, made Douglass an offer to "take over Haury and his salary and . . . make it possible for him to continue his tree-ring work." At the time, Douglass thought this a sound proposition, especially since many economic markets were in free-fall and the future funding situation in Tucson was tenuous at best. Judd, never failing to lose focus on his own research, rejected the proposed arrangement because he felt that since Haury had been doing work for the National Geographic Society, he should continue to be paid with NGS funds until they were no longer to be had. Gila Pueblo remained flexible in its scheduling and decided to wait until

Haury's services were available. Douglass later conveyed to Judd the details of an unmatchable invitation extended by Gila Pueblo: "They are offering Haury a position there at any time he is ready to take it up at a substantial advance in salary, and entire freedom, for the present anyway, as to whether he works with me over there. His line of work will be the application of tree-ring studies to archaeology" (November 27, 1929).

Gladwin's first written offer to Haury came in a letter dated December 16, 1929: "After talking to Dr. Douglass when he was here [in Globe] the other day I wanted to write to you to make you a definite offer which you may use in giving our proposal consideration. In joining our staff you would be entirely free to pursue your chosen line of research and we will furnish every facility within our power. We will, of course, publish any reports which you may prepare. Your salary, for the first year, would be $250 per month with your house in addition. It is our sincere hope that you will join us."

Haury wrote Gladwin on December 18, 1929, thanked him for the offer, and postponed any decision. He reminded Gladwin that he was committed to work with Douglass in Tucson for another two to three months. Gladwin replied that he did not need an immediate answer; in the meantime, Douglass mulled over Gladwin's proposal. By the end of January and in the face of funding cuts from NGS, Douglass concluded that Gladwin's offer to "take Haury on [and] keep the archaeological aspect going" amounted to "a great kindness" tendered by Gila Pueblo.

The matter of Gila Pueblo's proposal to Haury was again dropped until May 10, 1930, when Gladwin wrote to Douglass and told him that Gila Pueblo was willing to pay Haury $3,000 per year. He assured Douglass that Haury would be free to work under Douglass's direction in tree-ring analysis and interpretation as long as the work applied to southwestern archaeology. Gila Pueblo's schedule was becoming less flexible, however, and this time Gladwin stipulated that Haury had to make a decision by July 1, 1930. Gladwin suggested that the three of them meet to finalize Haury's research agenda, and he guaranteed that Haury's research would be published by Gila Pueblo in the Medallion Paper series. Perhaps more important from Haury's perspective, Gila Pueblo offered to fund his graduate studies at Harvard to the tune of $125 per month, or half his usual salary.

The Gila Pueblo offer must have seemed too good to be true. The Great Depression had just begun, and prospects of employment at the University of Arizona were dubious at best (Martin 1960). By May 16,

1930, Haury's departure for Gila Pueblo was a foregone conclusion. National Geographic Society funding for tree-ring research was depleted, and Douglass had no additional prospects for archaeological tree-ring analysis. Haury told Gladwin that he wanted to spend one year at Gila Pueblo, then two years at Harvard working on his Ph.D., after which time he would "consider it an obligation and privilege to spend at least three years at [Gila Pueblo], in return for the grant."

Haury accepted Gladwin's offer by telegram on May 29, 1930, and though the arrangement was paved with good intentions, it is clear that sentiments had somehow soured between Douglass and Gladwin and that there was potential for permanent damage to relations if the interested parties did not remain sensitive to each other's goals. Correspondence indicates that Kidder acted as a mediator between Douglass and Gladwin; he also contacted Haury for information regarding the strain in relations.

On May 26, when it was clear that Haury would accept the Gila Pueblo offer, Douglass asked Kidder if he knew of a student who could replace Haury, adding that he thought Haury might have left because he was not guaranteed fieldwork opportunities for the summer. Three days later, Douglass wrote Kidder that Gladwin's "plan would deprive me of a reliable and relatively experienced and promising assistant." He lamented the fact that Gila Pueblo's planned use of Haury would restrict him to applied archaeological problems rather than allowing him to become a generalized "student of the . . . tree-ring problem in its archaeological phase" as he would if he stayed at the University of Arizona. Unknown to Douglass, however, Haury had already decided on his own that he did not want to spend his life looking through a microscope at tree-rings (Thompson 1995:646).

In early June 1930, Kidder tried to point out the positive aspects of the new arrangement to Haury, who obviously had much to gain:

> There is no question as to the importance of tree-ring work, nor of its close connection to archaeology, but it is not a thing which, with your present fine start, you are likely to neglect, and I think the end results should be best if you work for the archaeological rather than the meteorological end, the latter process would probably be inevitable were you to be associated directly with Dr. Douglass. . . . Furthermore, I understand that Mr. Gladwin's proposition allows you to come to Cambridge, and this I consider of first importance. (June 3, 1930)

Trying to placate Douglass, Kidder wrote, "Gladwin is at times quixotic but I have always found him thoroughly sound at bottom, and I

feel sure that he wishes to do everything in his power to advance archaeological science irrespective of his own personal plans" (June 3, 1930).
As we shall see in Chapters 4 and 5, it appears that Kidder erred in this
assessment of his old friend. Indeed, signs of Gladwin's dendrochronological ambition and challenges to Douglass's authority and proprietor-
ship of tree-ring dating were becoming evident as early as June 5, 1930.
Gladwin wrote to Haury seeking clarification of his research plans:

> I should like, of course, to pave the way towards carrying back the
> early [tree-ring] dating, but find it difficult to make plans until I know
> the future of your relations with Dr. Douglass, and, also, to what
> extent you will be guided by his direction. It seems to me that, if you
> are going to work in an intimate relation with Dr. Douglass, part, at
> least, of your summer will be spent with Earl Morris. He is now off on
> a trip with [Charles] Bernheimer and will not return until the first of
> July, after which time he will be up in the Mancos–La Plata country,
> [Colorado]. On the other hand, if you are going to work independently
> of Dr. Douglass, you might feel more inclined to penetrate a new area,
> such as Sagi [Tsegi], [or] the Grand Gulch country of southeast Utah,
> in search of early beams. As you know, I do not want to pin you down
> to tree-ring work, but if we are not going to work in close relationship
> with Dr. Douglass, it is going to be necessary for us to build up our
> own fundamental series.

In attempting to facilitate the development of Douglass's tree-ring
chronology before A.D. 700, Gladwin tried to co-opt Douglass's primary
dendroarchaeological research goal. Douglass first communicated this
goal to Morris on September 19, 1929, and Nusbaum on April 29,
1930. Nevertheless, it appears that Douglass gave at least tacit approval
to Gila Pueblo's work on this problem in a letter to Gladwin dated May
15, 1930, in which he outlined tentative work schedules for the future.

On June 18, 1930, Emil W. Haury arrived at the Gila Pueblo field
camp at Tusayan Ruin near Navajo Point at Grand Canyon National
Park. Gladwin wrote Douglass that "it is a great relief to know that you
harbour no resentment over [Haury's] decision to join the staff of Gila
Pueblo." Years later, Haury explained his decision:

> I had four options [continue teaching his peers at Arizona, con-
> tinue working on tree rings with Douglass, take a job at the United
> States National Museum, or take the job with Gila Pueblo]. I wasn't
> ready to teach, I had had enough of squinting through a microscope
> to look at tree rings to tell me that that's not going to be my life's
> work, and I didn't quite cotton to the idea of going east into a different

environment, so I looked at the old Gila Pueblo. And Dr. Douglass told me, since he had worked with the astronomer Percival Lowell, at Flagstaff, who was a monied man and put up the observatory there, that when you are working for a private outfit be prepared for certain kinds of difficulties and trouble. You have no recourse. You are subject to the whims of those individuals. (February 27, 1983, Interview Transcript, p. 7, Arizona State Museum Archives)

Douglass's words proved prophetic.

EARL MORRIS AND CHRONOLOGY EXTENSION

Earl Morris had been a collaborator in Douglass's tree-ring research since 1916, longer than any other anthropologist except Wissler. He was a great admirer of Douglass's work and many years later recounted Douglass's first visit to Aztec Ruin: "I had a good sized stack of timbers too short for re-use [in the restoration of Aztec Ruin]. I turned [Douglass] loose on that woodpile and he was busy as a beaver all day. That evening, by lantern light in my small room in the ruin, he spread out samplings he had taken and explained how he was building up a sequence of over-lapping tree-ring patterns. I could see he was working on something big, and from that day I became an ardent collector of wood" (quoted in Kidder 1957:393; see also Lister and Lister 1968:40, 156). Whether this passage contains the sort of poetic license found in the "Legend of HH-39" does not matter; it is clear that Morris was in awe of Douglass's work. Morris made significant contributions to the development of archaeological tree-ring dating throughout his career by supplying Douglass with huge quantities of high-quality specimens. Morris's feelings regarding the importance of Douglass's work never changed. Indeed, just before his death, Morris reflected on his contribution to archaeological tree-ring dating in a letter to Haury: "Although I served only as a gatherer of material, I feel that what I did toward the making, the building of the chronology possibly constitutes my most important contribution to southwestern archaeology" (April 25, 1956; quoted in Lister and Lister 1968:174). This is no small statement from a man who greatly advanced the identification and delineation of Anasazi culture history in the American Southwest.

Despite Morris's many contributions to the development of archaeological tree-ring dating, when it came to learning the results of Douglass's research in 1929, he was treated no differently than a member of the general public. National Geographic Society restrictions against the prepublication release of results prevented Douglass from giving the dates to even his closest professional colleagues, including Morris and Kidder. They had to wait until Douglass's article appeared in the December 1929 issue of *National Geographic* to learn the fruits of his labor. It is well that Morris understood the situation and did not become bitter, for he kept supplying Douglass with wood specimens in the months and years to come: in July 1929, he sent samples from Grand Gulch, Utah; in October of that year, he sent Douglass a spectacular sample, dubbed M200, from a kiva in Site 33 in Mancos Canyon, Colorado. Two years later M200 assumed a critical role in the effort to extend the Central Pueblo tree-ring chronology back before A.D. 700.

On October 27, 1929, Morris wrote Douglass that "the closing of the gap has me nearly rabid with curiosity" and offered his congratulations: "Profoundly I congratulate you on the accomplishment and look forward to the date of its announcement to the world. My every effort will be spent to see that material is gathered to carry the sequence back to post-Basketmaker," a period roughly coeval with Basketmaker III in the Pecos Classification, which Morris did not endorse. Morris also considered alternative means for obtaining Douglass's as yet unpublished dates: "I shall do my best to worm the gap dates out of Judd, but I fear it will be much like trying to elicit information from the Sphinx." Douglass lamented the fact that the proprietary nature of his relationship with the National Geographic Society required him to keep results from Morris: "The one thing which has seemed wrong to me about this dating business is that I did not have you nearby to talk it over, for you deserve it first of all. If I had been running this show you would have known but this has been a game in which I have been under obligations to cooperate. You talk with Judd [to obtain the dates in advance of publication] when you get to Washington" (October 31, 1929).

Approximately three weeks later, at about the time *National Geographic* was to be released, Judd succumbed to their pressure and released the dates to Kidder and Morris. The date list caught Morris by surprise, for the unexpectedly late dates for southwestern sites suggested a much shorter period of occupation and a much more rapid rate of cultural change than had previously been imagined. He wrote Douglass: "[I am] disappointed to find that [the dates] fall so late. . . . It simply means that in the potent ferment of the Great [Pueblo] Period [roughly Pueblo III in the Pecos Classification], change took place much faster than we expected." Morris also revealed his biases with regard to his beloved Basketmaker sites: "I do hope the earlier periods will not prove to commensurately shortened, else it would be hard to crowd the post-

Basketmaker [roughly Basketmaker III in the Pecos Classification] into the B.C.s" (November 22, 1929).

Douglass's discomfort with NGS's behavior with regard to release of the dates was severe enough that by September 1929 he had already made overtures to Morris for his continued support in the effort to extend the tree-ring chronology back from the current beginning date of A.D. 643. Douglass wrote: "I remember very well the matter we were speaking of out at Jeddito. The decks will soon be cleared for making an extension of the prehistoric series now [made] happily historic. . . . I would like exceedingly to see enough material to carry dating back into the B.C.s" (September 29, 1929). Douglass confided to Morris his desire to find alternative funding for additional tree-ring work: "I am very anxious to feel behind this work the support of a scientific institution rather than a popular one." Douglass's desire was sincere, for he subsequently sought funding from the Carnegie Institution, Morris's employer, and although his continuing relationship with Judd and NGS was not evidently chilled, it focused purely on the full publication of the Beam Expedition results, not on new dating applications.

Morris wrote Douglass on April 10, 1930, inquiring about the plans they had made the previous winter for chronology extension to earlier periods. Morris was going to be in the Carrizo and Lukachukai mountain ranges of Arizona–New Mexico as director of the Eighth Bernheimer Expedition and would therefore be sending new specimens. He subsequently submitted samples from Broken Flute Cave in Canyon del Muerto as well as sites in the Lukachukai Mountains (see Figure 18).

One year later, in June 1931, Morris repeated his inquiry regarding their plans for chronology extension, noting that he was beginning to work on his report on the archaeology of the La Plata–Mancos district (Morris 1939), focusing on the Basketmaker III and Pueblo I periods. He wanted any dates or relative chronologic information that Douglass could provide. In closing, he noted that he would like to make plans for a "Beam Expedition" into the La Plata country to search for old specimens. Douglass responded briefly on March 6, saying that he would work on the samples soon and requesting that Morris not fail to collect samples the coming summer.

It is at this point that the interdisciplinary dynamic between archaeologist and dendrochronologist becomes most interesting, complex, and confusing, as Morris and Douglass convey their understandings, relate their misgivings, clarify their questions, and negotiate solutions in the

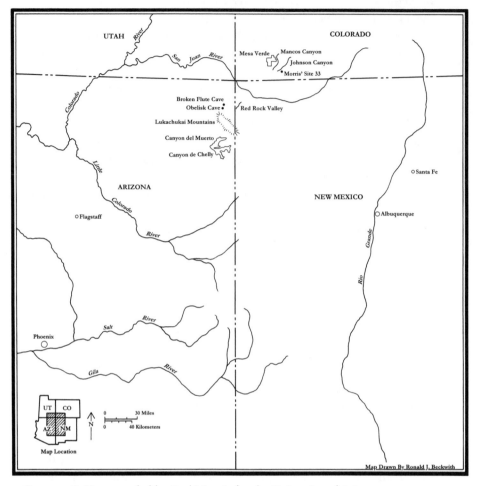

FIGURE 18. Sites sampled by Earl Morris for the University of Arizona, 1920–1945.

effort to extend the tree-ring chronology back to the beginning of the common era. In retrospect, we can be thankful that Morris and Douglass lived in different cities and communicated through the post, for the intriguing dynamic in which they were engaged almost certainly would not have been recorded in detail had they conversed face-to-face.

Research into the earliest portion of the Central Pueblo Chronology (CPC) actually began in October and November 1927. At that time, Morris visited Canyon de Chelly and Canyon del Muerto in northeastern Arizona specifically to collect beam specimens for Douglass (Morris

1927). In a progress report to Douglass on October 27, 1927, Morris stated:

> Mummy Cave should yield 25 specimens. [Jean] Jeançon [and the First Beam Expedition in 1923] sectioned only the beams in the first story. Sliding Ruin should produce quite a few [specimens]. . . . I do not plan to make much of a search for timbers of post-Basketmaker [i.e., Pueblo I] age this time. The work of getting those that fall within the Pueblo horizons ends sooner than I expect, this because I am in a hurry owing to some digging I must do at Aztec [Ruin] after my return. . . . I am anxious to have your impression as to the burned post-Basketmaker timbers I sent in from the La Plata [region of southwest Colorado]. . . . I am sure I could get funds to do [the research] were there a reasonable prospect of determining thereby the time relation of the post-Basketmakers to the Great Pueblo periods.

By November 6, Morris had secured 185 tree-ring specimens, about half of which were assigned, on the basis of associated archaeological evidence, to his post-Basketmaker period (roughly Basketmaker III in the Pecos Classification) and half pre-Pueblo (roughly Pueblo I).

At a minimum, Morris in 1927 collected samples from White House Pueblo and Sliding Ruin in Canyon de Chelly and from Mummy Cave, Cave 1, and architectural features in the Mummy Cave talus pile in Canyon del Muerto. He considered the Mummy Cave talus pile materials critical to his effort because they came from a post-Basketmaker (i.e., Basketmaker III) occupation and should, on the basis of his archaeological analyses, crossdate with the post-Basketmaker sites he had been excavating in the La Plata district of Colorado (Morris 1939). He related the exciting implications should these sites be dated: "Could the time count be carried back definitely from RD [the relatively dated tree-ring chronology] as exemplified by Pueblo Bonito, to Basketmaker III, the fact would constitute the most monumental contribution to southwestern archaeology that has ever been made. And then when RD is tied onto the modern series of known age. Well, that would be almost too ideal to fall within the range of human experience" (December 18, 1927).

The ring sequence in specimens from the room located in the Mummy Cave talus pile gave Douglass a new undated chronology, which he called Early Pueblo Dating (EPD), as well as a second undated sequence that he referred to as Old Pueblo Dating (OPD). Douglass thought the OPD sequence might soon join onto either the EPD sequence or the later Chaco Canyon/Pueblo Bonito (i.e., Central Pueblo) sequence, and indeed OPD is never referred to after 1927.

In September and October 1929, Earl Morris led the Seventh Charles Bernheimer Expedition to the region between the Mancos and La Plata Rivers of southwestern Colorado. The expedition excavated a "huge transitional Basketmaker III–Pueblo I site south of Mancos Canyon directly opposite Mesa Verde. [The site] has a slab lined kiva 63 ft in diameter" (Morris 1929). The site was designated "Site 33," and the Great Kiva yielded a well-preserved pilaster that Morris packaged in plaster, labeled M200, and shipped to Douglass on October 24, 1929. Douglass did not have an opportunity to examine the specimen until 1931.

When Douglass finally examined M200, he discovered it possessed a beautiful 356-year, climatically sensitive ring record. He immediately recognized that the sequence did not fit in his Central Pueblo Chronology, the earliest portion of which was dated to A.D. 643. Douglass intoned the then archaeologically prevalent notion that cultural lag might be confusing the attempts to find early specimens: "Pueblo I in [the] Flagstaff area could easily be of the time of Pueblo II at Chaco." The dominant culture history paradigm in southwestern archaeology at the time used the notions of culture area and diffusion to explain differences visible in the archaeological record; Douglass's (1929) tree-ring chronology simply made such assertions testable by allowing calendar dates to be assigned to the sites in question. Thus, prehistoric relationships could be calibrated.

On the basis of the archaeological evidence, Morris felt that the M200 sequence should fall later than the Mummy Cave (EPD) dating. Morris wrote Judd: "I should be very much surprised if [M200] proved to be as old as the material from the slope of Mummy Cave. . . . It would be not at all a matter of surprise to me if the oldest timbers that we will eventually be able to secure were cut sometimes [sic] previous to the beginning of the Christian era" (June 5, 1931). To rectify the situation, Morris sent Douglass another four boxes of specimens from Site 33 that he thought, on the basis of archaeological evidence, were more likely to crossdate with materials from Cave 1 and the Mummy Cave talus room from Canyon del Muerto.

On July 7, 1931, Douglass reviewed these developments for Kidder:

> I talked a great deal about further specimens from talus at Mummy Cave with Earl Morris and strongly urged the advantage of further collections at that point if possible. I now have three large charcoal sections from Basketmaker III ruins between La Plata and Johnson Canyons. I have not been able to crossdate them with Chaco material as yet, but I am not sure that cross-dating is excluded. . . . I have two

chronologies [EPD and OPD] of 130 and 155 years from the Mummy Cave talus and they look very promising for the building of a very long chronology to a very early date.

Later in 1931, Morris submitted an additional 64 specimens, probably from Obelisk and Broken Flute Caves in Red Rock Valley, which represented the final installment in the summer's tree-ring collections. He again tried to clarify his interpretation of the archaeological evidence and its meaning with regard to the Canyon del Muerto tree-ring dating. Morris reasoned that the cists found in the Mummy Cave talus pile should be oldest, that the "pre-Kiva" in Cave 1 should be next oldest, and that the large room in the Mummy Cave talus should be the most recent, though he admitted that the latter two might in fact be contemporaneous. In addition, he warned Douglass that prehistoric beam reuse might confuse their interpretations of the tree-ring data (October 26, 1931).

One week later, Kidder asked Douglass if he had had any success with Morris's Pueblo I specimens, for "my tongue is hanging out with excitement about that stuff" (November 2, 1931). Douglass had by that time succeeded in joining the EPD and OPD sequences into one 300-year chronology, now referred to as the Early Pueblo Dating, but he still could not join that sequence with the M200 sequence.

In a progress report to Morris dated November 10, 1931, Douglass introduced a third high-quality tree-ring sequence, referred to as "179D." This specimen was collected by Morris in 1927 in Johnson Canyon and had a 300-year sequence independent of the Canyon del Muerto EPD dating. The 179D sequence crossdated with a portion of the M200 sequence, however, though neither 179D nor M200 crossdated with the dated tree-ring chronology.

Douglass asked Morris for additional comments regarding his understanding of the relationship between the various early undated ring sequences then in hand. Morris replied to this plea for archaeological interpretation on November 14, 1931, with not one but two letters. In the first, he stated that he saw no archaeological reason to place the EPD (Mummy Cave Basketmaker) sequence earlier than the 179D (Johnson Canyon Basketmaker) sequence and reasserted that the M200 (Site 33 Mancos) specimen came from a transitional Basketmaker III–Pueblo I context in the Mesa Verde region. On reflection, however, Morris related in the second letter that to get to the Mummy Cave talus room, he had dug through Pueblo II period sherds and not Pueblo I sherds, and that the EPD tree-ring sequence might therefore fall archaeologically later than he had originally suspected. He suggested that

Douglass try crossdating the EPD with the dated Central Pueblo Chronology up to about A.D. 1000. He then expressed his concern with the implications of such a late dating: "While I hope it is not so, because I would prefer to see the life cycle of Southwestern culture lengthened rather than shortened, there may be a chance that EPD will fall into Pueblo II or the Pueblo I–Pueblo II transition."

The dendrochronological situation in 1931 was therefore analogous to that of 1927. Douglass and Morris had two undated "floating" chronologies (composed roughly of the EPD and OPD and the M200 and 179D sequences, respectively) whose relationship had to be determined on the basis of archaeological evidence. They suspected that Gap 1 fell between the EPD sequence and the 179D sequence and therefore would be represented by sites occupied between Morris's Basketmaker (ca. Basketmaker II in the Pecos Classification) and Post-Basketmaker (ca. Basketmaker III) sites. Similarly, Gap 2 was indicated between the Johnson Canyon (M200 and 179D; ca. Pueblo I) sequence and Douglass's dated (CPC) tree-ring chronology.

Douglas acknowledged that he was willing to acquiesce to Morris's interpretation of the archaeological evidence one week later: "If you say that archaeologically the EPDs from the [Mummy Cave] talus room are subsequent to the 179DS and the JCDS [M200] from Johnson Canyon, then it must be so" (November 21, 1931). He also requested a map of the Four Corners region to try to make spatial sense out of a temporal problem, in the process again invoking cultural lag as an explanatory device.

Douglass and Morris thus faced an extremely difficult task in the fall and early winter of 1931. They had a series of archaeologically contemporaneous, nearly contemporaneous, and temporally differentiated sites with tree-ring sequences that did not crossdate among themselves as well as they expected, especially in light of Morris's archaeological assessments. They could not return to the field to gather more data and were therefore forced to thresh the archaeological and dendrochronological nuances in geographically separate laboratories: Douglass was in Tucson, and Morris commuted between Boulder, Colorado, and Washington, D.C. Other archaeologists, including Kidder and Judd, were consulted during this time, but as of late November 1931, Morris and Douglass were "passing the buck" to each other, neither one willing to declare that his evidence was definitive.

On December 1, 1931, Morris reiterated the argument made in his second letter of November 14, suggesting that Douglass not take too seriously his original assessment that the EPD should necessarily fall later than the 179D sequence, as he argued in his first November 14 letter. In retrospect, the problem was one of conflicting levels of resolution in their respective data sets. Douglass was trying to construct an annually precise, accurately crossdated tree-ring chronology while using as a guide Morris's archaeological evidence and interpretations that, almost by definition, cannot be resolved to a level of resolution finer than one or two human generations (see Baillie 1995). This is not to say that it is impossible to infer more refined temporal relationships on the basis of archaeological assessments, only that Morris's stratigraphic, ceramic, and architectural evidence could not be so resolved.

In January 1932, Douglass examined the specimens collected by Morris in Broken Flute and Obelisk Caves in Red Rock Valley in 1930 and 1931. Morris assured Douglass that the occupation of these Basketmaker III caves was contemporaneous, with a possibility that Obelisk Cave fell slightly earlier. He noted that both should nevertheless date earlier than the M200 sequence. On January 7, 1932, Douglass announced a breakthrough of sorts. Waldo S. Glock, Douglass's Carnegie-funded replacement for Haury, discovered crossdating between the Mummy Cave EPD sequence and an undated 450-year Obelisk Cave sequence, thus extending the EPD by about 200 years. He also tentatively suggested that the outer portion of M200 might terminate about A.D. 830. Morris replied the next day that if Glock's crossdating was correct, the occupation of Mummy Cave and the sites he tested in the Carrizo and Lukachukai Mountains would have to date after A.D. 600. He was incredulous: "I would be truly astonished. It would shorten the life cycle of Southwestern culture to an almost incredible degree" (January 8, 1932). Such a shortening of the southwestern chronology, he felt, would require much higher population densities and rapidity of culture change than most archaeologists had been willing to consider before the advent of tree-ring dating.

The spring of 1932 saw no additional progress in the effort to date these many archaeological chronologies, as Douglass focused most of his effort on cycle studies. He was still concerned with the problem of cultural lag, however, and seemed somewhat pleased that he did not have to deal with the interpretive aspect of the problem: "The lag of cultures, while moving from point to point, is going to develop into a line of great interest. It will be the problem of the archaeologists to say what lag may be appropriate in any one region" (Douglass to Morris, July 2, 1932).

During the summer of 1932, Morris collected and submitted to Douglass more than 400 tree-ring samples from a Pueblo I site, a

Basketmaker III site, and two Pueblo III sites in Canyon del Muerto and Johnson Canyon. He devoted special attention in October to finding sites transitional between Pueblo I and Pueblo II, sites that would therefore fill the gap between the Johnson Canyon and Central Pueblo chronologies, but he could not locate any sites that had burned and that would therefore contain preserved charcoal specimens.

Fall 1932 was not a banner season for Douglass and his tree-ring research, for he was forced to resume teaching, at age 65, because the Arizona state legislature felt that research should be eliminated at the university until the end of the depression (Douglass to Kidder, September 30, 1932; Martin 1960). Archaeologists were still appreciative of the work he had done: "I have been so greatly interested in your work and I feel, like all other archaeologists, so vastly indebted to you for having put our researches on so wonderfully sound a basis, that nothing you do is without the keenest interest to me. And I know that Morris feels the same way" (Kidder to Douglass, October 11, 1932).

Douglass renewed his analysis of the undated sequences in January 1933. Morris reiterated his surprise at Douglass's suggestion of an A.D. 830 date for the termination of the JCD dating, though this time he was willing to "alter his notions in accordance" with Douglass's determination, if Douglass was convinced of the dating.

The final undated tree-ring sequence that factors into the development of the Basketmaker chronology was collected by Morris in 1932 at a Pueblo I site near Bennett's Peak in the Lukachukai Mountains. He argued on the basis of archaeological evidence that the site was culturally contemporaneous with the Johnson Canyon Pueblo I sites and that the tree-ring sequence therefore should, in the absence of any cultural lag, crossdate with the JCD sequence (Morris to Douglass, January 16, 1933). Though Morris did not expect to get into the field in the summer of 1933, he did not want to miss a chance to assist Douglass in the quest to extend the chronology. In the loquacious style of correspondence between professionals with mutual respect, Morris wrote: "If at any time your mind fastens upon particular spots in the culture sequence from which you consider it would be especially desirable to secure timber sections, let me know, so that I can be endeavoring to figure out localities from which they might be obtained" (February 17, 1933).

Douglass kept working on crossdating the specimens, trying all possible ring-sequence comparisons and combinations. On March 17, 1933, he reported to Morris:

I have been reviewing with care the EPD and 179D and JCD sequences for the purpose of building a chronology. . . . I read the MLK [Morris's Carrizo-Lukachukai specimens] of 1931 with perfect ease in terms of the JCD sequence, suspected near 830 A.D. You may remember that the JCD ending was about 355 in its own sequence. . . . This would put the EPDs before the JCDs. Obelisk Cave probably gives only EPD. . . . The above in summary favors EPD as preceding 179[D], with a good crossdating, but dependent on a single piece (MLK-211), which, however is a full section of Douglas fir and a very fine record. . . . I have reviewed again the possible connection between JCD and our early Chaco chronology. The dating would put the end of JCD at about 830 A.D.

Morris replied with his usual enthusiasm and willingness to forgo preconceived notions in the face of dendrochronological data:

I am more pleased than I can express at the headway you are making in straightening out the relationships of the EPD, JCD, and MLK series. I shall look forward with pronounced eagerness to your findings after you have examined the material which may clear up the disagreement in the neighborhood of 740–760. . . . The relative dates in which the MLKs and JCDs fall are exactly as they should be. Of course I am surprised that the JCD series comes down to 830. But ideas I am willing to surrender to facts at any time. The source of M200 was beyond question a Pueblo I settlement and [Frank] Roberts's date of 790+ [from a Pueblo I site near Allantown, Arizona] from the same period surely indicates that your 830 correlation is correct. (March 20, 1933)

The Bennett's Peak specimens proved valuable in that they provided supporting evidence that Pueblo I sites, like those in Johnson Canyon, could date as late as A.D. 830. Morris also was not surprised by an A.D. 677 date that Douglass obtained for a Pueblo I site, for he noted that there were a substantial number of Basketmaker III sites in the area and that, as he noted on October 26, 1931, beam reuse was probably common. In a significant shift, Morris's incredulity at the surprisingly late dates gave way to bashful appreciation of Douglass's efforts: "It is tremendously gratifying that so many dates are coming forth. I often feel that those of us whose interest is primarily in archaeology make life a burden for you because of our insistence, and distract your thoughts from the more fundamental problems which are your central interest. If such be the case, I hope that our unending gratitude will to a slight degree balance our indebtedness" (April 5, 1933).

Douglass was soon able to report a tentative solution to the early chronology problem, particularly the Johnson Canyon Dating and the

Early Pueblo Dating. On April 10, he wrote Morris that the crossdating suggested that ring JCD 0 fits at EPD 73 for the calendar year A.D. 875. Thus the EPD sequence was in fact older than the JCD sequence, contrary to Morris's suggestion based on the coarsely resolved archaeological data. Most impressive, however, was that one particularly sensitive specimen from Obelisk Cave offered a reliable ring record back to A.D. 10.

Morris commented on Douglass's findings on April 14, 1933, and again expressed surprise: "The way in which the entire mass of this material is falling into order is of course what I greatly hoped for. But nevertheless it is truly astonishing that you have been able to piece together nature's record for so great a span of years. I had not even surmised from your previous letters that the sequence might be extended back as far as the year 10 A.D." Morris was indeed pleased by the antiquity indicated by the crossdating.

Douglass was now confident enough in the crossdating to inform Kidder that the sequence warranted publication. He made it clear that he wanted the Carnegie Institution to publish the results, for Morris was employed by Carnegie, he had supplied the beams, and Carnegie had recently funded portions of Douglass's research (April 12, 1933). Kidder replied that he too advocated publication and gleefully expressed his excitement: "I am more tickled than I can express at the splendid results you are getting with the early stuff. Isn't the whole thing grand?" (April 25, 1933).

Douglass and Glock spent the next two months strengthening some of the weak points in the EPD–JCD–CPC chronology, especially the period from A.D. 625 to 650. Douglass nevertheless wished for a chance collect additional specimens from Cave 1 and Mummy Cave in Canyon del Muerto, as well as Morris's sites "near Shiprock" (i.e., the Red Rock Valley and Lukachukai sites).

A letter from Morris to Douglass provides additional insights on the appreciation felt for Douglass's work, the confidence most archaeologists had in the results, and their stunning implications:

> The cumulative evidence that tends to fix the upper limit of the [early tree-ring] series is a source of tremendous satisfaction. I shall be extremely glad when you have removed the last doubt in your mind about that lot of timbers, because I feel that it is the most important tie that we will ever have between the late and early phases of the [Basketmaker–Pueblo] cycle. . . . All the way along your actual dating has corresponded perfectly with the relative sequence that has been established by our [i.e., the archaeologists'] angles of approach. Your

findings have shortened the process beyond our expectations, *but they have done nothing but corroborate the order of events.* (June 15, 1933; emphasis added)

The next written contact between Douglass and Morris occurred in October 1934. At that time, Morris sent Douglass another shipment of beams he had collected in the summer of 1934 at sites in Johnson Canyon ruins and the La Plata Valley. Douglass was able to report that one of the specimens, "D-1," gave an excellent record from A.D. 740 to 836. More important, he reported that he was obtaining corroborative evidence for the early portion of the chronology from Basketmaker III specimens from a site near Allantown, Arizona, excavated by Frank Roberts of the Smithsonian Institution between 1931 and 1933.

Later that month, Douglass reported that a pinyon specimen from Allantown, dated by student Carl Miller and verified by Douglass, produced a splendid ring sequence from A.D. 640 to 870, with an especially good sequence around 700. This dating was critical because the turn of the eighth century had been a major weak point in the chronology. Unfortunately, archaeological evidence from the site was confusing, and Douglass again called on Morris's expertise. Apparently, Roberts designated the house from which the pinyon beam was extracted Pueblo I, on the basis of architectural evidence and the presence of Fugitive Red Ware, but also present was some grayware that might be Basketmaker III. Douglass inquired of Morris how such a situation might arise. Morris replied that it was not unusual to have architecture and ceramics characteristic of different Pecos Classification periods together at the same site. Again resorting to the notion of cultural lag, Morris stated that "it would appear that pottery development along the south edge [i.e., at Allantown] of the great northern center did not progress as rapidly as it did in the nuclear portion of the San Juan area" (November 4, 1934).

By March 1935, Douglass was able seriously to consider publication of the chronology before A.D. 700. By that time, he had "complete confirmation" of the chronology from a fine specimen (F3992) recovered by the Museum of Northern Arizona in Medicine Valley northeast of Flagstaff. This specimen contained what Douglass now referred to as the "Johnson Canyon signature" (A.D. 611–620). Interestingly, John McGregor, the Museum of Northern Arizona dendroarchaeologist who dated specimen F3992, apparently, and somewhat surprisingly, did not want to be involved in the publication of the early dates and early chronology, but Douglass was also reluctant to move back into the archaeological dating: "McGregor has told me to publish all these dates over my own name and not attempt to bring him into the dating game. That is good sense, but I do not want to do it beyond the building and verification of long and important chronologies that have a strong climatic value" (Douglass to Morris, March 21, 1935). McGregor's reluctance in this regard is indeed curious, because he had been publishing dates for MNA for some time (McGregor 1930, 1932, 1934; see Chapter 6).

Douglass published "The Central Pueblo Chronology" in 1936, and in the same issue of the *Tree-Ring Bulletin*, Morris offered extensive comments entitled "Archaeological Background of Dates in Early Arizona Chronology." These articles, taken together, provide a detailed, firsthand account of the early extension of the Central Pueblo Chronology. Douglass took pains in his article to emphasize that although the Central Pueblo Chronology extended to A.D. 11, it was now available to date human occupation and construction only from the middle 300s because of poor sample depths in the earlier centuries. He also noted that a unique value of the chronology was the lengthy record of winter rainfall it offered (Douglass 1936:29). Morris and Douglass continued their correspondence throughout the 1940s, exchanging detailed ideas on specific relationships between archaeological and tree-ring data. They maintained sporadic contact in the 1950s, up to the time of Morris's death in 1956 (Lange and Leonard 1985). Douglass mourned: "He was one of the very favorite friends of mine for many years" (letter to Ann Axtell Morris, July 2, 1956).

ARCHAEOLOGICAL TREE-RING RESEARCH AFTER 1929

The extension of the Central Pueblo Chronology was by no means the only task Douglass had on his research agenda after 1929. He expended a great deal of effort attempting to establish archaeological tree-ring dating in other parts of North America and the world, creating exhibits to convey the subtleties of tree-ring dating to an interested public, publishing more fully the results of the beam expeditions (Douglass 1935a), and obtaining permanent financing for a laboratory of tree-ring research.[1]

The ultimately successful attempt to bridge the gap and date archaeological sites in the Southwest was a source of envy among archaeologists working outside the area, and they often submitted samples directly to Douglass or requested information on how to collect and analyze

1. The Laboratory of Tree-Ring Research was formally incorporated at the University of Arizona in 1937 and remains the primary provider of archaeological tree-ring dates in North America.

samples themselves. Donald Brand of the University of New Mexico requested sampling equipment from Douglass for his archaeological survey of northern Chihuahua, Mexico, in 1930. J. Charles Kelly sought advice from Douglass as he attempted to date specimens from southeastern Utah he collected while working with Julian Steward in 1929 and 1930. John Gillen submitted samples from Nine Mile Canyon in Utah. V. Gordon Childe visited Tucson to learn the principles of tree-ring dating in the hope that he could apply the technique to the archaeology of Egypt. M. R. Harrington of the Southwest Museum submitted samples from sites along the Virgin River in Nevada. Harlan Smith of the National Museum of Canada sent samples, as did John Angus of the New York State Archaeological Association. Carl Miller tried to develop a chronology for Colonial National Park in Jamestown, Virginia. Waldo Wedel submitted cedar samples from houses he was excavating along the Republican River in Nebraska, and the ever-collecting Morris provided pine boards from Guatemala. The most significant attempts to establish tree-ring dating outside the Southwest were by Douglass's students Florence Hawley (see Chapter 7) and James Louis Giddings (see Chapter 8) in the American Midwest and Alaska, respectively.

Harry T. Getty of the University of Arizona was hired by the National Park Service to collect and analyze samples from Mesa Verde National Park in 1932 and 1933 (Getty 1935a, 1935b, 1935c). Douglass later solicited funds from the Bureau of American Ethnology, the National Park Service, and the National Geographic Society for dating by Miller and Getty, but the depression kept these institutions from contributing. In 1935, the Carnegie Institution finally provided funding for two assistants, Getty and Gordon C. Baldwin, and Douglass removed himself almost entirely from archaeological dating. As can be seen in Figure 17, few archaeological sites were sampled for dendrochronological purposes by the University of Arizona after Getty's work at Mesa Verde. The bulk of archaeological tree-ring research was now conducted by three of his former students—Haury at Gila Pueblo, McGregor at the Museum of Northern Arizona, and W. Sidney Stallings at the Laboratory of Anthropology in Santa Fe.

CONCLUSION

Douglass's dendrochronological research after 1929 focused on chronology extension, student training, and the extension of tree-ring dating to new regions. Emil Haury independently verified Douglass's chronology and conducted the first detailed analysis of the dating capabilities of pinyon, ultimately concluding that the species could be used for dating purposes (Douglass 1935a:39–41). Through the untiring efforts of Morris and Douglass, the Central Pueblo Chronology was extended to A.D. 11, thus allowing sites from all the Pecos Classification periods to be accurately and precisely dated. Douglass's involvement in archaeological tree-ring research diminished throughout the 1930s, especially after publication of the Central Pueblo Chronology. Dating of archaeological specimens was performed by Douglass's students, though Douglass remained the authority to whom they turned for guidance when considering dendrochronologically difficult questions, such as the dating of Bluff Ruin and other early sites. Douglass died in 1962 (Judd 1962).

CHAPTER 4

Yang and Yin

Harold Gladwin, Emil Haury,
and Tree-Ring Dating at the
Gila Pueblo Archaeological
Foundation

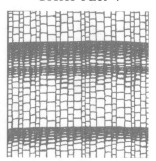

Archaeology . . . is nothing more than applied common sense.
WINIFRED GLADWIN AND HAROLD S. GLADWIN
The Red-on-Buff Culture of the Gila Basin

The Gila Pueblo Archaeological Foundation of Globe, Arizona, began in 1928 as the Medallion Society of Pasadena, California. On April 7, 1930, a trust was established to create and maintain an archaeological research and curatorial facility. Gila Pueblo's iconoclastic and energetic cofounder, director, and trustee, Harold Sterling Gladwin (Figure 19), had been a successful stockbroker on Wall Street from 1908 to 1922, at which time he sold his seat on the exchange and moved west. His first exposure to southwestern archaeology occurred on a camping trip with Kidder in 1924 (Haury and Reid 1985). He worked with Kidder at Pecos from 1925 through 1927, and in 1926 he became acting, or more accurately honorary, curator of archaeology at the Southwest Museum in Highland Park, Los Angeles.

Dendrochronological research at Gila Pueblo began in earnest with Haury's acceptance of employment on May 29, 1930 (Figure 20). Critical examination of Haury's tree-ring work while at Gila Pueblo, and the professional reaction to it, suggests that Gladwin and his institution receive less credit than they deserve for supporting Haury's tree-ring research, both administratively and financially. After Haury's departure for the University of Arizona in 1937, dendrochronological research at Gila Pueblo changed radically in both nature and scope. Although there are many problems with Gila Pueblo's dendrochronological methods and interpretations in the post-Haury era, Gladwin's tree-ring research raised some important questions, and archaeological dendrochronology may have been better off because of his critique. Table 4 provides a chronology of the work done at Gila Pueblo.

FIGURE 19. Harold Sterling Gladwin (1883–1983), founder and director of the Gila Pueblo Archaeological Foundation, Globe, Arizona. Courtesy of the Arizona State Museum.

TABLE 4. Timeline: Archaeological Tree-Ring Research at Gila Pueblo.

1928	Gila Pueblo Archaeological Foundation incorporated.
1930	Haury surveys Sierra Ancha and environs.
1932	Haury excavates Canyon Creek and other ruins in the Sierra Ancha.
1934	Haury publishes the now classic *Canyon Creek Ruin and the Cliff Dwellings of the Sierra Ancha.*
	Gladwin develops a ring-width measuring machine.
1936	Haury and Morris make field trip to Red Rock country.
1937	Haury resigns post at Gila Pueblo, becomes head of the Department of Archaeology, University of Arizona.
1939	Gladwin refuses Haury permission to publish tree-ring dates from White Mound Village.
1940–1941	Deric Nusbaum conducts extensive dendrochronological fieldwork for Gila Pueblo.
1944	Gladwin severs communication with members of the Douglass "school" after prolonged debate on tree-ring dating, dates, and their interpretation.
1950	Gladwin donates Gila Pueblo archaeological collections to the Arizona State Museum.
1957	Gladwin donates Gila Pueblo's dendrochronological collections to the Laboratory of Tree-Ring Research.

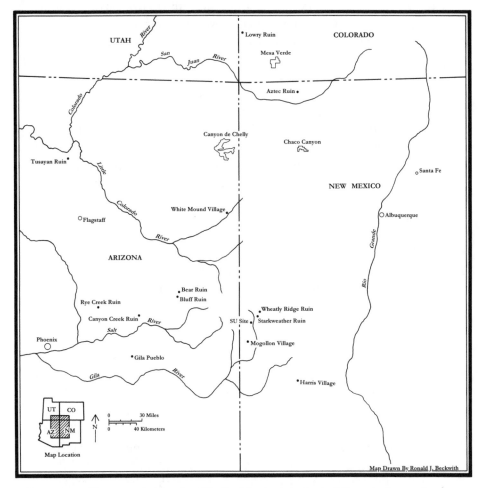

FIGURE 20. Sites sampled by the Gila Pueblo Archaeological Foundation and mentioned in the text.

DENDROCHRONOLOGY UNDER EMIL HAURY, 1930–1937

Although Gladwin's 1930 overtures to Haury included promises that he be able to pursue tree-ring dating in a close working relationship with Douglass, it is clear that Gladwin's own dendrochronological ambitions, if realized, would co-opt Douglass's goals for the next phase of archaeological tree-ring chronology development, that of extending the chronology back before A.D. 700. As Gladwin told Haury, he was especially desirous of "pav[ing] the way towards carrying back the early dating. . . . I do not want to pin you down to tree-ring work, but if we are not going to work in close relationship with Dr. Douglass, it is going to be necessary for us to build up our own fundamental series" (June 5, 1930). Later that summer, Gladwin turned his attention to the application of tree-ring dating south of the Colorado Plateau, an area that, until then, had not enjoyed the benefit of absolute dates. He directed Haury to spend August and September of 1930 conducting a survey of the Mogollon and upper Salt River drainages: "One of the main purposes of [this] work will be the attempt to correlate the tree-ring chronology of the country lying south of the Mogollon Rim with the established Flagstaff series" (Gladwin to Carl Guthe, July 12, 1930). Gladwin had spent several years conducting an exhaustive survey of the southern Arizona deserts (Gladwin and Gladwin 1929a, 1929b, 1930) and therefore hoped to add a temporal dimension to his studies through Haury's tree-ring analyses.

At the end of July 1930, Gladwin reported to Haury that he had obtained a permit to collect beam material on all national parks, monuments, and public domain lands. Though he did not want the permit to change Haury's archaeological plans, he thought it might come as "welcome news" if Haury wanted to take samples while surveying. Gladwin then added a couple of sentences that may have given Haury pause about his new employment situation: "It is such a queer feeling of relaxation to turn the burden of responsibility over to you that I am afraid you will have to grow accustomed to it. . . . Remember always not to take things too hard or too seriously; we shall do ever so much better work if we can keep it a pleasure" (September 3, 1930). Gladwin again tried to define the parameters of their relationship: "My conscience is beginning to prick me and I am wondering if you feel that I have completely deserted you. I hope not but rather that you realize the compliment implied in leaving you to work out your puzzles unmolested." Their work relationship seems to have gelled by late October 1930, when Gladwin admitted that "excavation has no charm for me at all. I don't enjoy it and I get bored very easily. . . . [I] can't express to you what a joy it is to be able to ask you to share so much of our responsibility" (October 19, 1930). Haury probably enjoyed this arrangement, for he was able to undertake fully funded archaeological field research to a degree that remains the envy of many young archaeologists today.

In early fall of 1930, Haury conducted an archaeological and, to a lesser degree, dendrochronological survey of the Sierra Ancha and surrounding vicinity in east-central Arizona, collecting sherds from 140 ruins "that practically date themselves thru pottery" (Haury to Gladwin, October 19, 1930). Surprisingly, however, he encountered more than 20 cliff dwellings, an archaeological phenomenon he had not expected to find so far south. Haury applied to Byron Cummings, chair of the Arizona Archaeological Commission, for a permit to excavate one of the most promising of those cliff dwellings, the Rye Creek Ruin.

Haury was busy at Gila Pueblo during the winter of 1930–1931. Among the more mundane tasks of artifact sorting, cataloging, and tabulation, he tried to determine a suitable dissertation topic, for he was to enroll at Harvard in the fall of 1931. He prepared for publication his contribution to the Third Beam Expedition (Haury and Hargrave 1931) and made plans for fieldwork in the summer of 1931. He dated the many tree-ring specimens he had collected the previous summer at the Sierra Ancha sites, the Tusayan Ruin near the Grand Canyon, and the Gila Pueblo ruin. One immediately pleasing result for Gladwin was Haury's successful dating of the Gila Pueblo ruin, on which the modern facility of Gila Pueblo was built (Haury 1935b). Its 185-year tree-ring record was surprisingly similar to the northern Arizona chronology and therefore demonstrated that sites as far south as Globe, Arizona, could be dendrochronologically dated (Haury to Morris, February 20, 1931).

In these efforts Haury must have been confident and encouraged, for his work was endorsed by powerful figures in southwestern archaeology. With regard to Haury's archaeological dating, Douglass wrote: "I have checked over the ring records from Echo Cliffs 13-1 ruin, which you call Tusayan Ruin, and feel satisfied with a certainty of 9 [out of 10 on Douglass's unpublished and no longer used date-rating system] that your dating is correct. . . . I congratulate you very much on the results which you have obtained in the Sierra Ancha region. By way of putting it on record and in your hands I would state that I find your dating correct on one or more specimens in each of the following ruins: [Arizona] C:1-16, -45, -40, -21, -25, -44, -38, -14, -08, C:2-8 [Canyon Creek Ruin], and Echo Cliffs 13-1 [Tusayan Ruin]" (February 11, 1931).

With regard to the publication of the beam expedition results (Haury and Hargrave 1931), Douglass wrote: "I have just received the Smithsonian Publication No. 3069, 'Recently Dated Pueblo Ruins in Arizona,' autographed by you and Lyndon [Hargrave]. I cannot tell you how much this pleases me, and the fact that you each autographed this copy makes it doubly valuable. It is true I have looked over the manuscript but I shall read this again with a great deal of pleasure, and pride also because I had something to do with it" (September 23, 1931). The predoctoral Haury must have taken great pride in receiving such a compliment from the near-retirement Douglass.

As far as Haury's proposed dissertation at Harvard was concerned, Judd wrote:

> I quite agree with Dr. [Alfred] Tozzer that a subject treating of tree rings and [southwestern] archaeology would prove most instructive and worth while. Dr. Douglass, I believe, has in contemplation an article he mentioned to us in the summer a year ago, "A Key for Archaeologists in the Interpretation of Tree Rings." Whether or not he writes such an article I do not see that it necessarily need interfere with your proposed thesis. For the subject suggested you would have to give attention to the interpretation of tree rings, explain how they are read, what rings can be relied upon, etc., etc. The Douglass chronology has so completely substantiated the deductions of Nelson, Kidder, Morris, Roberts, and others as to the sequence of ceramic types in the sw that your dissertation if built upon these and other observations should quite meet the commendation of the faculty. (January 7, 1931)

Haury decided to reject dendrochronology as a research topic in favor of an analysis of archived artifacts collected by Frank H. Cushing and Frederick W. Hodge on the Hemenway Expeditions of the late 1880s (see Haury 1995). The tree-ring dissertation he had first proposed was not restricted to a detailed analysis of the technique itself, however, or to the development of a key for interpreting dates. He was interested in considering "the implications of the knowledge gained" as a result of tree-ring dates and dating (Haury 1995:718). In the absence of such a firsthand account, I consider this question here.

Haury's employment at Gila Pueblo made his research subject to the whims of his employer, Gladwin, just as Douglass's research had been subject to the whims of astronomer Percival Lowell in Flagstaff three decades earlier (Webb 1983). Gladwin, however, never pressured Haury in the selection of a dissertation topic. Though Gladwin identified his goals for tree-ring analysis at Gila Pueblo, his own research in the early 1930s focused on the spatial definition of the "Red-on-Buff" culture of the southern deserts (Gladwin and Gladwin 1929a, 1929b, 1930). He was therefore not disappointed by Haury's decision to analyze the Hohokam materials collected by Cushing and Hodge. In fact, Gladwin argued that by focusing on the Hemenway collections Haury's effort might be more beneficial to Gila Pueblo as an institution and Haury as an individual than would a tree-ring dissertation under Douglass's tutelage: "The Hemenway collection in connection with your thesis does not surprise me at all. When I first heard that they had given you the job of going over the material, it seemed to me the obvious thing to do, and I think that the general science of archaeology will derive greater benefit from an intelligent analysis of Cushing's work than from the excavation of one more cliff-dwelling, however important it may be" (January 12, 1932). Gladwin later added that aside from benefiting archaeology in general, Haury's dissertation would allow him to make an independent name for himself: "I believe that an analytical treatment of the Hemenway collection will be regarded as more distinctly the product of your own efforts than the application of Dr. Douglass's method to the tree-rings of the Sierra Ancha" (February 9, 1932).

Haury enrolled at Harvard University in the fall of 1931 and apparently took with him the chronology plots necessary to undertake archaeological tree-ring dating. Paul Martin of the Field Museum of Natural History sent specimens from Lowry Ruin, in southwestern Colorado, to Haury in October. While at Harvard, Haury was able to spread the dendrochronological gospel to his classmates and tried to teach an unnamed student the basics of sample collection before the latter went to conduct fieldwork in Ireland. Haury also examined wood in the Peabody Museum from Swiss lake-dweller and Egyptian sites.

In 1932, Haury returned to excavate Canyon Creek Ruin in the Sierra Ancha with a "multidisciplinary" team (Haury 1934:v) consisting of Russell Hastings, a recent graduate of the University of Chicago and new employee at Gila Pueblo; Solon Kimball, a fellow graduate student at Harvard who later became a prominent social anthropologist; and Daniel Jackson, a Pima Indian. Although Haury was disappointed by the lack of stratified deposits at Canyon Creek, results of his dendrochronological analysis were no less than spectacular. After taking three dozen tree-ring cores back to Gila Pueblo for analysis, Haury informed Gladwin that he could identify the sequence, date, and sometimes the likely season of construction events at Canyon Creek:

> The beam material is all dated and out of it have come some rather interesting results. Cutting dates range from 1326 to 1348. In five rooms the dates of the major beams agreed within each room so that construction dates for them seem practically certain. Summer cuts out-number those trees on which the last ring is completely formed. The rooms at the ends of the pueblo and those built out in

front gave more recent dates than the inner rooms, as would be expected. In the one case where both first and second story rooms dated, the upper one was constructed a dozen or so years later than the lower room. Twenty-nine of the thirty-six specimens collected dated. (August 12, 1932)

Haury's dendrochronological analysis at Canyon Creek is the first sophisticated analysis of archaeological tree-ring dates within their architectural contexts, and as a result his interpretations went beyond the simplistic one-to-one correlation between ring sequences and "periods of building," as Douglass had proposed in 1922. The detailed contextual data Haury gathered also allowed him to move beyond statements regarding construction sequences and their dates. Although these are worthy goals of any dendroarchaeological analysis, Haury demonstrated that tree-ring data facilitate complex behavioral interpretations as well. Specifically, he made some inferences regarding the wood-use practices of the prehistoric inhabitants of Canyon Creek, who had apparently used windfalls as sources for construction timber (Haury 1934:19). The heavily scarred surfaces of the major roofing beams indicated that they had been "dragged or rolled for some distance" after cutting (Haury 1934:55). Haury suggested that prehistoric migrations between A.D. 1327 and 1343 explained the sudden appearance of the cliff dwellings in the Sierra Ancha, especially since the San Juan region had been abandoned less than half a century before (Haury 1934).

The Canyon Creek Ruin and the Cliff Dwellings of the Sierra Ancha was published as Medallion Paper 14 (Haury 1934) and remains a classic in the field. One of its key contributions was the understanding that tree-ring dating could be used to do more than simply "date" a site. Haury recognized this as early as 1931 when, in the presentation of his research at Whipple and Pinedale ruins in Show Low for the Third Beam Expedition in 1929 (Haury and Hargrave 1931:6), he made it clear that "an attempt is made to correlate the archaeological observations derived incidental to the search for charcoal with the data obtained from the charcoal specimens themselves." In other words, Haury realized that, in addition to dating sites, tree-ring dates can inform on topics such as environmental and behavioral reconstructions.

Haury's convincing dendroarchaeological analysis of Canyon Creek Ruin was also important because the concurrence among architectural, archaeological, and tree-ring data provided skeptical archaeologists with concrete reassurance that tree-ring dating and archaeological analysis need not lead to excruciatingly complex interpretive problems, such as those Douglass and Morris faced in the attempt to develop the early chronology (see Chapter 3), or the ones Douglass, McGregor, Colton, and Hargrave encountered in dating Pueblo I occupations around Flagstaff (see Chapter 5). J. O. Brew of the Peabody Museum congratulated Haury on his Canyon Creek analysis:

> Your "Dating" section is superb. I refer this time not to the manner of presentation, which is straightforward and clear, but to the results. It is the most convincing exposition I have yet encountered. Before I had reached your mention of it in the last sentence I had checked over the dates of 2nd storey, outer, and inner rooms on the ground plan and had found that they came out right. This is truly a beautiful thing, Emil. As you know my skepticism of the validity of tree-ring dating in the hands of a competent analyst has evaporated. That skepticism is not transferred to the operator and has to do with the danger of the technique as applied by half-baked or unscrupulous individuals. The credentials and references of a man claiming to read tree-rings cannot be too carefully examined and checked. It is to be hoped that Dr. Douglass, in a desire to assist his pupils in their efforts to rise, does not place the seal of competence upon them before their technique or their sense of responsibility merits it. For their responsibility is great when others place specimens in their hands and rely upon and *publish* the results of the analysis. Perhaps you would be so kind, when next you write, as to send me a list of the people you consider thoroughly competent in this work. Please do not hesitate to do this because of fear lest you be unfair to some. If you know a man to be incompetent who is, as we might say, "in public practice," I hope you will say so. Otherwise, if a name which I know does not appear on your list I shall merely infer that you have not sufficient knowledge of his work to permit a judgment and can promise you no unauthorized "reading between the lines." (April 25, 1934; emphasis in original)

It is important to reiterate that Haury's research at Canyon Creek and the Sierra Ancha ruins was administratively, financially, and editorially supported by the Gila Pueblo Archaeological Foundation and Harold S. Gladwin. Gladwin has a reputation of being a member of the lunatic "fringe" of southwestern archaeology in general (Williams 1991) and archaeological tree-ring dating in particular (see Webb 1983:161–171). Gila Pueblo and Gladwin deserve as much credit for Haury's success at Canyon Creek and elsewhere as the National

Geographic Society and Neil Judd deserve for Douglass's success in bridging the gap. Nevertheless, in the rush to criticize Gladwin's archaeology, and later his dendrochronology, Gila Pueblo's early contributions to archaeological tree-ring dating, via Haury, are often overlooked. Credit is certainly due.

Haury was as busy with tree-ring research in 1933 as he had been in 1932. He analyzed pinyon specimens collected by Gladwin near Coolidge, New Mexico, in 1932. On C. Burton Cosgrove's recommendation, he tried to help Mr. Roscoe Ellison of Pueblo, Colorado, learn how to date archaeological specimens from the Cloverdale district of southwestern New Mexico, because "it would be a good move to interest a pothunter in something besides collecting specimens" (Cosgrove to Haury, January 23, 1933). Haury also gained assurances from Brew and Douglas S. Byers, who were excavating at Alkali Ridge in southeastern Utah and Waterfall Ruin in northeastern Arizona, respectively, that they would submit wood samples to Gila Pueblo. Finally, Haury was analyzing wood he collected at Mogollon Village in 1933 and wood collected by Paul Martin at Lowry Ruin in 1931.

By mid-1934, and certainly by 1935, tree-ring analysis became more complicated for Haury as archaeologists became more sophisticated in their interpretation of tree-ring dates. Archaeologists to whom Haury had returned dates began to consider the archaeological implications of those dates and what they might mean for the interpretation of individual sites as well as entire regions. Douglass was not involved in archaeological tree-ring dating at this time, except to verify dates derived by his students. Douglass's assistants at the University of Arizona did a meager amount of archaeological dating, but they were botanists (Glock) or anthropologists (Getty), and Douglass had not had a full-time assistant for archaeological dating since Haury left in 1930. It was therefore to Haury that most archaeologists turned for tree-ring dating and interpretive advice, and indeed Douglass considered Haury the senior scientist in this regard. The dating of Lowry Ruin demonstrates some of the problems with which Haury and others had to contend.

Paul S. Martin of the Field Museum of Natural History in Chicago excavated Lowry Ruin and surrounding sites in southwestern Colorado between 1930 and 1934 (Martin 1936). In the process he submitted tree-ring samples to three different laboratories, in part because he did not know which laboratory was engaged in commercial, though apparently pro bono, archaeological dating (Ahlstrom, Breternitz, and Warren 1985). Martin submitted samples to Douglass at the University of

Arizona in 1931, W. Sidney Stallings at the Laboratory of Anthropology in 1933, and Haury at Gila Pueblo in 1934, and he kept some in Chicago, where they remained unanalyzed until the early 1980s (Ahlstrom, Breternitz, and Warren 1985).

Douglass initially derived a date of A.D. 989 for one of the Lowry Ruin specimens. This date did not in and of itself raise many eyebrows, but when Haury checked Douglass's dating of the 1931 samples at Gila Pueblo in 1934, he verified that date but also derived two cutting dates at A.D. 1106. He inquired of Martin as to their archaeological context; Martin assured him that the 1106 dates made sense according to the masonry sequence and ceramic assemblages at the site. Early the next year, Martin received dates on the shipment he had sent to Stallings in 1933, and problems arose. Douglass's 989 date, since then redated to 987, came from a room from which Stallings had dated a specimen at 1090. Without considering the possibility that the earlier-dated beam may have been reused, Martin asked Haury if there was some way that the earlier noncutting date could be "stretched," by adding missing rings, to reach 1090. Otherwise, Martin felt there would be "a conflict in building dates which I cannot understand and which I shall have to reconcile in some other way, if possible" (January 14, 1935). Haury replied that it was unlikely that the specimen was missing about a hundred rings and suggested three possible sources of error in the dating of the specimens: Stallings's date of 1090 was incorrect, the Douglass/Haury date of 987 was incorrect, or the log from which the early date was derived was a reused beam. He deemed the third possibility most likely. Martin countered that the beam-reuse hypothesis did not appeal to him because there was too much architectural evidence that all the rooms were built at one time. In this, Martin confused the dendrochronological implications of beam reuse, which is not necessarily evident architecturally, with use of a beam for repair, which is more likely to leave an architectural scar.

The matter seems to have been tabled until late in 1935, when Martin asked Haury for permission to publish dates he had been given by Douglass for the great kiva at Lowry. Haury dutifully deferred official approval to Douglass. Martin replied that he would ask Douglass for approval but noted that his patience was limited and he could not wait long for date verification. Impatience with Douglass was not uncommon among archaeologists during the 1930s, and procedures approved by the First Tree-Ring Conference in Flagstaff in 1934 (Glock 1934a; see Chapter 5) were part of the problem, for the adopted protocol required that all archaeological tree-ring dates be approved by Douglass before publication. Douglass was a busy man and already at retirement age; many archaeologists felt that the verification requirement unnecessarily delayed their publications.

In the end, Martin published dates for the great kiva and other portions of the site, but he did not stress tree-ring dates in his discussion of the construction sequence at Lowry (Martin 1936). The sequence was reconstructed on the basis of "bonding and abutments, . . . faced and unfaced walls, . . . similarities in masonry techniques, . . . pottery sequences, and . . . general impressions" (Martin 1936:194). "Convincing" tree-ring data "supplemented" his analysis, but he warned that "a date obtained from single logs is not sufficient for fixing a period" (Martin 1936:201, 198). He concluded that "it is probable that the Lowry Pueblo was constructed over a comparatively short period of time" (Martin 1936:200). Over the course of the next two years, three tree-ring publications offered different dates for Lowry Ruin: Stallings (1937:3) listed a range of A.D. 1090–1104 ± 1, Haury (1938:3) listed dates of A.D. 1085+x–1086, and Douglass (1938:11) listed a date of A.D. 987+x. It should be no surprise that Martin was frustrated by the lack of consistency in these data, but tree-ring dating, analysis, and reporting was still in its infancy and had not yet been standardized.

MORRIS, HAURY, AND THE RED ROCK COUNTRY

As noted in Chapter 3, Earl Morris was an ardent collector of wood, and he appears in the dendrochronological literature as the apolitical field man, ready to supply tree-ring samples and archaeological expertise to dendrochronologists but somehow remaining above, or at least removed from, the technical difficulties and professional differences that affected dendrochronological research. Morris's primary obligation was to Douglass and the development of the early pueblo chronology, but he did not hesitate to send duplicate samples to other tree-ring labs, especially Gila Pueblo and the Laboratory of Anthropology. As early as July 1930, he sent Haury samples collected by the Eighth Bernheimer Expedition in the Carrizo-Lukachukai Mountains of northeastern Arizona. Morris's fears that the specimens were too complacent or too short for use were well founded. Although the samples did not yield dates, Haury officially thanked Morris "on behalf of Gila Pueblo" for submitting them (September 26, 1930). Morris subsequently sent Gila Pueblo 35 duplicate specimens from Aztec Ruin to enhance its meager reference collections.

As early as 1930, Gladwin had been interested in collecting tree-ring specimens from standing ruins in northern Arizona, and indeed Gila Pueblo was awarded a permit to collect the specimens on federal lands in July of that year. In 1931, Haury wanted to take a trip with Morris to northeastern Arizona to collect tree-ring specimens from Basketmaker sites. Gila Pueblo applied to the Department of the Interior for a collecting permit in December 1931, but the application was rejected, at least in part because the authorities did not see the need for duplicate specimens to be located in both Tucson and Globe, which are only 130 miles apart. A permit was instead granted to collect borings from above-ground dwellings that were not on National Park Service lands, provided that cores were obtained near walls, the core holes were plugged, saws were not used, and a report was filed in triplicate. Because these conditions were not satisfactory to Gila Pueblo, the Haury-Morris expedition did not occur until several years later. Nevertheless, Morris's 1931 advice to Haury on the proposed trip conveys the older man's spirit of cooperation as well as the potential dangers of collecting in ancient ruins:

> Glad to know you are going to northeast Arizona to collect beam specimens. If you do get into Canyon de Chelly you will find a few sections to be obtainable in the Sliding Ruin and there should be piled up near the east end of the White House a few coniferous sticks that I left there. Provided you will get up del Muerto as far as Mummy Cave, you will find many timbers scattered about within its shelter. What you might find higher up [Canyon] de Chelly I do not know. . . . At one time I made a trip into these canyons for no other purpose than to secure timber sections for Dr. Douglass and I took a sample of absolutely every piece of pine, spruce, pinyon, and cedar that I could find. If you do work in Mummy Cave and attempt to take sections from the roof timbers or other timbers of the tower, be very careful about putting any jar or stress on that front wall. As we found when we put in the brace rods there, the whole structure is in a decidedly dangerous condition. (May 20, 1931)

This is the last written communication between Morris and Gila Pueblo regarding tree rings until 1935. From 1931 through 1934, Morris and Douglass were deeply involved in the work on the early chronology, and Douglass asked Morris to withdraw from interactions with Gila Pueblo until that task was completed. Douglass wrote to Morris on May 4, 1931, to complain about Haury's decision to leave for Gila Pueblo, saying, "Mr. Gladwin took him away by larger efforts

and set me back a year in time and more than a year in progress."
Douglass added that he was under the impression that Morris was sending specimens to Gladwin and Haury and noted that although he did
not necessarily wish to monopolize archaeological tree-ring work, he
wanted to accomplish their chronology-building task as quickly as possible. Morris seems to have understood Douglass's message, and written
correspondence with Haury ceased until October 5, 1935, when they
once again began laying plans for a beam-collecting trip to northeastern
Arizona.

The tension between Douglass and Gladwin resurfaced when
Douglass visited Gila Pueblo on November 10, 1934, to learn more
about Gladwin's own tree-ring research, including a ring-width measuring device Gladwin had his machine shop construct. In a draft letter to
Morris on November 23, 1934, Douglass conveyed his well-founded
protectionism from, and perhaps a touch of envy of, Gladwin:

> I visited Gila Pueblo on Saturday, November 10, and had a num-
> ber of talks with Mr. Gladwin. I felt that he had no hesitation in ask-
> ing for advance information on any detail connected with my dating
> work. Perhaps my trip over there was a mistake, as he placed me in
> an embarrassing position. He has the [financial] means to carry
> through any project that he wants. If I give him certain bits of infor-
> mation, he is quite able, if he wishes, to jump in and take some of the
> cream without being the least entitled to it. This is not saying that he
> would do it. I understand that you and Mrs. Morris are going to
> spend some time there this winter. Would you be willing to avoid giv-
> ing any information as to the location of the earliest [Basketmaker]
> material, whose dates I have already communicated to you? This
> refers especially to Obelisk Cave and Mummy Cave. At least, could
> you make this reservation, until you and I have had a chance to talk
> this matter thoroughly?

Morris informed Douglass that the Gladwin matter rested squarely
on the former's shoulders; he would tell Gladwin as much or as little as
Douglass wanted. This was probably a moot point, however, for Haury,
and by extension Gladwin, almost certainly already knew the location of
the Basketmaker sites. Morris then added a curious caveat that effectively ignored an archaeologist's responsibilities in the use of dendrochronological information and indeed downplays his own role in
helping Douglass develop the early chronology: "Those of us who secure
the material in the field should have nothing to say about it thereafter. It
is you who have the knowledge and skill to make something out of what

to the rest of us would have less meaning than an equal quantity of good fresh kindling wood" (December 4, 1935).

Ultimately, Douglass decided to withhold his as yet unpublished early chronology from Gila Pueblo. He explained his reluctance in a letter to Gladwin: "Probably in all this chronology work the greatest privilege I have had has been the chance to go ahead deliberately enough to be sure on every point before letting it out. That would have been much more difficult if others had been in the same field and perhaps developing a sense of competition for the results" (December 9, 1934).

On May 12, 1935, Haury wrote to Douglass again requesting information on his progress with the early chronology. Douglass's handwritten notes on the back of that inquiry provide some insights: "Haury (and Gladwin especially) want the master chart extending back so they can date some pieces from near Durango sent them by Martin (?) [probably I. F. "Zeke" Flora; see below]. Haury describes a fine sequence some 110 years long, mean ring size about 2–3 mm but sensitive. He will send me a skeleton plot of that piece and if I find it contributes to the chronology at or near 700 A.D. or even 500 or especially at 350 A.D. and before, then I use it. If it does not then I send him a plot or something so he can try dating it. . . . He will respect its use." Haury later submitted to Douglass two skeleton plots of the Colorado wood specimens in question, though he recognized and understood Douglass's sensitivity. He wrote: "Please rest assured that my desire to have the early chronology is only to hasten the work of getting early dates and, as with everything else, all such material would naturally be referred to you before any information is released" (May 31, 1935). Douglass subsequently sent Haury a copy of his chronology back to the A.D. 400s.

Morris had in 1935 renewed his efforts to donate duplicate samples to Gila Pueblo, as plans were again in the making for a Haury-Morris trip into the Arizona Red Rock country to collect duplicate samples. This time, Kidder endorsed their trip as a precaution against the inadvertent loss of Douglass's collection, which was tenuously housed in the baseball stadium at the University of Arizona.[1] Kidder also suggested that a duplicate set of specimens be deposited with Haury at Gila Pueblo, for, after Douglass, Haury was "the best tree-ring dater in the business" (Kidder to W. M. Gilbert of the Carnegie Institution, September 3, 1935). Kidder, a member of the Board of Directors at the

1. The collections were moved to their current location under the football stadium in 1937.

Laboratory of Anthropology in Santa Fe, added in a postscript that he would like to see a third duplicate collection donated to that facility.

Apparently, the need for duplication was felt in many quarters, as it had not been in 1931, and various high-level administrators in relevant federal agencies became involved in Gila Pueblo's permit application process. Floyd E. Dotson, chief clerk for the Department of the Interior, personally submitted the Haury-Morris fieldwork proposal to the requisite federal agencies, including the Office of Indian Affairs. Jesse Nusbaum, director of the Laboratory of Anthropology, lobbied C. E. Faris, superintendent of the Central Navajo Agency, on the merits of the project.

Morris obtained the permit for the Red Rock country trip in March 1936. Sometime after the American Association for the Advancement of Science meetings in Flagstaff in May of that year, he and Haury began the long-awaited field trip. On his return trip to Flagstaff, Morris suffered one of the unusual consequences of fieldwork that have afflicted many an archaeologist in the Four Corners region. He tried to obtain lodging in Gallup, New Mexico, only to find that a Hollywood film crew occupied most of the hotels. After much searching he found a room and later noted that the waitresses at the Harvey House restaurant offered him free food because they thought he was an actor. He denied their "questionable compliment" and proceeded to pay for his meals with pride intact.

Gila Pueblo's renewed interest in the development of the Basketmaker chronology began in 1935 when I. F. "Zeke" Flora, a self-described pothunter from Durango, Colorado, initiated a long-term relationship with Morris, Haury, and Gila Pueblo when he submitted archaeological wood from Basketmaker III sites that he and others had pillaged in southwestern Colorado. Flora apparently submitted at least one duplicate specimen from Ignacio 7:2, a Basketmaker III site located just outside Durango, to both Douglass and Haury, who independently dated it to A.D. 650. In 1935, a date of 650 was considered solidly Basketmaker III, but the material culture from that site indicated that it was Basketmaker II. The specimen and site therefore aroused the interest of Gladwin and Haury, for no pure Basketmaker II sites had yet been dated, and the date of the transition between Basketmaker II and Basketmaker III was still unknown. Haury explained the situation to Douglass:

> You will recall the 649 date from a piece of wood sent you by Flora
> of Durango, Colorado, reputed to be from a Basketmaker II cave. I
> have been in further touch [with] Flora to get more information on the

subject. From the collection of material we have from the cave and from his description, I see no reason to doubt the identification as to period. Consequently the date becomes of considerable interest as it is the latest for Basketmaker II, confirming a suspicion some of us have had that there was a lag in that area. Two days ago Flora sent down another piece picked up on site C-3 excavated by Roberts on the Piedra. Flora had himself looked the piece over and had placed it about 770. My check shows 774 with a good set of rings. Roberts placed the site as Pueblo I although the pottery looks very much like Basketmaker. What do you think of a note in the *Tree-Ring Bulletin* covering at least the Basketmaker II date? (March 29, 1936)

Flora caused an ethical dilemma for Haury, Morris, and others, one that archaeologists still deal with today. Although he was a talented field archaeologist and self-taught dendrochronologist of sorts, he was also a self-aggrandizing professional pothunter whose 1951 business card offered a brief résumé:

> Hobbies—Grave Robber, Game Exterminator, Mummy Excavator
> Professions—Dendrochronologist, Archaeologist, and Horologist
> Outstanding Failures—Movie Actor, Author and Writer, and Laborer
> Aspirations—Making A-Bombs, Counterfeiting, and Dermogating [?].

Despite his unorthodox (and often illegal) activities, Morris described Flora as "an inveterate digger and as keen an observer as one is likely to come across. It is a pity that some arrangement cannot be made to let him go on in a legitimate way. . . . It may be the wrong thing to do, but I am loath not to encourage anyone as interested as Flora is" (letter to Haury, May 20, 1936). Haury concurred: "As for Flora, I appreciate your position regarding him very much. Flora sent me a great deal of wood and he has done much work on it himself. I have recently checked two pieces from him that he has dated correctly, one a piece dating 774, from Robert's Piedra site. He has been very receptive of my ideas as to how to handle the wood and, since he has been so very good about sending the material down, I too am loath to discourage him" (May 28, 1936).

"With the bold abandon that is characteristic of the amateur" (Flora 1940:1), Flora made a trip to Gila Pueblo in October 1936 to work with Haury on the wood he had collected around Durango. He later noted that he wanted to challenge Gladwin's assertion that the Durango sites should postdate A.D. 700 (Flora 1940). Flora and Haury continued their dendrochronological correspondence throughout 1937, and their effort resulted in a joint paper on the Basketmaker III dates from the Durango area later that year (Haury and Flora 1937), despite Flora's protestations that he need not be listed as a coauthor (Flora to Haury, July 21, 1937). Flora most often contributed summaries of his research to *Sherds and Points*, an amateur archaeologists' circular out of Durango. The tone of this publication indicates disdain for professional archaeologists, and by appearing on the byline with Haury in the *Tree-Ring Bulletin*, Flora became associated with establishment and professional archaeologists, thus potentially compromising his stature as an independent amateur.

The working relationship between Gila Pueblo and Flora persisted until early 1940. For reasons that are not entirely clear, relations soured between them, as well as between Flora and Morris. Gladwin concluded that Flora possessed "a devious mind" and severed relations with him on March 1, 1940 (Gladwin to J. Nusbaum, March 8, 1940). Scholars interested in Flora can read about him in the August 1940 issue of *Time* magazine in an article entitled "About This Man's Town," in which Flora claimed that he had excavated the oldest dated ruins in the Southwest, near Durango. *Life* magazine had been planning a similar article on Flora and had rejected semibiographical articles on Haury and Morris, who were far less flamboyant and prone to exaggeration and who therefore made for less sensational copy. In response to *Life*'s slight and *Time*'s "glorification of a notorious pothunter," Jesse Nusbaum rallied professional southwestern archaeologists to protest formally to the editors, though his call to arms was largely ignored. Despite the severance of relations with Gila Pueblo and Morris, Flora continued to submit tree-ring specimens to Douglass until late 1943.

Between October 1936 and June 1937, not much progress was made on the Red Rock Basketmaker III collections, but Haury was able to report dates in the early A.D. 600s for Basketmaker III samples from Broken Flute Cave in Red Rock Valley and dates in the 700s for samples that he and Ted Sayles, also employed by Gila Pueblo, collected in 1936 at White Mound Village, another Basketmaker III site, near Houck, Arizona. Morris was less interested in these results, for he already knew the dates for full-blown Basketmaker III occupations as a result of Douglass's research some years earlier. He was still interested in determining the date of transition from Basketmaker II to Basketmaker III, however, and therefore wanted to know whether Haury's dates from Obelisk Cave in Canyon del Muerto corroborated Douglass's Obelisk Cave specimen that dated to A.D. 477. Haury reported that nine specimens from Obelisk Cave dated between A.D. 473 and 489 and that "this will give us some notion as to where the dividing line between Basketmaker II and Basketmaker III should be drawn" (June 17, 1937).

The material culture of one component in Obelisk Cave was purely Basketmaker II, with an overlying Basketmaker III ceramic assemblage, so Morris reasoned that the Basketmaker II–Basketmaker III transition must have occurred before A.D. 478, at least in that region. Haury was pleased with the results and suggested that Morris contribute these findings to the *Tree-Ring Bulletin*, though he never did.

During his tenure at Gila Pueblo, Haury received other job offers. In June 1935, Donald Brand of the University of New Mexico offered Haury $1800 per year to become curator at the new Museum of Anthropology. On Christmas Eve 1935, Judd unenthusiastically informed Haury that there was an opening at the United States National Museum for an assistant curator, paying $3200 per year, but added that "the opportunity for fieldwork is not great." Even if Haury wanted to leave Gila Pueblo, he was under verbal, if not contractual, obligation to Gladwin to remain there for at least three years after earning his Ph.D. Haury therefore could not seriously entertain offers until the spring of 1937, and it may be more than mere coincidence that Byron Cummings announced he would retire from the University of Arizona at the time Haury again became eligible for the job market.

Cummings and Douglass had been friends and colleagues for more than twenty years and were both beyond retirement age in the mid-1930s (Thompson 1995). Haury had been a prized student and cherished colleague of both men in the late 1920s and early 1930s. Though Cummings's and Douglass's professional relationship was never highly interactive, Cummings supplied Douglass with a host of graduate students over the years. He and Douglass must have discussed their plans for the future, and it seems likely that Haury's name came up in those conversations. Thompson (1995:648) states that Cummings went to Gila Pueblo in November 1936, specifically to ask Haury if he was interested in becoming head of the Department of Archaeology. No later than the second week of 1937, Douglass encouraged Haury to accept the position. Douglass's research had suffered when Haury left in 1930 and stood to gain if Haury returned in 1937, for together the two men could develop a successful tree-ring analysis program. Douglass wrote:

> We have here one of the great opportunities for distinguished and creditable local development in [the archaeology-dendrochronology] line for generations to come. You have the ability and character to make a great contribution not merely right here at the moment but for all time to come because here is the educational center and here should be a major center of development. You also have the acquaintance

with the tree-ring problem and its application to archaeology. . . . I am free to say that I am personally anxious to see someone here who will have understanding and sympathy with the development of tree-ring dating. This locality should be an immense center for that sort of thing, a clearing house not only for the southwest but for other parts of the world. If I find it possible to develop tree ring studies more fully on this campus a very fine cooperation could take place between the climatic values in ring records and the archaeological information in them. (January 10, 1937)

Haury shared Douglass's sentiments: "I do not hesitate to say, however, that the opportunity at Tucson has several very attractive facets to it, and at the same time I am fully aware of the advantages offered here. . . . Naturally, in revolving the whole thing in my mind, I have thought of the relationship of tree-ring work to archaeology, [and] felt there should be a closer bond than I believe exists at the present time and I would consider it one of the greatest opportunities to work out something along that line with you" (January 16, 1937). J. O. Brew of the Peabody Museum treated the situation with a bit more levity when he wrote to Haury in January 1937:

I have news. Did you know that Emil Haury is leaving Gila Pueblo? He is going to head the Department at Tucson. Oh, yes, it's all *settled*, he begins next fall. . . . This will take a lot off your mind. . . . I thought you might like to know. It's always best to have these things out in the open. So much less nervous strain. . . . Word is all over the country. Such is fame, Dr. Haury. So you might as well crawl out from under the bushel basket, though I imagine 'twould take at least a hogshead to secret you . . . . Meanwhile, good luck in your negotiations. Drive a hard bargain and get it all your way. You've got the goods, and they need you badly. (January 6, 1937; emphasis in original)

The difficulty in Haury's situation lay not merely in his allegiance to Gila Pueblo and his desire to work more closely with Douglass, for Cummings decided not to retire peacefully. The original plan had been for Haury to assume Cummings's position as both Archaeology Department head and director of the Arizona State Museum, but Cummings reneged and decided he wanted to retain the directorship of the museum, a situation that Haury deemed "impossible" (Haury to Gladwin, April 2, 1937). A compromise was established in which Cummings would retain the museum for one year, though this arrangement did not ease tensions between him and Haury thereafter (Thompson 1995).

Gladwin had had his own difficulties with the potentially irascible Cummings less than a decade earlier. Cummings, chairman of the Arizona Archaeological Commission, was well known for his irritation with, and sometimes downright hostility toward, out-of-state institutions that removed antiquities from Arizona for display or study elsewhere. Gila Pueblo was especially scrutinized by Cummings and the commission in 1930 when accusations by Odd Halseth, the Phoenix city archaeologist, led to rumors that Gila Pueblo was simply a front for a massive pothunting effort. Gila Pueblo was subsequently exonerated, but there remained no love to be lost between Cummings and Gladwin (see Haury 1988:25–29). Gladwin sarcastically suggested to Haury one possible solution to the situation created by Cummings's desire to remain affiliated with the Arizona State Museum: "I have seen some of the editorials describing the old badger's [Cummings's] activities and for pure poppy-cock they are in a class by themselves. Have you thought of suggesting that he might be mounted as an exhibit, and so retain his connection with the museum?" (April 3, 1937).

On April 26, Haury submitted his resignation to Gladwin, effective September 1, 1937, though he hoped his relationship with Gila Pueblo would remain strong. Gladwin graciously accepted the resignation on May 11, 1937: "Our best wishes go with you. We hope you will find just what you are hoping for, and you can always count on us as friends who are deeply concerned in your success." One month later, Gladwin remained optimistic about cooperation among the Museum of Northern Arizona, the University of Arizona, and Gila Pueblo, though subsequent relations between the three institutions can hardly be called cooperative.

Haury's remaining duties at Gila Pueblo included completing the analysis of tree-ring specimens from the Red Rock region, as well as Brew's specimens from Awatovi, and a tabulation of all sites dated during his tenure at Gila Pueblo (Haury 1938; see also Haury 1935b). Haury added to these tasks by assuming responsibility for the fledgling *Tree-Ring Bulletin* during the Tree-Ring Society meetings at Flagstaff on June 28–30, 1937.

Haury spent the remainder of his career at the University of Arizona, serving as director of the Arizona State Museum and head of the Department of Anthropology until his retirement in 1964. He continued conducting archaeological fieldwork well after retirement, including reexcavation at Snaketown in the mid-1960s. Though he never again engaged in archaeological tree-ring work, he continued to be an ardent

supporter of the Laboratory of Tree-Ring Research. He died in 1992
(Smith 1987; Thompson 1995).

HAROLD GLADWIN'S TREE-RING RESEARCH, 1930–1941

Gladwin had collected tree-ring samples on his own as early as 1930. By
1932, his discomfort with the Douglass system induced him to initiate
his own study of archaeological wood and charcoal specimens. Between
1932 and 1941, Gladwin acquired a substantial tree-ring sample collection (Figure 21) and experimented with new quantitative techniques of
tree-ring analysis. The ensuing critique of southwestern archaeology and
its practitioners is well known (Webb 1983; Downum 1988) and often
includes ad hominem criticism of Douglass (Gladwin 1940a), Colton
and McGregor (Gladwin 1943, 1944), and even his former assistant
director, Haury (Gladwin 1946, 1948).

Harold and Winifred Gladwin, as well as Gila Pueblo secretary Edith
Sangster, audited Douglass's tree-ring class at the University of Arizona
in the spring of 1930 (Gladwin 1977). Thompson (1995:646) stated that
Gladwin did not complete the course, and as we saw earlier, there is evidence that he and his associates missed more than a few class sessions.

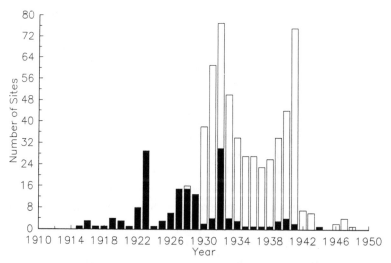

FIGURE 21. Archaeological tree-ring research by Gila Pueblo 1928–1943. Note the
peak at 1930 created by Haury's work in the Sierra Ancha, the peak in 1936
as a result of Haury and Morris's trip to the Red Rock country, and the peaks
in 1940 and 1941 created by Deric Nusbaum's collecting activity on Gladwin's
behalf.

Gladwin boasted of the fact that, after meeting with Douglass privately and challenging some of his assertions during the spring, "Dr. Douglass did not again attend the class but delegated the teaching of the rest of the course to his assistants at the Tree-Ring Laboratory" (Gladwin 1977:3). Gladwin's boast seems only loosely tied to the facts. Haury was Douglass's sole assistant in tree rings at the time, but his name appears on the first class session attendance sheet, so his status as an "assistant" is questionable. Gladwin's apparent revisionism therefore does not accurately reflect the facts of the situation, and it is clear that he missed at least three class periods that semester. We can therefore infer that Gladwin did not seriously attempt to learn the Douglass method, though he would later admit that he "did not possess the ability or type of mind to achieve dependable results" using the Douglass system (Gladwin 1940a:1). Perhaps he simply did not have the ability or type of mind to attend class on a regular basis. Whatever the case may be, Gladwin's critique of the Douglass system centered on the technique's subjective nature, his erroneous notion that tree-ring dates are *dependent* variables, and a basic misunderstanding about the relative interpretive utility of cutting and noncutting dates.

Gladwin's primary objection to the Douglass system was that the skeleton plot method of dating was "subjective" and that the dates could therefore be verified only by Douglass or a member of his "school" (Gladwin 1942:3). To a certain extent, Gladwin had a point, though he confused "unsystematic" with "subjective." Gladwin felt that a quantitative method of tree-ring analysis, based on ring-width measurements, would be more reliable and replicable, and he therefore set out to devise a quantitative technique. It is clear that in all of this Gladwin conflated the terms "quantitative" and "objective," but they are by no means synonymous. Indeed, it appears also that Gladwin's use of quantitative data was nothing if not subjective. To wit, on March 6, 1940, McGregor suggested that Gladwin see a statistician to help clarify problems with his methods, but Gladwin would not be swayed: "You are probably right about consulting a statistician, but I am so profoundly distrustful of this 'breed of pup' that I have laid down our own rule that a correlation is correct if it shows 90% agreement."

Gladwin also believed that archaeological evidence, or, more accurately, his interpretation of that evidence, should be considered more reliable than tree-ring dates when the two are in conflict (Gladwin 1943:68, 1945:18, 1948:175). That is, he argued that archaeological evidence is the independent variable whereas tree-ring dates are the dependent variables. Dendrochronological dating theory in the 1930s was only poorly developed, but the Douglass "school" at least considered the possibility of beam reuse, structural repair, and other contingencies that might lead to apparent discrepancies between tree-ring dates and the archaeological evidence. Haury was assistant director of Gila Pueblo when he published the first contribution to archaeological tree-ring dating theory (Haury 1935a), and Gladwin must have been aware of the increasing sophistication in the theory of tree-ring date interpretation. His unflinching adherence to archaeological data therefore seems downright peculiar given that tree rings are now considered archaeologists' best source of culturally independent dates (see Dean 1978a).

Gladwin's third objection to, or misunderstanding of, the Douglass technique relates to the distinction between cutting and noncutting dates, the latter of which he erroneously called "incomplete" (Gladwin 1945:30, 1943:55). Here Gladwin failed to recognize the distinction between "precision" and "accuracy." Noncutting dates are as "complete"—that is, "precise"—as cutting dates when they are properly crossdated. Whether they are "accurate" depends on what question is being asked (Ahlstrom 1985; Dean 1978a). Noncutting dates are accurate if one is interested only in the growth date of the outside ring on a particular specimen; they are less "accurate" if one is interested in archaeological questions, such as the date of a construction event or the abandonment of a village. Properly crossdated noncutting dates are never, however, "incomplete" (Dean 1978a).

In 1932, Gladwin paid a visit to Frank Roberts's Pueblo I site south of Allantown, Arizona. There Roberts and Gladwin discussed in general terms the interpretation of tree-ring dates. McGregor had recently determined, and Douglass had verified, the dating of several specimens from a Pueblo I pithouse near Flagstaff at A.D. 797 to 820. A masonry structure one mile south of the pithouse produced a date of A.D. 830, but it was firmly designated Pueblo II on the basis of its ceramic assemblage. This befuddled Roberts and especially Gladwin, who could not reconcile the fact that sites that were assigned to distinct Pecos Classification periods on the basis of their material culture could be essentially contemporaneous on the basis of tree-ring dates. Rather than consider parsimonious alternatives for the apparent discrepancy, such as cultural lag, beam reuse, structural repair, sampling error, and the nonmutually exclusive definitions of the Pecos Classification periods, Gladwin made the inferential leap that Douglass's dating was in error. He assumed that Roberts agreed with this inference and tried to manipulate the situation to Gila

Pueblo's advantage. As he told Haury, "I think he [Roberts] is beginning to feel as I do, and so I took advantage of his confusion and exacted a promise that he would send you some of his wood samples in [the] future. My own personal belief is that you are the only man who can really date wood and I don't think Douglass is able to do it, much less his recent satellites [i.e., students]" (August 13, 1932). How Gladwin, who repeatedly proclaimed his own incompetence with the Douglass system, could reasonably argue that Haury was more capable of cross-dating archaeological wood than Douglass, the founder of the technique, is difficult to determine. One assumes it must have been simply a question of institutional loyalty, for Gladwin turned against Haury as well once the latter left Gila Pueblo for the University of Arizona.

Gladwin elaborated his problem with the McGregor and Douglass dating of the Pueblo I and Pueblo II sites in a 20-page letter to Haury on February 1, 1933. Here he quoted freely from the manuscript of his forthcoming book *The Eastern Range of the Red-on-Buff Culture* (Gladwin and Gladwin 1935):

> During the season of 1932, tree-ring dates have been assigned to many additional ruins, of which three have a direct bearing on the point at issue. First, near Flagstaff, a Pueblo I pithouse is said by J. C. McGregor to bear the date 787 A.D., second, near Allantown, a series of Pueblo I pithouses, excavated by F. H. H. Roberts, has been dated by Dr. Douglass as ranging from 797 to 820 A.D. In both instances pottery showed these pithouses to belong to the northern, Kayenta culture. . . . The third instance was a small pueblo of the [Prudden] unit type, also near Allantown, also excavated by Roberts in 1932. This was given a date of 816 A.D. by Dr. Douglass and, as this building was a typical Pueblo of eight rooms, built on the surface of the ground, and obviously according to preconceived plan, it was difficult, if not impossible, to see how this site, containing pottery characteristic of Pueblo II to Pueblo III of the Little Colorado, could have been contemporaneous with pit-houses nearby containing Pueblo I pottery. . . . It would seem from this that either Dr. Douglass must be mistaken in his method of dating, or that there is something fundamentally wrong in the present concept of the evolution of culture in the Southwest. In the absence of any evidence to combat the growing list of dated ruins, it is necessary, we believe, to cast about for another explanation than that implied by the Pecos classification. (See also Gladwin and Gladwin 1935:266–268)

In this passage Gladwin illuminated his failure to acknowledge the independence of the tree-ring method as well as to understand the dendrochronological implications of beam reuse and structural repair. Tree-ring dates are "correct" if they fit his preconceived notions; they become "incorrect" when they do not fit his preconceived notions or if they were not provided by Haury. Gladwin then generalized the problem to an extraordinary degree. The relatively small Pueblo I/Pueblo II dating problem somehow led to the conclusion that "something [was] fundamentally wrong" with the current understanding of southwestern prehistory. Significantly, Gladwin framed the issue in terms of "combat" against both Douglass's tree-ring dating and the Pecos Classification. The passage demonstrates Gladwin's willingness to place blame on others while remaining free of fault himself, an attitude that is somewhat characteristic of the "purveyors of pseudoscience" (Williams 1991:16). This attitude is exemplified in Gladwin's (1943) *Review and Analysis of the Flagstaff Culture*, as well as numerous subsequent publications.

Gladwin's belief that Haury was the only member of the Douglass school capable of accurate dating led him to direct Haury to "make every effort" to obtain samples from other investigators. He reminded Haury that all Douglass's samples collected under federal permit were legally available to them for study "without it being considered a favour" (March 31, 1933).

In May 1934, Gladwin decided to take matters into his own hands, and he related to Haury that he was beginning the "preparation of wood samples" to build up "my original [tree-ring] series" (May 3, 1934). Two weeks later, he reported "unexpected success" in the preparation of wood samples and that workers in the local machine shop were constructing a ring-measuring machine. On June 18, Gladwin expressed his desire and intent to learn more about the physiological aspect of ring growth. He outlined for Haury his master plan for dating southwestern sites:

> My present plan for dating is to attempt to establish a composite (or key) measured plot for about eight zones in the southwest. These zones follow fairly accurately our archaeological branches. In other words the Kayenta Culture area seems to include trees which show better cross-identification than when trees from Flagstaff are compared to those from McNary [Arizona]. After all, our archaeological branches are primarily drainage areas. . . . What is your opinion? At present I recognize Chaco, Kayenta, Salado, Cibola, Mesa Verde, and Rio Grande zones. There will undoubtedly also be a Mogollon and a Chihuahua zone. (June 23, 1934)

Haury was intrigued by, and diplomatic with regard to, his boss's research design: "I have never been quite satisfied by the present system of dating wood from one area with a plot based on trees at some distance and for that reason your present attempt to work out zones will go far to relieve my own mind. It should also do the same for others who may be in doubt as to the reliability of the method. You can count on me for any help that I may be able to give you and I hope that you will let me know when new developments appear" (July 4, 1934).

Gladwin worked on his dendrochronological techniques throughout 1934. His newly discovered interests in tree physiology induced him to take cores weekly from an unfortunate Engelmann spruce, though he would later dilute his sampling schedule to once a month. He eschewed climatological research, for he found it too "taxing," but years later he listed for McGregor all the climatic variables with which he sought tree-ring correlations, including precipitation, temperature, length of growing season, number of cloudy days, sunspots, ultraviolet radiation, and solar radiation (May 11, 1940). In August 1934, despite attestations of "unexpected success," Gladwin refused Haury's offer to publish an account of his method in the *Tree-Ring Bulletin*; he would refuse all such subsequent offers and did not publish his techniques until six years later (Gladwin 1940a, 1940b). Interestingly, Gladwin invited Douglass to come to Globe to review his methods, for, as he said, "I am tremendously encouraged by the progress we have been making but I do not wish to go any farther until we can earn your approval" (September 12, 1934). Douglass visited Gladwin's laboratory on November 10, 1934, and though he politely expressed approval of Gladwin's "increment" plot and "splendid" measuring machine in a thank-you note, he also expressed discomfort with their meeting in a letter to Morris (see Chapter 3).

In late December 1934, Gladwin circulated for peer review the galley proof of *The Eastern Range of the Red-on-Buff Culture* (Gladwin and Gladwin 1935), an interesting event for two reasons. First, the circulation of papers for peer review is a practice for which the usually bombastic Gladwin may have set the precedent, at least in the Southwest. Second, and more important, Gladwin wanted to publish a date range of A.D. 800–850 for the Pueblo I phase of the Kayenta Culture in the Flagstaff region, despite the fact that the 1934 Tree-Ring Conference had adopted a resolution that dates were not to be published until they had been confirmed by Douglass and published in the *Tree-Ring Bulletin*. The Pueblo I dates Gladwin sought to publish had not been so verified. To be fair, he had not attended the 1934 Tree-Ring Conference and therefore might have been ignorant of the protocol. He could also legitimately argue that he had never formally agreed to the protocol, but it seems likely that he knew of these restrictions, because Haury was still on staff at Gila Pueblo. Colton and Douglass both notified Gladwin that he was going to be in violation of the Tree-Ring Conference protocol if he went to press (Colton to Gladwin, November 28, 1934; Douglass to Gladwin, December 10, 1934). Gladwin replied that he had obtained the Pueblo I date in a personal communication from Douglass (Gladwin to Colton, December 5, 1934); he felt that the date was therefore public domain. Douglass subsequently deferred judgment on the matter to Colton, whose institution had paid for the excavations on which the samples were gathered and who therefore retained priority for their publication (Douglass to Gladwin, December 10, 1934). Colton warned Gladwin that Douglass was still uncertain about the dating, for some of the specimens in question seemed to date equally well at points some 200 years apart in the chronology (Colton to Gladwin, December 20, 1934). Inexplicably, Colton gave Gladwin permission to publish the date range (see Colton to Douglass, December 20, 1934). Douglass, however, informed Gladwin that his interpretation of Colton's letter was that Colton wanted to be the first to publish the Flagstaff-area Pueblo I dates and therefore recommended that Gladwin omit the dates from his manuscript (Douglass to Gladwin, December 28, 1934). Gladwin ignored Douglass's advice but did gain Colton's approval on the exact wording before publication (Gladwin to Colton, February 5, 1935).

This episode reinforced Gladwin's belief that the verification protocol adopted by Douglass and his students, rather than leading to reliable and replicable results, amounted to nothing more than censorship: "I am really most disappointed about the tree-ring conference as I had hoped that we might be able to tighten up the censorship. I am rather inclined to think that, while Douglass is a darned good scientist, he is not as good when it comes to administering his problem. I cannot see how he will have time to adequately check results from the entire Southwest when his whole time belongs to Carnegie for another type of work" (Gladwin to Haury, May 15, 1935).

Gladwin and Douglass represent the two opposing poles in archaeological publication philosophy. Gladwin felt that archaeological research must be published promptly (if not prematurely) and saw no problem in revising previously published data and their interpretation when he deemed it necessary (see, for example, Gladwin's 1942 revisions of Gladwin, Haury, Sayles, and Gladwin 1937). Douglass, on the other hand, was extremely cautious and would not publish data until he was absolutely if not "infernally sure" of their veracity (Douglass to J. L. Giddings, May 22, 1939). Douglass was also reluctant to engage in personal debate and attack in print. He typically answered his critics' charges indirectly, through publication of new studies instead of direct responses to inflated charges. For instance, Douglass's (1941a, 1941c, 1942) contributions on the techniques of tree-ring analysis were inspired by, and indirect responses to, Gladwin's methodological publications (1940a and 1940b). Douglass's philosophy in this regard is delineated in a 1942 letter to McGregor, who advocated a direct rebuttal to Gladwin's attack on the "Flagstaff Culture" (Gladwin 1943; see Chapter 5). Douglass wrote: "I think the less notice taken of such work, the better. I have usually tried to answer attacks of that sort by some very explicit illustrations in the next article I write" (November 10, 1942).

In May 1935, Gladwin revealed to Haury some of the intricacies of his developing method of tree-ring measurement and analysis. The following quotation from Gladwin's letter to Haury is somewhat confusing, but the resulting publication of his technique, *Tree-Ring Analysis: Methods of Correlation* (Gladwin 1940b, 1944), is not a model of clarity either. In the last sentence, one of the basic differences in Gladwin's and Douglass's approach to the problem becomes apparent. Where Douglass used core-to-core ring-width variability to his advantage in crossdating, especially in the identification of locally absent or missing rings, Gladwin sought uniformity in cores from the same tree, in trees from within a stand, and in stands within a district:

> A new approach may evolve out of this work, based primarily on measured rings. . . . The most promising angle thus far is the ability to divide all trees into not less than three different classes depending upon their variability. A tentative system would be that if a tree showed an increase or a decrease [in ring growth] of one millimeter in any one year, it would fall in a certain class in which all differentials of .5 mm or less would be ignored. If it showed no differential over .5 mm, differences of .25 mm or less would be ignored. Possibly something may come of it as I think it is necessary to determine some standard of avoiding minute changes which are visible in one core but which may not be uniform throughout the circuit. (May 7, 1935)

Up to this point, the bulk of Gladwin's analyses had been performed on ring-width measurements supplied him by Douglass, even though he had collected living-tree cores on his own and had experimented with different surfacing and measuring techniques. Gladwin felt no qualms about asking Douglass for samples collected with public funds, and

Douglass usually gave Gladwin duplicate samples as well. Douglass drew the line, however, when Gladwin asked to him to send his original ring-width measurements and plots. Gladwin, with abundant finances, solved this problem by offering to pay one of Douglass's students fifty cents an hour to copy them.

By June 1935, Gladwin's need for data led him to impose on Douglass once more. On May 1, 1935, Gladwin had asked Douglass for copies of his sequoia ring-width measurements, which he was "anxious to use"; on June 9, he requested of Douglass "detail sheets" of the growing conditions of each tree for which he had obtained measurements, and a day later he asked Haury to "keep at" Douglass for the information. Douglass supplied the "Flagstaff and Sequoia" measurements on June 13, but Gladwin seems to have equated his reluctance to do so with recalcitrance. Although there may have been a touch of the latter, Gladwin behaved as if Douglass's only professional commitment was to supply Gila Pueblo with tree-ring data. In view of the fact that Gladwin obtained samples and data from the Laboratory of Anthropology as well (Stallings to Douglass, July 29, 1935), it is perhaps not surprising that Gila Pueblo did not undertake massive sample-collection expeditions until late 1939. Gladwin did not like fieldwork; why should he waste time and money making collections when he could easily obtain duplicates from other researchers?

Between 1935 and 1938, Gladwin made periodic progress reports to Douglass, often inviting him to come to his tree-ring laboratory in Santa Barbara, California. During this time, Gladwin confided to Haury his general feelings about the state of southwestern archaeology, but for the most part this was a period of reduced communication among Douglass, Haury, and Gila Pueblo, especially after Haury's departure for the University of Arizona in 1937. Haury kept asking Gladwin to publish in the *Tree-Ring Bulletin*, but each time Gladwin refused. In these refusals, Gladwin was always polite and rarely failed to include a note that while "progress was being made" and results were "better than expected," he nevertheless preferred not to broadcast his results until he was "perfectly satisfied" (July 11, 1938), though the criteria for his satisfaction were never explicitly identified. By December 1938, Gladwin seems to have become "perfectly satisfied," for he wrote to Haury that he was ready to submit his new technique for examination and would therefore like a "junta" with Colton, McGregor, Douglass, and Haury. Invariably, Gladwin noted that although he could not make the trip to Arizona, he would welcome the others to his laboratory, now in Santa Barbara. He thus found it acceptable to disrupt four schedules instead of one; the "junta" never occurred.

In March 1939, the ramifications of these attempts at tree-ring dating became more serious, for Gladwin refused to allow Haury to publish dates from White Mound Village. Gila Pueblo had paid for the excavations in 1936 and Gladwin argued that he was nearly ready to publish his own report on the site, with dates, but that report did not appear for six years (Gladwin 1945). Up to this point, even as he tried to impose his research needs on Douglass and others, Gladwin had not obstructed the dissemination of scholarly research. In the case of White Mound, he was technically within his rights because Gila Pueblo had paid for the excavation, but one is tempted to question the sincerity in the explanation of his denial to Haury. Gladwin wrote: "You will understand, I am sure, that . . . my purpose is to validate our own work and is in no way designed to cast any doubt on the Douglass chronology. We all earnestly hope that the Douglass chronology will be confirmed by the methods which we are employing" (March 22, 1939). Gladwin had previously argued that Douglass's samples were legally available to interested scholars because they had been collected under federal permit; one wonders if Haury was tempted to make the same argument, for White Mound Village is on the Navajo Reservation, and federal permits would have been required to dig there as well. Surely no harm would have been done to science had Haury been allowed to publish the dates. This episode tarnishes the credibility of Gladwin's assertions regarding the purpose of his own tree-ring research.

Gladwin's stubborn attitude regarding meetings with other scholars continued in 1939. He wrote to Colton and McGregor on April 19, 1939, to express again his willingness to meet and discuss, but his attitude changed when Colton informed him that plans were in the works for a full-fledged tree-ring conference in a location central enough for dendrochronologists Florence Hawley of the University of New Mexico and Sid Stallings of the Laboratory of Anthropology to attend. On May 17, 1939 (and again on June 22), Gladwin informed Haury that he and assistant Jack Denison were not prepared to discuss their technique and results in such a large conference. In backing out of the proposed conferences, Gladwin almost always legitimized his reluctance by describing his situation as analogous to that faced by Douglass many years earlier. The following is representative: "We find ourselves in very much the same position as Douglass in 1929. The modern series stretches back, in decreasing numbers of trees, to about 1400. . . . We have Morris's [sic] series from Aztec, as you know, but most of these records are comparatively short, and I would give my eye teeth for a few long records from Chaco Canyon. . . . I had hoped that we might have a conference this summer, but Jack [Denison] and I have been talking it over and have agreed that we want to be more sure of our ground before calling such a meeting" (Gladwin to Haury, May 17, 1939). Thus Gladwin could argue that he was not shying away from his December 30, 1938, offer to meet, nor the seven other offers he extended to meet with Douglass, Colton, and Haury, over the previous four years. Instead, he simply had to bridge the proverbial gap. The key verb in the passage above occurs in the last sentence: Gladwin wanted to "call" the meeting, thereby dictating its location and terms. Gladwin's disdain for public conferences was well known (Haury 1988:41), but the correspondence provides additional evidence of the many stipulations he placed on meetings of any sort.

Despite his refusal to meet with members of the Douglass "school" and to grant Haury permission to publish the White Mound results, Gladwin expanded the scope of his tree-ring research in 1939. He finally initiated a massive beam-collection effort that would duplicate, at least in terms of the archaeological specimens, the collection in Douglass's possession at the University of Arizona. If successful, he would no longer be hostage to Douglass's busy schedule and would not have to borrow specimens. First, however, he had to convince Jesse Nusbaum of the National Park Service that such sample replication was necessary. Eight years earlier, Nusbaum advocated rejecting "as a matter of policy" Gladwin's application for a permit to replicate Douglass's collections. Gladwin now felt that he was in a better bargaining position because he had an alternative tree-ring method that "avoid[s] the personal element" of the Douglass system, would help test the validity of that system, and would make tree-ring dating available to the archaeological proletariat:

I am writing to obtain a permit to collect specimens from some of the sites in the prehistoric sw. . . . I am doing my damnedest to put tree-ring dating on a firmer basis. When a tree-ring date is released, it is the most positive kind of information with which an archaeologist has to deal, and I do not think it can be overemphasized that such a date should be correct beyond any reasonable question of doubt. In my opinion, this is not true at the present time. . . . Furthermore I am extremely anxious to evolve a method which will make it possible for *all* institutions to do their own dating, provided they have the equipment to measure rings. I am strongly opposed to the present set-up

whereby tree-ring dating is limited to a few institutions. (Gladwin to
Nusbaum, May 19, 1939; emphasis in original)

It probably did not hurt Gladwin's case that Nusbaum's stepson Deric
had been offered employment on the proposed collecting expedition as
well. The senior Nusbaum replied in a "personal and unofficial" letter
to Gladwin on August 31, 1939, that he believed that the "stage is now
set for favorable consideration of a formal application for the project."
Gladwin submitted his formal application to the Department of the
Interior on September 4, 1939, and the permit was granted three
months later.

In a series of personal notes dated September 2, 1939, Gladwin outlined his concerns about the independent wood collection. He argued
that "mistakes" had been made but did not attempt to demonstrate that
mistakes existed dendrochronologically. The dates were mistakes
because they did not fit his preconceived notions about the archaeological evidence:

> Our position as to collections [sic] wood is that we shall be glad to
> build up an independent series, if such a series can be obtained without
> bickering. Our work should confirm the Douglass dating, and such
> confirmation can do no one any harm. . . . Kidder, Morris, Haury,
> Colton have all expressed their approval of multiple wood collections
> as good insurance against damage or destruction of the Douglass col-
> lection. . . . We feel strongly that a subject as definite and important as
> a tree-ring date should be subject to confirmation. Mistakes admittedly
> have been made, and I suspect the accuracy of the 900 A.D. date for
> Mogollon Village (Haury) and the 1030 A.D. date for St. John's Poly-
> chrome at Roberts' Great Kiva near Zuni (Douglass). . . . If there is no
> objection we desire to collect wood a) whenever available, b) to pre-
> serve it from destruction, c) to reinforce our own chronology, d) to
> confirm the Douglass chronology. (Emphasis in original)

Deric Nusbaum conducted fieldwork for Gila Pueblo from
September 4 through at least October 13, 1939, but collected only modern cores while engaging in a modest public relations effort. He discussed the goals of the Gila Pueblo tree-ring research with personnel
from the Museum of Northern Arizona as well as with Morris, Glock,
and personnel from the School of American Research in Santa Fe. After
negotiating numerous bureaucratic hurdles, including the submittal of
an additional nine copies of the application and a list of sites to be visited, Gila Pueblo received a collecting permit from the Department of the
Interior on December 28, 1939, effective until New Year's Day, 1941.

Nusbaum immediately began an archaeological sample-collection effort that continued throughout 1940.

While Nusbaum was in the field, Gladwin once again appealed to Douglass for a personal conference. This time he was deferential: "I believe that we are on the right track as regards the measurement of tree rings and the correlation of deviations, but your opinion, based on your experience and greater knowledge, would be of the utmost value to us, and it would give me great pleasure to be able to show you our instruments and methods" (March 17, 1940).

In late summer 1940 Gladwin began working with material collected by Deric Nusbaum in the Rio Grande Valley and immediately encountered the same problem Douglass had faced in the 1920s and Stallings had addressed in 1931 (see Chapter 6): that of the Rio Grande pines and their unique climate signal. Gladwin proposed two solutions. Gila Pueblo could either construct a Rio Grande chronology on its own or appeal to Stallings for the loan of the specimens used in his chronology (Stallings 1933). Gila Pueblo received increment cores from Stallings in 1935, and though Gladwin suggested he would do anything in his power to get the specimens "short of digging up the valley to duplicate Stallings' wood," he decided to leave the decision to Deric Nusbaum, who was in a better position to judge the politics of the situation (July 22, 1940). Gila Pueblo pursued the Rio Grande chronology no further.

By late December 1940, Gladwin gave Deric Nusbaum a progress report that included results of his analysis and interpretation of the White Mound material. Again, there was a perceived conflict between archaeological and tree-ring evidence.

> Our worst crisis has come with a date of 680 (?) for one of the houses at Nesbitt's Starkweather Ruin which Emil [Haury] dated as 927!!! This seems to have the making of trouble, as [Paul] Nesbitt has already published the date. The trouble here seems to have been that Nesbitt had a very mixed site with a long occupation; some small pit-houses, some surface houses with masonry walls, and a small pueblo nearby. He is all cock-eyed on his classification of pottery, particularly Reserve and Tularosa, and I don't know yet what to make of it. I am quite sure of a date about 680 as we have an excellent correlation with White Mound, but there may be an addition or subtraction of a year or two as we are going over all of our White Mound material again. I cannot see anything at 927 A.D. . . . . I also think that we shall be able to work out some dates for Martin's SU material, probably in the 600s. (December 27, 1940)

Once these dating problems were "resolved," Gladwin was able to reinterpret the entire prehistory of the Southwest:

All told, we are getting along well, particularly since we have revised our ideas of the southern [i.e., Hohokam] sites being earlier than the northern. My guess is that there will be no southern dates any earlier than 500 A.D. and maybe 600 A.D. In which case we shall have to make allowances for a Mexican trek similar to that of the Zuni: They must have gone by boat to the Mississippi, then up the Red or the Canadian, this would have brought them to the Cimarron and then they could have moved in to the 4 Corners and finally worked south to the Mogollon and Hohokam. (December 27, 1940)

Deric Nusbaum submitted his report to the secretaries of the Department of the Interior and the Smithsonian Institution on January 14, 1941. In it he included a list of sites from which beams were sampled at Mesa Verde National Park and various national monuments: Natural Bridges, Navajo, Canyon de Chelly, Chaco, and Aztec. From 32 sites—10 in Canyon de Chelly, 11 in Chaco Canyon, 9 at Mesa Verde, and 2 at Aztec—Nusbaum collected 616 samples, of which 230 (37 percent) dated according to the Gladwin system. Nusbaum conducted additional beam-collecting expeditions for Gila Pueblo in Chihuahua, Mexico, in May 1941; Mesa Verde National Park in August, September, and October 1941; and Navajo National Monument in November 1941. By the end of 1941, Gladwin had accumulated a massive specimen collection and had published Medallion Papers outlining the methods and instruments of his tree-ring analysis (Gladwin 1940a) and methods of correlation (Gladwin 1940b). He could now turn his attention to the interpretation of the dates obtained and the reinterpretation of southwestern prehistory.

The narrative regarding Gladwin's reinterpretations really begins in the early and mid-1930s when Haury conducted fieldwork for Gila Pueblo in the mountainous region of west-central New Mexico at Mogollon Village in 1931 and 1933 and Harris Village in 1931 and 1934. Haury's (1936) account of that research in Medallion Paper 20 details his interpretation of the chronological relationships between Harris and Mogollon villages and the rest of the Southwest. Although the number of tree-ring samples is not great from either site, when the tree-ring dates were considered in light of attendant material culture, Haury could make reasonable inferences regarding their chronometric placement. At Harris, a large village with more than 100 pithouses spanning the Georgetown, San Francisco, and Three Circle phases of the

Mogollon sequence, most of the tree-ring specimens were juniper, which at that time could not be dated. At Mogollon Village, where growing conditions were more similar to those of northeast Arizona and northwest New Mexico, tree-ring dating was more successful (Haury 1936:116). The presence of well-dated intrusive pottery, especially Lino Black-on-Gray and Red Mesa Black-on-White, led Haury to reason that Mogollon Village was not occupied later than a period roughly coeval with Pueblo I and that Harris village probably contained an occupation as late as the Pueblo II period (Haury 1936:117). Synthesizing these data, Haury concluded: "In terms of the northern [Anasazi] chronology, the basic Mogollon Culture was dominant, possibly, in Basketmaker III, certainly in Pueblo I (Georgetown and San Francisco Phases). Pueblo II can be recognized as a period of change and assimilation (Three Circle Phase) rising, in Pueblo III, to full force as the Mimbres Culture" (Haury 1936:128).

Haury's desire to tie in the Mogollon sequence with the better-dated Anasazi sequence to the north and to date the Hohokam sequence to the west and south is exemplified in an unpublished manuscript, probably written in 1937, in which he detailed the decision to work at White Mound Village:

> Recent discussions pertaining to the Mogollon Culture of the Southwestern United States have called attention to the very important angle of the relationships of this group with neighboring peoples. Patently, marginal areas are fertile fields for deriving information bearing on this problem. It was mainly this reason which persuaded Gila Pueblo, in the summer of 1936, to excavate a small village site known as White Mound situated about 30 miles west of Gallup, NM, in the valley of the Puerco River. . . . Tree-ring dates are of some interest as they reflect the survival of Basketmaker III into the eighth century A.D. . . . Dates [are] all derived from Pinyon charcoal. [The] range of dates is small—700+x to 802, with a large cluster at 786, for Room 4, the material culture of which seems to indicate a mixture of Basketmaker III and Pueblo I traits. Roberts has full Pueblo I at Allantown about 3 miles from White Mound, by the mid-ninth century, thus we date the Basketmaker III–Pueblo I transition at about 800 A.D.

Haury also worked in 1937 on the report of excavations undertaken during the winters of 1934–1935 and 1935–1936 at the Hohokam site of Snaketown. The White Mound excavations had direct bearing on the absolute chronology Haury proposed for Snaketown on the basis of intrusive tree-ring-dated ceramics. In addition, Paul Nesbitt of Beloit

College in Beloit, Wisconsin, had been excavating Mogollon sites during the 1930s, specifically the Mattocks Ruin in the Mimbres Valley of New Mexico from 1929 through 1931 (Nesbitt 1931) and the Starkweather Ruin near Reserve, New Mexico, in 1935 and 1936 (Nesbitt 1938). Despite the feeling at Gila Pueblo that Nesbitt's Starkweather excavation was largely a pothunting exercise (Haury to Gladwin, July 18, 1934), his tree-ring specimens played an important part in Haury's determination of the Snaketown chronology. As he told Roberts, "a recent date that I obtained for Nesbitt from his summer work near Reserve, New Mexico, from a Three Circle Phase house is 927, confirming the suspicion that my Mogollon dates of about 900 were at the tag end of the San Francisco phase. With this, and other facts that have come up, I would reconsider the dating as given in my report to the extent that the Georgetown phase would extend some centuries prior to 700. But all this is subject matter to be argued out with the shovel" (November 20, 1936). Later in this letter Haury noted that, when all of evidence was considered together, the Snaketown chronology (from earliest to latest the Vahki, Estrella, Sweetwater, Snaketown, Gila Butte, Santa Cruz, and Sacaton phases) "looked good" with phase lengths of about two centuries each. This was comparable to the Anasazi phases to the north (Nesbitt 1938:4). Haury argued that Snaketown therefore had an occupation span of 1,400 years (Gladwin, Haury, Sayles, and Gladwin 1937) with the following dates:

Sacaton Phase	A.D. 900 to 1100
Santa Cruz Phase	A.D. 700 to 900
Gila Butte Phase	A.D. 500 to 700
Snaketown Phase	A.D. 300 to 500
Sweetwater Phase	A.D. 100 to 300
Estrella Phase	100 B.C. to A.D. 100
Vahki Phase	300 B.C. to 100 B.C.

In the summer of 1939, Nesbitt excavated Wheatly Ridge Ruin near Reserve, New Mexico, to attempt once again to characterize the Mogollon culture and determine its relationship to previously defined Anasazi and Hohokam cultures. Nesbitt sent his tree-ring specimens to Haury for dating at the University of Arizona, with an enclosed honorarium of $25 for the graduate student who would date the material (September 28, 1939). As of March 1941, no dating had been accomplished, so Nesbitt contacted Gladwin. Nesbitt had no prior reason to doubt Gladwin's work, for Gladwin had confirmed Haury's dating of the Starkweather specimens from A.D. 862 to 927, with one specimen dating

A.D. 575–684 (Nesbitt to Haury, March 5, 1941). Gladwin reminded
Haury of these results, adding that he had obtained dates of A.D. 681–
697 for the combined Georgetown Phase at Harris and Starkweather
ruins, a phase that Haury thought dated much earlier. He then implied
for the first time that change was in the wind for the Hohokam chronology: "The whole problem of sites below the rim is beginning to crystal-
lize, and it now looks to me as if it will be necessary to raise [i.e.,
shorten] the Snaketown chronology, and as things stand at present, I
think the Vahki Phase will be raised to about 500 A.D." (Gladwin to
Haury, March 14, 1941).

Haury quickly questioned the architectural context of the dates
Gladwin quoted, for Nesbitt had told him that the A.D. 684 date was for
a late Georgetown or early San Francisco Phase house and therefore
should not drastically affect the phase sequence (Haury to Gladwin,
March 18, 1941). To make matters worse, Haury's Snaketown chronology, based on his and Douglass's tree-ring dates from other sites, was
getting longer, not shorter. Haury's excavations at the Bear Ruin in the
Forestdale Valley revealed the presence of intrusive Hohokam Gila Butte
Red-on-Buff ceramics at a site dendrochronologically dated to ca. A.D.
675 (Haury 1940a, 1940b, 1940c). If his original estimate of 200-year
phase lengths and the interpretation of the Bear Ruin intrusives were
even remotely correct, the Vahki Phase should date closer to 200 B.C.
than A.D. 500, as Gladwin suggested. Gladwin replied that the issue was
far from settled, but he appeared to have already made up his mind that
"some major revisions [in southwestern chronology] are needed"
(Gladwin to Haury, March 21, 1941).

In late spring or early summer 1941, Haury sent Gladwin the Bear
Ruin tree-ring specimens he had dated to A.D. 676 ± 10 and A.D. 677 ± 2
(Haury 1940b). Gladwin dated these using his own ring-width measurement and correlation techniques and on June 28 dropped a dendrochronological "bomb" on Haury: according to Gladwin's calculations,
these specimens dated somewhere between A.D. 750 and 850. Haury was
disturbed by Gladwin's revelation, though less by the changes implied for
the interpretation of prehistory than by the implications for archaeological tree-ring dating as a chronometric technique:

> Needless to say, the dates you have placed on the [Bear Ruin] ma-
> terial are somewhat disturbing in that they do not agree with our
> dates. Would it be possible for you to supply the information on the
> individual specimens as to just where each one falls within the century
> you mention. I do not believe that your dates, if right, will materially

affect the archaeological picture inasmuch as I have put an estimated date of 600 to 800 on our Forestdale phase. But the disconcerting feature is that it is possible to assign two dates to the specimen by the two methods used. My report has already gone through galley and I am afraid there is nothing I can do about introducing any changes. (July 14, 1941)

Several days later, Gladwin provided Haury with a list of dates for the Bear Ruin charcoal and informed him that he was now engaged in a complete reworking of the Mogollon tree-ring material, including specimens from Mogollon Village, the Harris Site, Starkweather Ruin, Wheatly Ridge Ruin, the SU site, and Bear Ruin (July 18, 1941). Haury asked Gladwin to return the Bear Ruin specimens, not simply the list of dates, so that he might go over his dating again (August 9, 1941); they were returned on September 2. On August 9, Gladwin sent to Haury, at Paul Martin's request, specimens from the SU site in west-central New Mexico, adding that though he had had difficulty with the Mogollon material, he again thought revisions were necessary, because "[it] looks to me as if all dates for southern sites, prior to 850 A.D., need to be revised. I think SU dates late 700s or early 800s."

Gladwin added later that he thought some of the White Mound Village materials "are at the root of our troubles" (August 17, 1941). Whether or not this was true, it was certainly an astonishing coincidence that the troublesome dates came from the very site for which Gladwin had refused Haury permission to publish his own tree-ring dates in 1939. Because Haury did not therefore have priority in print, it was much easier for Gladwin to personalize the debate in terms of "Haury's word against mine" rather than "Haury's verified and published dates versus Gladwin's unverified and as yet unpublished dates." By preventing Haury from publishing the White Mound dates two years earlier, Gladwin thus changed the structure of the debate in 1941. Whether his action in this regard was premeditated will never be known.

In August 1941, Gladwin sent Douglass about a hundred of the specimens he had so far dated. Given the severe implications of Gladwin's dating of this collection, Douglass dropped all his other projects to examine the specimens. He was not pleased with what he saw, and explained his concern to Haury:

I have worked a week on the hundred specimens that came from Mr. Gladwin, which by the way did not include the one No. 18 which gave the chief date on the 1939 dig at Forestdale. That is, I did not find a single specimen that had anywhere near that number of rings, some

86. The numbers marked on the specimens that came back ran from 1945 to 2039 with a number of duplicates. So I had no real assurance that these were the same pieces that you secured in 1939. But I have no reason to think otherwise. They had been cut into half-inch-thick sections which were so frail that they were largely broken and I spent many hours in gluing them together. *The surfaces on them were utterly impossible to use and I believe could never have been capable of giving reliable data.* I had to resurface them with fresh razor blades in order to see the rings. That used up blades pretty rapidly for the charcoal had, I think, been mounted in something like putty for cutting them into sections; the putty was partly filled with sand particles so that secondary surfaces usually available for studying the rings were put out of commission and the sand made razor cutting difficult. I regretted very much that any part of the original specimens was removed unnecessarily for we have always depended on looking the entire piece over to find the very best presentation of the ring sequence. I hope that no more charcoal specimens of any value are subjected to that treatment. I saw no signs that suggested to me any dates in the 800s.

Yesterday [Carlton] Wilder was in my office and I asked about the missing pieces and especially your old No. 18 which was the one I saw at Forestdale in 1939. He could not find that but he did bring over a collection of some 25 pieces that were not sent to Mr. Gladwin but which had been overlooked by [Frederick] Scantling. That lot averaged much better than the group that came back from Mr. Gladwin. I believe I found one date in a brief once-over that does not disagree with the former estimate.

In looking these over I think of one point of caution. While it is probable that many of these pieces were small logs and as charcoal really retain most of the original sapwood and thus give near cutting dates, it is very difficult often to estimate the nearness of the original outside and thus to judge the amount of annual rings lost on the outside. So if dates even as late as 750 should show up, I would not consider it as indicating error in that former dating. (August 21, 1941; emphasis added)

This passage identifies the main reason Douglass declined to answer Gladwin's charges directly. After examining the specimens Gladwin had "dated," Douglass realized that Gladwin's surfacing methods precluded the identification of ring boundaries, and that no matter what Gladwin thought he might have been measuring, he was not measuring ring widths. Comparison of their methods and results therefore amounted to the comparison of apples and oranges—hence Douglass's refusal to engage in debate with Gladwin.

On September 2, 1941, Gladwin related to Haury that he was making headway on the White Mound material but that most of the correlations, especially those for dates before A.D. 740, were too tenuous to be accepted; these dates, not coincidentally, contradicted Gladwin's belief in a short and relatively recent Mogollon chronology. He then expressed dismay that Martin had taken the liberty to publish a date of A.D. 450 for the SU site (Martin 1941a), which supported the longer and earlier Mogollon chronology. Gladwin argued that the situation was "extremely unfortunate as [Martin] is making confusion worse confounded" (September 2, 1941). Haury replied that he could not comment on the situation immediately but mentioned that he would soon see Martin and would ask him the source of the 450 date in person (September 17, 1941).

As noted above, Gladwin took over the dating of Nesbitt's Wheatly Ridge Ruin samples in late 1941 or early 1942 when it was clear they could not be dated in a timely fashion at the University of Arizona. The following exchange of letters regarding their dating is informative not only for the implications of that dating but also for suggestions of the deteriorating relationship between Gladwin and Haury. Nesbitt wrote to Haury expressing his understanding of Gladwin's dating:

> I am surprised that Gladwin did not inform you of the results which he obtained for the Wheatly Ridge specimens. I was very much surprised with the findings. The dates are in the main contemporaneous with those obtained at Starkweather, whereas I expected a time difference of 50–100 years. Wheatly Ridge, you will remember, was almost pure Three-Circle [Phase], while Starkweather was San Francisco [Phase] in character. From the standpoint of time, I now believe these two phases can be allocated to one time period. (March 4, 1942)

Haury expressed his understanding of the fundamental flaw in Gladwin's specimen preparation:

> I am not surprised that Gladwin didn't report the outcome of his work. He has not been in the habit of reporting such things of late. As a matter of fact, I sent him specimens from Forestdale [probably from Bear Ruin] which we had dated as a matter of courtesy and he began to tell everybody else of his results before he told me. The interesting fact in connection with this is that his results did not tally with ours, the dates being a century or a little more later. I feel that he is making a fundamental error in his technique of sandblasting the surface of the

specimens to read the rings. When he returned our specimens we found that his count varied as much as five to fifteen years in sequences of 75 years. Obviously it is impossible to get comparable results if the ring patterns themselves are not correct.

I am saying this not in a carping sense nor by way of implying that your dates are wrong; but if you hear rumors that the Forestdale dates are too early, that is the basis for it. Douglass has since re-examined the Forestdale wood and finds the early dating to be correct and has strengthened the same by additional dating criteria. I don't know just how the thing is going to straighten itself out. I hope the time will come again soon when we can get together in the field and thresh things out. (March 9, 1942)

By April, lines were being drawn in the dating "controversy" as Gladwin became more impatient with the publication of dates that did not agree with his preconceptions, including dates for Martin's (1941a) SU site and Douglass's (1941b) dating of samples from the Forestdale Valley. Nevertheless, he intoned to Haury that his research would avoid further "confusion":

We think it is necessary to publish our revisions [of the Snaketown chronology] since several recent papers have been based on our original estimates of chronology etc. and there is danger of growing confusion. . . . You will notice I have scarcely mentioned the Bear Ruin [dates]. My reasons for this are that I do not want to be held responsible for what may develop into a major controversy. As I said to you in Cambridge—I am sorry that I do not agree with your conclusions in regard to this site—nor do I agree with Douglass' dating. These are questions which I shall be glad to discuss with you whenever you wish, and, in my opinion, this would be very much better than for us to stage a knock-down drag-out fight in public. (April 27, 1942)

Over the next several months, Haury corresponded with a number of archaeological colleagues and informed them of Gladwin's research and its implications. The tone and content of the letters varies with the closeness of the relationship and the expertise of the receiving archaeologist. It is obvious, however, that Haury had not yet read Gladwin's (1942) revision of the Snaketown chronology when he wrote the letters from which the following quotations were extracted. Haury wrote to his Harvard classmate Brew in May: "Gladwin is about to break out his revisions which is interesting reading but I fear will confuse the issue instead of clearing it, as he intends. We have some tentative tree-ring results from our Bluff site work of last summer and while these are not sure enough yet to release because all specimens haven't been reviewed, there is some promise of getting early dates—and the site has a little pottery" (May 18, 1942). Haury explained the implications for Hohokam chronology to his colleague Malcolm Rogers in June: "Gladwin is about to come out with a revision of the Hohokam chronology which makes little sense to me. He wants to push Vahki up to 600 A.D. This doesn't make sense because we have Santa Cruz pegged at about 800. The Gila Butte intrusives at Forestdale with tree-ring dates in the late 600s and early 700s leaves the Snaketown, Estrella, and Vahki Phases to be squeezed in between this time and 600" (June 11, 1942).

In September, Haury had obviously seen Gladwin's revisions of the Snaketown chronology when he wrote to his friend and fellow Mogollon student Paul Martin, and his frustration is evident: "What did you think of Gladwin's Snaketown III? I don't know how in hell he gets that way or how he is going to laugh off some of the dope from both your and my [Mogollon] digs. I take great exception to his pat fifty year phase interval established for the Wingate-Chaco area [phases] and applying this as a measuring stick to the developmental phases of a wholly different culture in a different environment" (September 1, 1942).[2] The next day, Haury wrote directly to Gladwin: "I think you realize that on some points I do not agree with you but fortunately this still is a country where we may disagree amicably. It is going to be very difficult to reconcile your revised dating with the findings in our oldest site in the Forestdale Valley [the Bluff Site, at that time dated to ca. A.D. 310 or 320]. But on that score I feel that we need to do a great deal more arguing with the shovel rather than verbally." In another letter to Martin, Haury was less formal:

The gist of the whole thing is that the Snaketown chronology is collapsed so that the Vahki Phase is now dated from 600 to 650 A.D. Now it is a hell of a stretch of the imagination to see how we can cram the Estrella, the Sweetwater, the Snaketown, and the Gila Butte phases by 700 A.D., the dates we got at Forestdale [at the Bear Ruin]. Gladwin puts the Gila Butte phase at 800 to 850 A.D. which is completely at variance with our evidence. My chief criticism is that Gladwin has completely thrown overboard the Flagstaff dates; that he has established on not too precise evidence a pat fifty year phase for the Chaco,

2. This comment is especially interesting in view of the fact that Haury used exactly the same technique with pat 200-year phase intervals to obtain his first Snaketown chronology (see Gladwin, Haury, Sayles, and Gladwin 1937).

Mesa Verde, Kayenta, and Mimbres branches and is using these intervals as a measure of development in the totally different culture and a
totally different environment and, damn it, I don't get it. . . . Somebody
is going to have to answer this report because I think it has some implications which, if accepted, will be very destructive. All of this would be
well and good if his proposals were backed by some solid new evidence
but they are not. It is a good example of armchair bulldozing.
(September 16, 1942)

In March 1943, Haury and Gladwin finally met to discuss the situation face to face, but their meeting does not seem to have been productive, for Gladwin argued that the debate now hinged on the A.D. 310
date at Bluff Ruin (Gladwin to Haury, March 15, 1943; see also
Douglass 1942, 1944; Haury 1942). Haury countered that the issue lay
not in the dating of any particular sample but rather in the method of
tree-ring analysis in general. He confided to Brew that he was glad he
was no longer employed by Gladwin and was therefore in a position to
argue with him (March 25, 1943). In the meantime, Gladwin took it on
himself to inform, behind Martin's back, Orr Goodson, acting director
of the Field Museum of Natural History, that Douglass's dates for the SU
site were incorrect, that they should date to the last half of the eighth
century, and that "there has been a tendency to exaggerate the antiquity
of ruins of this character. This applies particularly to the Bluff Site, near
Forestdale, for which Dr. Douglass has recently published a date of 310
A.D. [Douglass 1942]. I have reason to believe that Dr. Douglass is in
error, and that the Bluff Site will eventually belong to the same general
horizon as other ruins of this kind, at a date of about 700 A.D. or slightly
later" (March 25, 1943). Gladwin's tactic seems to have backfired, however, for Goodson discussed the letter with Martin, and together they
determined that the specimen Gladwin had dated from the SU site was
from a Three Circle (i.e., late) Phase pithouse that really should date in
the early 700s. Gladwin thus inadvertently induced Goodson and
Martin to prove that Douglass's and Gladwin's dates for "ruins of this
character" were not in conflict with the archaeological data, especially
since most of the SU site was attributed, on the basis of archaeological
evidence, to the Pine Lawn Phase, which is stratigraphically earlier than
Three Circle. Martin summarized these developments, and his plans, in a
letter to Haury on March 30, 1943:

> I must say I am filled with a certain amount of unholy glee at hav-
> ing caught Gladwin on the hip because, as the Director [Goodson]
> points out in his letter to Gladwin, the wood which Gladwin dated for

the su site is from a Three-Circle pit house, and to have it dated in the early 700s is wonderful! . . . When I last saw you in 1941 Gladwin had told Nesbitt that the su site dated in the early half of the 8th century, and he assumes, because he didn't know where the wood came from, that that date holds for Pine Lawn phase or the Mogollon-like materials he has been excavating. . . . He undoubtedly will persist in his own thinking and in statements he will make to others in saying that the su site dates at about 725 A.D. and will neglect to state that this wood came from a Three-Circle house and is not, therefore, representative of Pine Lawn phase. . . . In order to spike his guns and beat him to the draw, I shall publish a Three Circle date from the Reserve area, and will not indicate that there is any controversy. . . . This ought to make the old boy gnash his teeth in rage. In this way I shall let most disinterested archaeologists know what is going on and will prevent the notion from becoming widespread that the su site is late and would date at about 725 according to Gladwin.

Haury approved of Martin's plans and noted with incredulity that Gladwin was now producing dates on the basis of measurements taken from photographs:

Gladwin wrote to me the other day, since I saw him in Globe, to the effect that he had measured the rings of the Bluff Site specimen illustrated by Douglass in the TRB [Douglass 1942], and he pompously informs me that according to his method he finds better correlations at a considerably later time. Who in God's name does he think he is anyway? The idea of thinking that it's possible to do this sort of thing without access, not only to the specimen illustrated, but to all the specimens which make up the collection. It seems to me that in coming out with things like this, Gladwin is going to hang himself. (April 2, 1943)

This type of debate raged on with varying degrees of intensity into 1946, but the final straw for Haury seems to have been when Gladwin asked him to pick sides—either to endorse Douglass's dates and techniques or to endorse Gladwin's. Gladwin had originally asked Haury to serve as a "referee" between him and Douglass because Haury was familiar with both men and their work (Gladwin to Kidder, September 12, 1944), but later he perceived Haury's refusal to side with him as blatant disloyalty. This kind of essentialist combativeness is typical Gladwin. It ignored the possibility that both researchers might have positive contributions to make, and it helped Gladwin legitimize his approach and at the same time assail the hegemony of the Douglass system without the need to engage its practitioners further.

Haury tried to explain the situation to Kidder on April 26, 1943, noting that "[Gladwin's] unorthodoxy has been very good for us all . . . [but] I cannot convince myself that his dating method is better than Douglass' or that Douglass has made the mistakes which he claims. I am particularly suspicious when the critical job of ring counting and measuring is left to [his] assistants who report that the whole technique was learned in two hours." Haury added some weeks later that he would try to keep his mind open with regard to Gladwin's techniques and the ongoing debate, but after having worked for Gladwin for seven years, he felt that such restraint was not going to be easy. He also refused to acquiesce to Gladwin's surprising demand that, were Haury to go to Santa Barbara to examine Gila Pueblo's dating, he would have to work from paper records instead of the original specimens (Haury to Sayles, July 2, 1943).

Nearly a year later, Gladwin sent Haury a letter that clearly illustrates another of his favorite demagogic tactics, that of Gladwin-as-martyr. He set the stage by reducing the debate between the Douglass camp and the Gladwin camp to one over differences in the interpretation of the Bear Ruin and Bluff Ruin dates, not in their use of radically different analytical techniques. In so doing he attempted to deflect attention from problems in his dating method. Although it was Gladwin who chose to rewrite the prehistory of the Flagstaff area, the Chaco area, and portions of the Mogollon area, it was also he who had "run foul" of the dendrochronologists responsible for that dating. That is, he contended, he felt they were not interested in the dates he had produced and were instead engaged in personal attacks. Finally, Gladwin claimed he was being persecuted by graduates of the University of Arizona and the Douglass "school" as a whole. Gladwin nevertheless tried to placate Haury. Once again, he did not try to delineate the "mistakes" dendrochronologically but simply expressed faith that certain dates were wrong:

> Lines are being drawn and I do not like to see you [Haury] and myself on opposite sides of the fence. . . . When I tackled the job of trying to unscramble the archaeology at Flagstaff from tree-ring dates which seemed to me to be wrong, I of course ran foul of Hargrave and McGregor. More recently in dealing with the archaeology of the Chaco Branch, I find that I have run foul of some of [Florence] Hawley's tree-ring dates which I believe to be wrong. . . . As the Chaco report nears completion I am already planning a review and analysis of the entire Mogollon problem based primarily on our work in the San Simon Valley, but also involving correlations with all cultures below the

Mogollon Rim. It is already obvious that in so doing I shall again run foul of Douglass and his tree-ring dates for the Bear Ruin and the Bluff Site. . . . It is becoming more and more apparent that my differences of opinion are largely confined to the graduates of the University of Arizona. This may possibly be explained as due to the teachings of Dr. Cummings, but I think it is more probably the result of Dr. Douglass' teachings in dendrochronology. (May 23, 1944)

Gladwin reiterated these sentiments in a letter to Haury on July 10, 1944, but added a completely unrealistic demand: "Since I do not agree with Douglass' dating, I am now taking the position that when the accuracy of *any* date is questioned, the operator shall be required to submit the evidence upon which the date is based. . . . I will deal with archaeological evidence if you agree that such evidence shall serve as a control of tree-ring dating rather than vice versa as has been customary" (emphasis in original). Gladwin failed to recognize that dendrochronologists had been "required to submit the evidence upon which the date was based" since the Tree-Ring Conference of 1934 stipulated that dates had to be verified by another qualified dendrochronologist before they could be published. As we have seen, however, Gladwin felt this practice was invalid and amounted to "censorship" rather than verification. Haury replied that he would not jettison his faith in the Douglass system nor would he accept Gladwin's contention that archaeological evidence should be the control for tree-ring dating. Indeed, Haury felt that such a practice would negate the very independence of tree-ring dating in archaeological chronology. Gladwin replied that he would not again waste their time trying to solve the problem, and they would simply have to agree to disagree (August 24, 1944). In a letter to Kidder three weeks later, however, Gladwin was less than diplomatic about the Douglass/Haury system, and his martyr complex shone through:

My efforts to induce Haury to act as a referee were prompted chiefly by his familiarity with both Douglass and myself. In his last letter to me, of which he sent a copy to you, he declared himself unequivocally as favoring tree-ring dates over archaeological evidence, and as far as I am concerned, this completely disqualifies him. From now on, I am all through with trying to appease anyone and in the final chapters of the Douglass Medallion [Gladwin 1947] I will not pull any punches. There is not a shadow of a doubt in my mind that serious mistakes in dating have been made by Douglass and the individuals who have associated with him and I also believe that these mistakes have been directly responsible for distorted perspectives and interpretations of

Southwestern archaeology. Rightly or wrongly, I have persuaded myself that it is my especial job to try to correct these distortions, since I happen to have stumbled upon an independent method by means of which the dating of the Douglass School can be challenged. This is merely an essential step, however, in clearing the ground of the archaeological hot-dog stands which have sprung up around Flagstaff and along the Mogollon Rim, and which will have to be disinfected before they can be introduced into decent Southwestern society—I propose using DDT, which, in this case, stands for "Damn Douglass' Tree-rings." (September 12, 1944)

With this statement, whatever semblance of a working relationship that existed between Gladwin and Haury was gone. No correspondence was exchanged between them for two years, though they did see each other in October 1945 after Ted Sayles was dismissed from Gila Pueblo and was hired by Haury as assistant director of the Arizona State Museum. Feelings were equally as harsh then as before (Antevs to Haury, November 3, 1945, and Haury to Kidder, November 9, 1945). Gladwin graciously sent Haury the page proofs for his revision of the Tusayan Ruin dating (Gladwin 1946), but Haury tersely replied that since it had been 15 years since the fieldwork was performed, he no longer remembered the facts regarding that excavation and therefore could not comment (October 2, 1946). In other words, Haury refused to engage in further debate with Gladwin.

CONCLUSION

Just as the National Geographic Society receives deserved recognition for its support of dendroarchaeological research led by Douglass and Judd during the 1920s, Gila Pueblo should be recognized for its administrative, financial, and to some degree scholarly support of Haury's dendrochronological research between 1930 and 1937. During that time, Haury made some significant contributions to archaeological tree-ring dating method and theory (Haury 1934, 1935a), without which a number of archaeologists would have remained skeptical of tree-ring dating in general.

Gladwin began experimenting with quantitative methods of tree-ring analysis during Haury's tenure, but his efforts grew in intensity and scope after Haury's departure in 1937. Gladwin based his stinging criticisms of Flagstaff archaeology, the Douglass method of tree-ring analysis, the Hohokam chronology, and other interpretations of southwestern archaeology on his own tree-ring methods and dating. Ignoring for the moment whether Gladwin's technique was methodologically flawed, which it was, it is unfortunate that his peculiar demagoguery precluded constructive engagement between the Douglass "school" and the Gladwin "school," for some of his criticisms of the Douglass technique, in spirit if not in letter, were echoed by other archaeologists of the day. Douglass was the court of last resort for verification of all archaeological tree-ring dates, but he was also an extremely busy man and in the 1930s had reached retirement age. This structure delayed the release of important archaeological and dendrochronological data to the point of frustration for many archaeologists (e.g., Antevs 1946a, 1946b; Dutton 1941). The production of tree-ring dates was thus a tightly controlled endeavor, and one gets the feeling that Gladwin would have been comfortable with the process if only he had been in control. Unfortunately for Gladwin, patience, practice, and persistence can lead to expertise in the Douglass method of tree-ring dating, but stubborn determination and unlimited finances do not.

In December 1950, Harold S. Gladwin donated Gila Pueblo's archaeological collections, valued at approximately one million dollars, to the Arizona State Museum in Tucson, thereby doubling the size of that institution's holdings (Martin 1960). As difficult as this donation must have been, Gladwin recognized that the ASM was the logical place for the collections. He explained his decision to Colton: "I am sure that no one could be as well qualified as Emil [Haury] and Ted [Sayles] to make the best of the material since they actually did most of the work" (January 3, 1951). Gila Pueblo's dendrochronological samples, equipment, and records remained in Gladwin's possession until 1957, when he donated them to the University of Arizona as well. With this donation, Gladwin remained equally gracious: "It gave me a great deal of pleasure . . . to learn that the records and equipment which were sent to the University may be of some value to you. Your Laboratory of Tree-Ring Research has become an institution of the greatest value, not only to the University of Arizona but also to climatologists and archaeologists all over the world, and I am very proud to be able to share in some degree its success" (Gladwin to Douglass, December 10, 1957). Gladwin died in 1983 at the age of 100 (Haury and Reid 1985).

CHAPTER 5

Volcanoes, Ruins, and Cultural Ecology

Tree-Ring Dating at the Museum of Northern Arizona

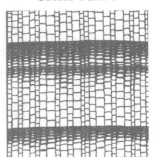

The Museum of Northern Arizona was established in 1928 by Harold S. Colton (Figure 22) and Mary-Russell F. Colton in conjunction with the Flagstaff Woman's Club and the Flagstaff Chamber of Commerce (Downum 1988:98). The museum was founded partly in reaction to outrage stemming from Jesse Walter Fewkes's export of Elden Pueblo artifacts to the Smithsonian Institution.

Harold Colton, by training a zoologist, had been conducting systematic archaeological surveys in the Flagstaff area since 1916 and was interested in providing the local citizenry with its own collection of artifacts and specimens that could be used to explore the relationships between human behavior and the environment (Downum 1988:100). Employees of the Museum of Northern Arizona (MNA) made significant contributions in this regard, especially after John C. McGregor (Figure 23) was hired as dendrochronologist and curator of archaeology in 1930. MNA's archaeological tree-ring dating over the next decade focused on the dating and archaeological definition of Pueblo II, and then Pueblo I, sites in the Flagstaff area, the dating of the eruption of Sunset Crater and, perhaps most important, the dating of ceramic types which still provides the basic chronological framework for northern Arizona (Downum 1988). Table 5 gives a chronology.

ARCHAEOLOGY AND TREE-RING DATING: LYNDON HARGRAVE AND JOHN McGREGOR

One of the first employees hired by Colton was Lyndon Lane Hargrave, formerly a student of biology at the University of Arizona and the lead member of the National Geographic Society's Second and Third Beam

FIGURE 22. Harold Sellers Colton (1881–1970), founder and director of the Museum of Northern Arizona. Courtesy of the Museum of Northern Arizona.

FIGURE 23. John C. McGregor explaining the principles of tree-ring dating to an unidentified colleague. Courtesy of the Museum of Northern Arizona.

TABLE 5. Timeline: Archaeological Tree-Ring Research at the Museum of Northern Arizona.

1928 Museum of Northern Arizona founded.

1929 Lyndon Lane Hargrave hired as assistant director.

1930 John C. McGregor hired as curator of archaeology and dendrochronologist.

Colonel Lionel F. Brady discovers Black-on-White sherds on volcanic ash from Sunset Crater; dating of that eruption becomes a research focus.

1931 January: Colton suggests Sunset Crater eruption may have left a mulch that facilitated agriculture in the eruption area.

May: McGregor and Douglass discover and crossdate "Type 1" dating.

1933 March: McGregor named curator of dendrochronology.

June–August: Hargrave leads Rainbow Bridge–Monument Valley Expedition (RBMVE).

August–October: Hargrave leads excavations at Wupatki Pueblo.

1934 June 11–12: First Tree-Ring Conference, Museum of Northern Arizona. *Tree-Ring Bulletin* founded, sampling protocol established, and date verification procedures adopted. Hargrave leads RBMVE.

1935 May: "Trees: Recorders of History and Climate" symposium at the Southwest Division Meeting of the American Association for the Advancement of Science, Santa Fe, New Mexico.

1936 Fieldwork focuses on delineating culture history rather than dating Sunset Crater.

1937 Haury becomes editor of fledgling *Tree-Ring Bulletin*.

Colton and Hargrave publish *Handbook of Northern Arizona Pottery Wares*.

1940 Gladwin begins his critique of Flagstaff-area archaeology.

1942 McGregor leaves MNA to become director of the Illinois State Museum.

1945 Colton (1945) and Douglass correctly date the eruption of Sunset Crater.

1950 Museum of Northern Arizona donates tree-ring collections to the Laboratory of Tree-Ring Research.

Expeditions of 1928 and 1929, respectively. Hargrave was hired as assistant director of the Museum of Northern Arizona on February 1, 1929. Ten weeks later, however, Colton was pressured by Douglass and Judd to release Hargrave for the summer to act as the senior field member of the Third Beam Expedition (see Chapter 2). Colton acquiesced and released Hargrave, who graciously saw his absence from the museum as an opportunity for McGregor, his old friend and fraternity brother. Colton asked Hargrave to recommend an able replacement, and McGregor's name came immediately to mind. Hargrave told McGregor that Colton might offer him the job of acting assistant director of MNA in his absence, and Hargrave "depended" on McGregor to accept, partly because he hoped McGregor would do a better job in the office than he had, for Hargrave felt more at home in the field. In early May, Colton offered McGregor a job, but it was a temporary position as acting curator of archaeology rather than acting assistant director. McGregor rejected Colton's offer for reasons that are not entirely clear, and the museum seems to have made it through the summer without an assistant director. MNA's fieldwork, however, was largely postponed until the following year (Downum 1988).

On December 5, 1929, shortly after Douglass's *National Geographic* contribution was released, Hargrave complained to Douglass that he had not been properly credited by Douglass and the National Geographic Society for the independent ceramic and architectural chronologies he had established and which had been used to target sites by the Second and Third Beam Expeditions. He was especially chagrined because Florence Hawley had recently published her own ceramic chronology based on the analysis of prehistoric ceramic paint composition (Hawley 1930), and she had therefore received public recognition that Hargrave felt he had been denied by the omission in Douglass's (1929) article. Douglass explained that the manuscript he had submitted to *National Geographic* had been cut by more than one-third by the editors and that all names had been removed from the text, including Hargrave's and that of his employer, the Museum of Northern Arizona. These omissions violated the negotiated terms regarding Hargrave's release from MNA to the NGS Beam Expeditions, as described in Chapter 2. Hargrave later stated (1935b:18) that the Beam Expeditions would have been "random walks" without the framework provided by his ceramic chronology.

Mary-Russell Ferrell Colton pointed out to Judd the *National Geographic*'s lack of reference to MNA. Judd downplayed her concerns, somewhat patronizingly stating that the "omission is just one of those miserable little accidents that will occasionally occur [even] in the most efficient of editorial offices" (January 2, 1930). In a more formal letter to Harold Colton the same day, Judd explained that the December *National Geographic* article "fails to express the obligation we all feel toward the MNA for its courtesy last summer in loaning Mr. Hargrave to us." Douglass later promised Colton that he would "endeavor to make up for this deficiency in every way possible" (January 7, 1930), but Colton felt that no additional apologies were necessary (Colton to Douglass, January 14, 1930).[1]

In April 1930, Hargrave and Colton finished plans for five months of fieldwork in Deadman's Flat northeast of Flagstaff in the upcoming season (Downum 1988:106; Hargrave 1930:1). Their goal was simple: "To investigate Pueblo II, a little-known period in Southwestern archaeology" (1930 at the Museum 1931:2). When it came to personnel issues, Hargrave again thought of his friend McGregor, who was completing Douglass's tree-ring class in Tucson. Hargrave wanted McGregor to serve as his assistant, and in June, McGregor joined the MNA staff as curator of archaeology and dendrochronologist. He immediately began work on the many charcoal samples collected during Hargrave's fieldwork in the Medicine Valley in May.

On June 1, 1930, Hargrave, assisted by Katharine Bartlett and a team of excavators, examined a number of Pueblo II sites (Hargrave 1930:1; Downum 1988:106). Their work began along Lower Walnut Creek and then moved to Wilson Pueblo and Medicine Cave northeast of Flagstaff (Figure 24). They tested or excavated at least 16 sites, including Medicine Fort (NA 862) and Medicine Pithouse (NA 1680), two sites that would later figure prominently in Gladwin's critique of MNA's work (Gladwin 1943). Dendrochronology absolutely affected their research design, for

---

1. Editors at *National Geographic* apparently also added some "human interest" anecdotes to make the article more appealing to the typically white, middle-class, moderately educated population that composed the bulk of their readership (Lutz and Collins 1993). Included in this regard are the title, "The Secret of the Southwest Solved by Talkative Tree-Rings," which was not Douglass's; the 10 photographs of Native Americans and their ceremonies that are irrelevant to dendrochronological research; and reference to HH-39, "the history within [which] held us spellbound; its significance found us all but speechless; we tried to joke about it, but failed miserably" (Douglass 1929:767). Douglass never wrote that passage (Douglass to Kroeber, September 17, 1931), and indeed the origins of the "legend" of HH-39 can be found on page 767 of the *National Geographic* article (Douglass 1929).

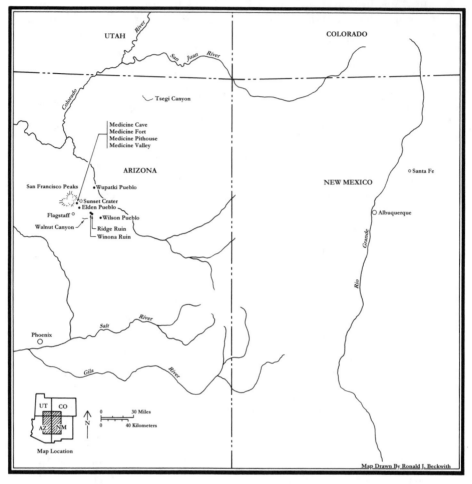

FIGURE 24. Sites sampled by the Museum of Northern Arizona and mentioned in the text.

they excavated only burned structures in which construction beams could reasonably be expected to have been preserved in situ (Hargrave 1930:3; Figure 25). On the basis of archaeological evidence and the Douglass tree-ring chronology, Hargrave estimated the date for the Pueblo II dwellings at between A.D. 500 and A.D. 700 (Hargrave 1930). This estimate, though not too far from the actual dates later derived by tree-ring analysis, followed archaeologists' tendency to the overestimate the age of southwestern ruins by at least a couple of centuries.

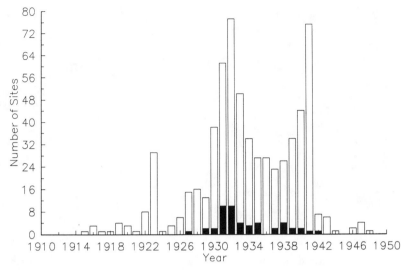

FIGURE 25. Archaeological tree-ring research by the Museum of Northern Arizona 1927–1942. Note the peak in activity in 1931–1932 as researchers attempted to date Pueblo I and Pueblo II occupations around Flagstaff and the eruption of Sunset Crater.

The 1930 fieldwork on the definition of Pueblo II occupations was quickly overshadowed by the discovery that a volcano had erupted during the time of prehistoric pueblo occupation in the Flagstaff area (Downum 1988:107). In June, Major Lionel F. Brady found black-on-white sherds lying directly on the surface of volcanic ash from the most recent eruption of Sunset Crater. He made the not unreasonable inference that people must have been in the Flagstaff area during or shortly after the eruption. McGregor subsequently discovered an ash lens in the fill of a pithouse he was excavating at site NA 1296; Hargrave found a similar lens in site NA 860A (Figure 26). Hargrave also excavated site NA 1653, near where Brady had discovered the sherds, and found two pithouses that were sealed beneath thick deposits of ash. Dating the eruption of Sunset Crater thus became a major focus of MNA's tree-ring research (Brady 1932; Downum 1988:108). Colton expressed to Douglass the importance of the 1930 tree-ring samples: "In our work this summer we have accumulated a vast amount of good pine charcoal from pithouses ranging from Basketmaker III to Pueblo II and early Pueblo III. I hope that you will be able in the near future to go over this material for I feel it will carry your chronology back several hundred years" (September 11, 1930).

FIGURE 26. Hargrave in an unidentified pithouse, possibly at site NA 860, northeast of Flagstaff. The "black sand" layer of volcanic ash from the most recent eruption of Sunset Crater is clearly evident in the profile.

While working on the dendrochronological analysis of the 1930 specimens, McGregor wasted no time developing his own publication record. In the fall he published "Tree-Ring Dating" in the MNA's *Museum Notes* (McGregor 1930), in which he provided a basic overview of Douglass's technique and its applications. Douglass would ordinarily have been proud of his student's achievement, but Douglass's long-time friend Brady offended him by telling McGregor, in Douglass's presence, that his article was the best ever written on tree-ring dating (Douglass to Colton, October 24, 1930). Judd recommended that Douglass consider McGregor's article and Brady's comment as stimuli and requested that Douglass ignore all new wood collections and focus on finishing his detailed report of the Pueblo Bonito dating (November 15, 1930). Douglass did not heed Judd's recommendations, and his report was not finished for another five years (Douglass 1935a).

In January 1931, results of McGregor's dendrochronological analysis of the 1930 specimens were being verified by Douglass. Hargrave checked McGregor's and Douglass's conclusions against the archaeological evidence, just as Morris was doing with the Basketmaker III specimens from northeastern Arizona (Chapter 3). Hargrave wrote McGregor:

> I am pleased to learn that Dr. Douglass is getting results and that he is delighted with the material. I have checked the numbers of his last group, namely: NA 917, 894, 906, and 919, and find that all are from

the large pithouse by the fort. I would have expected the cutting dates to be close. So far there has been no crossdating between any two sites, and recognizing archaeological differences between many of them, I must agree with you that a hundred years is far short of the time covered by the beam material we have collected. A hundred years for the [Medicine] Fort is ample. . . . I am anxious to have him work on some of the other sites. (January 14, 1931)

Hargrave also seems to have directed Douglass away from potentially erroneous dating on the basis of contextualizing archaeological evidence:

Regarding [Douglass's] thought that possibly the Lower Walnut specimen might crossdate with the [Medicine] Fort material, I can hardly agree with him. I was a member of the party and did some hard work grinding the core out. I am familiar with the pottery complex, and it is much later than that of the Medicine Cave region. In fact, the entire division of Pueblo II characterized by small masonry houses intervenes between the Lower Walnut specimen and the Fort. The specimen in question is a core from a pine beam in an early Pueblo III kiva in a cave. The pueblo closely associated with this beam is even later than the Wilson pueblo. With this evidence, that has been substantiated so many times in the field, I would be greatly surprised if a crossdate is found. (January 14, 1931)

When informed of Brady's June 1930 discovery of sherds on the Sunset Crater ash, as well as the discovery in 1930 of pithouses filled with ash, Douglass immediately expressed interest in the new dating problem and application. He hoped he might find an assistant to help him in the Sunset Crater research, especially because McGregor had chosen to stay in Flagstaff rather than return to Tucson during the 1930–1931 academic year. He wrote Colton: "The possibilities of your discoveries last summer of ruins with volcanic ash in them are tremendously attractive and I am anxious to work that line to the very limit, for it is a most important one. John McGregor has done good work with those specimens, and I regret that he will not have time to register this coming semester for special work in them" (January 22, 1931).

Colton replied that the Sunset Crater problem had become even more interesting. The foundation for Colton's "Black Sand Hypothesis" (Colton 1960) is clearly evident in the following passage: "Our work on the Sunset ash fall has taken another twist. We find that in the area where there was a light fall of ash late Pueblo II and early Pueblo III sites are abundant. Outside of this area of the fall they are scarce. This suggests that the ash made a mulch which made agriculture, by Hopi methods, possible over a limited area. . . . After the winds stripped the land of ash, putting it into the canyons and the lee side of mesas, the country in late Pueblo III again became uninhabitable" (January 28, 1931). For the first time, a prehistorian offered an ecological explanation for changes evident in the prehistoric southwestern archaeological record, following by only two years Douglass's identification of the "Great Drought" as a causal agent (Douglass 1929).

Dating the eruption of Sunset Crater proved to be an exceedingly difficult task but ultimately one of the major successes of the MNA tree-ring dating program (McGregor 1936). An initial estimate (Colton 1932) placed the eruption quite early, between A.D. 700 and 875. A second estimate narrowed the possible range to between A.D. 875 and 910 (McGregor 1936). This estimate was later changed to between A.D. 1046 and 1071 (Colton 1945) on the basis of a Gladwin-induced reanalysis of MNA's archaeological and dendrochronological data. As Downum (1988) points out, these revisions, rather than indicating McGregor's incompetence or the invalidity of the Douglass method of tree-ring dating (cf. Gladwin 1943), provide an excellent example of the self-correcting nature of scientific research, especially in sciences such as archaeology, in which the database is by definition incomplete, and dendrochronology, a cumulative science in which dating becomes better with the addition of more samples to a given tree-ring chronology. An excellent example of the latter is the "Type 1" chronology identified by Douglass in late spring 1931.

Douglass reported to Colton the discovery of a new, undated, and apparently old, floating chronology that he designated "Type 1" dating: "As perhaps you know there is [another] chronology which I call 'Type 1' of very distinctive characters, which so far I have been entirely unable to locate [in the Flagstaff chronology]. John McGregor tells me that he found this same fact in looking over [Flagstaff-area] specimens last summer. I had the same experience at Oraibi and after long study found that the unknown preceded the known by 213 years. It may occur where a site has been occupied for a long time" (May 4, 1931).

On November 7, Douglass informed Colton that he had not yet succeeded in dating it but suggested that it might tie into the dated sequence in the early 700s, and he hoped that some of the specimens collected during the summer that had not yet been examined might yield a clue. His wish came true, and one week later Douglass submitted a detailed, if somewhat unrefined, report to Colton entitled "Flagstaff Type I: An

Example of a Major Dating Operation." In it he related the dating of this sequence and its implications for archaeological tree-ring dating in general:

I have solved [Flagstaff] Type 1 dating and it is late instead of early. It involves building dates of 1067 for Medicine Fort (NA 862) and North Pit (NA 1238), and a date as late as 1114 for NA 2002, which I understand is somewhere out in Lower Dead Man's Flat. . . . The errors in this sequence were all concentrated at about 920 A.D. in a region which we had covered by perhaps only one specimen. This shows how duplication of specimens eliminates errors. . . . This chronology was first observed in the group of Flagstaff specimens brought down [to Tucson] by John McGregor, and examined by me in early January 1931. The pieces came chiefly from Medicine Fort, Site 862, and Medicine Fort Pit, Site 1680, and North Pit, Site 1238, all in Medicine Valley. Extensions were made both forward and backward so that Type-1 in my visit of November 1931, has become extended to 230 years in length. . . . Almost every major dating operation has resulted in a sequence later than expected. This is partly from a lack of systematic and tedious work on skeleton plots. It is very much quicker and easier to recognize some particular feature and much time is spent in that particular way. If there is a preconceived notion of the age, as there always is, it may place this attempt at a wrong point in the chronology. . . . Ring 1067, which is a very conspicuous drouth ring, was the principal basis of my first cross-dating between Aztec and Pueblo Bonito, over ten years ago, and in fact was the foundation of the work at Chaco Canyon. . . . We have here a very fine chronology extending from 877 to 1114. By means of the early charcoal from Medicine Valley it goes back in fine detail to about 735. We thus have two sequences from the east side of the San Francisco Mountains. The other is the Wupatki sequence which begins somewhere near 950, if I remember correctly, and extends to about 1180. . . . This is a good example of how building up a separate chronology and letting it grow in the certainty that it is essentially correct and has an important value. The more it grows and the longer it gets and the greater number of pieces in it adds to its value. In due time it fits in. All this shows again the fundamental value of cross-dating. One might almost say that crossdating is more important than dating. (November 14, 1931)

This rather coarse document is important for several reasons. First, one of the sites from which the specimens came, Medicine Fort, figured prominently in Gladwin's (1943) critique of work in the Flagstaff region.

Second, Douglass illustrates the potentially biasing effect that preconceived archaeological notions can have on tree-ring dating, thereby
touching on the independence of tree-ring dating with respect to archaeological sites. Third, Douglass for the first time explicitly stated that dendrochronological "crossdating is more important than dating."
Archaeologists pining for dates for their sites often find this difficult to
accept (see examples in Baillie 1995), but crossdating is now an established principle of dendrochronology. Finally, Douglass identifies the
importance of sample replication, or in his words, "duplication." Put
another way, the dendrochronologist must find good crossdating in multiple samples from the same area to be confident in her or his results.

Although Douglass was pleased with this accomplishment, the dating of the Type 1 chronology confirmed, in Colton's words, "our worst
fears" about Pueblo II dating in the Flagstaff area because the derived
dates came out so late in time (November 25, 1931). Hargrave
(1930:3) had already publicly announced his speculation that the sites
would date between A.D. 500 and 700; actual dates placed Pueblo II at
roughly A.D. 900 to 1100. Thus it appeared that Hargrave was not
even close in his original estimate. On the other hand, many archaeologists in December 1929 had to cut by 50 percent their published estimates for ages of southwestern sites, so Hargrave made out
comparatively well. Colton was not embarrassed by this revision, and
he was especially pleased that McGregor and Douglass arrived at the
Type 1 solution independently, thereby validating the result, however
unlikely it may have initially seemed. After some reflection and a
return to the archaeological data, the implications of the Type 1 dating
no longer seemed quite so unreasonable to Hargrave either. Colton
wrote Douglass:

> When John dated pithouse NA 2002 as late as 1116 we [archaeolo-
> gists at MNA] thought it improbable. Since then Lyndon has studied the
> pottery from the site and found a part of a Tusayan polychrome bowl
> which had been imbedded in the floor. Tusayan Polychrome was not
> found associated with any other pithouse. Also sherds of an unnamed
> black-on-white which characterize the transition from Pueblo II to
> Pueblo III were abundant. We must conclude that some people were
> still living in pithouses even while others a few miles NW were building
> masonry houses. . . . The dates of Medicine Fort NA 862 fit better into
> the scheme of things. It means that masonry came into use in the
> region after 1000 and was used in the construction of granaries and
> forts before masonry dwelling rooms were built. (November 25, 1931)

McGregor provided another perspective on the perplexingly late dating of Pueblo II in the Flagstaff area:

> With the discovery of these astonishingly late dates we were thrown into an uproar, but now have gone after a more careful study of pottery types and are more reconciled to it. It is giving us some very neat problems and some information which is most valuable on the effects of peripheral culture. This is certainly going to prove most valuable to archaeology and will rather certainly shake some definitely preconceived ideas. I am more anxious than ever to get an abundance of dates throughout the Hopi Country and north to Kayenta. I should like to build up separate chronologies like this for the various regions, and feel that is our best problem at present. (McGregor to Douglass, November 27, 1931)

In his last sentence McGregor foreshadows a longer-term aspect of the evolution of archaeological tree-ring dating: the development of increasingly localized archaeological chronologies. Until this time, archaeological tree-ring chronologies in the Southwest had not been differentiated. Douglass developed a pan-Southwest tree-ring chronology, the "Central Pueblo Chronology," which he used to date Pueblo Bonito and other sites in the 1920s (Douglass 1929, 1935a). By the end of 1931, however, several more localized chronologies had been or were being developed (see Stallings 1933; Chapter 6). The addition of locally specific chronologies made it possible to derive more dates because the vagaries of local ring sequences were better understood. Keeping the unique or unusual ring sequences in each chronology properly named and differentiated was nevertheless becoming more and more difficult, and McGregor felt the time was right for a conference of dendrochronologists to discuss these developments. He suggested the idea for a conference to his counterpart, Sid Stallings at the Laboratory of Anthropology in Santa Fe, who responded with a comical note on the arbitrary nature of typological designations:

> You are quite on good grounds in calling the original [Central Pueblo] sequence the Douglass series. It no doubt will be confusing to some for a while, but there [are] such few dendrochronologists that a change [in nomenclature] should be easy. In my report on Pecos which I am writing at present, I have at times referred to the Douglass series as the CP chronology (standing for Colorado Plateau) and have lumped the general features of the area covered by this chronology as CP characteristics. Of course your work is bound to bring in new aspects and problems, of which I, knowing the CP area only from

general characteristics, must be ignorant. The CP title, by the way, has been used purely arbitrarily—[it is] just a handle, and mean[s] just about as much as a "Crushed-Mouse Red-on-Buff" would. . . . Your suggestion for a conference of tree-ring workers is a good one I think—but I have an additional suggestion, or rather an alternative. I have been trying to get Dr. Douglass to Santa Fe to check the Rio Grande chronology, and very possibly he will get here this spring. How about shifting the place to Santa Fe instead of Flag? Of course, this would depend on where Douglass would be likely to be. But in either place I hope it goes through. As instigator, let me know how the plans progress. (January 18, 1932)

Although the first formal conference of dendrochronologists would not occur for another two years, the subject of nomenclature seems to have been worked out, with chronologies designated by the areas they served (i.e., "Rio Grande," "Central Pueblo," "Flagstaff") rather than by the dendrochronologist's name (i.e., the "Douglass Series"). Stallings nevertheless wrote to Douglass on October 21, 1932, seeking clarification on this matter. In so doing he outlined exactly what McGregor meant when he referred to his Flagstaff series. The "Flagstaff series" was the tree-ring sequence in the area around the San Francisco Mountains from A.D. 1000 to 1100, which was radically different from the same century's ring sequence in the Central Pueblo series, in part because of the Sunset Crater eruption.

As far as fieldwork in 1931 was concerned, efforts were as intense as those of 1930. Hargrave led an excavation team to Medicine Cave on May 1 to continue the fieldwork begun the previous year. On May 8, he reoriented the search to focus on sites in Medicine Valley that had been covered by the Sunset Crater ash. Some seven hundred tree-ring specimens were collected from 48 pithouses and masonry structures in Medicine Valley that were either tested for charcoal or completely excavated (1931 at the Museum 1931). Though the specimens did not lead to an absolute date for the eruption, Colton was able to bracket the eruption date (erroneously) between A.D. 700 and 900 on the basis of archaeological and tree-ring evidence (Colton 1932; see also Downum 1988).

MNA's 1932 fieldwork concentrated first in cliff dwellings in Walnut Canyon and then moved to additional sites in the Flagstaff area including Turkey Tank Fort (NA 113), Turkey Tank Caves (NA 117), Clarke's Caves (NA 811), Jack Smith Alcove Houses (NA 408, 409, 1295), Elden Pithouse (NA 1531), Bonito Terrace (NA 1570), Coyote Range Pithouse

(NA 1959), NA 2055, 2056, 2057, 2058, and Bonito Park (NA 1814) (Hargrave 1932). Although the excavators were still unsuccessful in dating Sunset Crater (McGregor 1932), they again collected a large amount of Pueblo I and Pueblo II beam material. They inferred that they were closing in on the true date of the eruption by bracketing it ever more closely, and the feeling at the end of 1932 was that the eruption occurred sometime between A.D. 1000 and 1100.

In March 1933, McGregor became curator of dendrochronology at MNA. Douglass suggested that his first official task be an intensive and applied reanalysis of already dated material which would yield the true date of the Sunset Crater eruption. He informed McGregor that this was "a perfectly gorgeous subject, one promising to strike important conclusions with a minimum amount of labor . . . [if] worked out with conservative and conscientious judgment" (May 8, 1933). Douglass later expressed his desire that McGregor use the dating of the eruption of Sunset Crater as a master's thesis (June 15, 1933). McGregor entered graduate school at the University of Chicago in the fall of 1933 but did not pursue the subject as a master's degree candidate.

MNA's fieldwork before June 1, 1933, concentrated on Wupatki Pueblo, northeast of Flagstaff (Colton 1933a). From June 1 to August 1, Hargrave directed the Rainbow Bridge–Monument Valley Expedition, carrying out a reconnaissance survey of southeastern Utah and northeastern Arizona (see Crotty 1983). Hargrave and others then returned to Wupatki for more excavation from August 1 to October 1. Because digging was concentrated at Wupatki and survey crews were no longer testing many sites for tree-ring specimens, the sheer number of samples processed by MNA dropped dramatically, although it was still high: 744 specimens were cataloged in 1933. This brought the three-year total for MNA to 3,286 (1933 at the Museum 1934; see also Colton 1933b).

McGregor was granted a leave of absence from the museum to pursue his graduate studies and was gone for the winter of 1933–1934 (1934 at the Museum 1934). His idea for a tree-ring conference was not, however, lost on his colleagues. Haury echoed McGregor's concern for standardization in the presentation of tree-ring data and endorsed the idea of a conference, but he lamented the fact that he had been out of tree-ring dating for nearly two years and felt that he would not have anything new to contribute. In 1934, Jesse Nusbaum of the National Park Service suggested that a tree-ring conference be called to address grievances with regard to destructive sample collection practices on

National Park Service land. Whatever the final reason for its calling, the First Tree-Ring Conference was held June 11 and 12, 1934, at the Museum of Northern Arizona (First Tree-Ring Conference 1934; Colton 1934; Douglass 1934a; Glock 1934b).

With Douglass serving as chair, the First Tree-Ring Conference approved the following agenda:

(1) Requirements in permits by Government
(2) Checking dates before publication—(a) errors made (b) credit for dating
(3) Photography of ring sequences—will have photos and probably models to show.
(4) Recommendations regarding advanced courses
    (a) Archaeology
        Doubles and false rings, charcoal and dating estimates, sapwood-heartwood contact and wearing, illumination and photography, pinyon reading and wood identity
    (b) Cyclology
        Tabular records, curves, etc., smoothing, cross-dating and correlations, growth climate relations
(5) Reports of difficulties by each worker
(6) Discussion of suggested problems

Attendees included Douglass and his assistant, Glock, from the University of Arizona (though Glock officially represented the Carnegie Institution); Stallings for the Laboratory of Anthropology; McGregor, Colton, and Ned Spicer for the Museum of Northern Arizona; Haury for Gila Pueblo; Louis Caywood for Mesa Verde National Park; and Gordon Baldwin of the Arizona State Museum (First Tree-Ring Conference 1934). Dendrochronologists notably and inexplicably missing from the conference were Florence M. Hawley, who at the time worked for both the University of New Mexico and the University of Chicago, and Harry T. Getty of the Arizona State Museum. Fledgling dendrochronologist Harold Gladwin also was not present.

Significant results of the conference include the establishment of the *Tree-Ring Bulletin* for the prompt and standardized release of tree-ring data of all kinds, a formal statement delineating how tree-ring samples should be removed from archaeological beams, and the agreement among all present that no tree-ring dates should be released without "the checking of two individuals," which meant the dendrochronologist who did the dating and Douglass, who did the verification. After the Second Tree-Ring Conference in 1935, Haury, McGregor, Hawley, Stallings, and

Getty were authorized to verify archaeological tree-ring dates for specimens from their respective areas (Getty 1935d).

Haury proposed a "uniform system of releasing dates," designed by Gladwin and Kidder, that apparently was not approved, for reasons that remain unclear (Haury to Gladwin, June 15, 1934). Douglass was named editor-in-chief of the *Tree-Ring Bulletin*, Glock was named assistant editor, Colton accepted the managing editorship, and McGregor became assistant managing editor (First Tree-Ring Conference 1934). The initial *Tree-Ring Bulletin* budget was established at $180, with $20 contributions from each of the institutions most interested in tree-ring dating—the University of Arizona, the Museum of Northern Arizona, the Laboratory of Anthropology, and Gila Pueblo. The remaining $100 was to be made up by the $1.50 annual individual subscription rate (First Tree-Ring Conference 1934). In another testament to the archaeological and general interest in tree-ring dating during the 1930s, McGregor reported on December 7, 1934, that the *Bulletin* had 80 subscribers, including subscriptions "from the most unexpected quarters and people."

MNA fieldwork in 1934 focused on further archaeological definition of the Pueblo I period around Flagstaff (Downum 1988). The dendrochronological goal of that research was to extend the San Francisco Mountains tree-ring chronology back "beyond the lower limits of Pueblo II . . . prior to about 800 A.D." (Spicer 1934:17). Approximately 175 charcoal specimens were collected in the vicinity of Baker Ranch, northeast of Flagstaff (Spicer 1934:18). Hargrave worked from early June to late August on the Rainbow Bridge–Monument Valley Expedition, a primary goal of which was to gather tree-ring and architectural data (Hargrave 1935a). Unfortunately, no tree-ring specimens were collected by the expedition that year, ostensibly because of a personnel shortage and the Tree-Ring Conference (Hargrave 1935a:26). A more likely reason is the controversy surrounding the expedition's sample-collection activities of 1933, which were severely criticized by Irwin Hayden of the Civil Works Administration (see Chapter 6).

In the spring of 1935, MNA's research contributed to the extension of Douglass's basic southwestern chronology. For the first time, the Pueblo I occupations north of Flagstaff could be solidly dated (McGregor 1935), as well as the Basketmaker III horizons on which Earl Morris had been working in northeastern Arizona. Haury, at the time still employed at Gila Pueblo, offered McGregor congratulations for his contribution in the Douglass-Morris effort, adding: "I am simply consumed with curiosity as to where Morris's Basketmaker II date falls. Let me know as soon as the gates are dropped" (March 20, 1935). In the same letter, Haury related some of the difficulties Douglass was having in finding time to devote to archaeological dating, but he also proposed a solution—a move by McGregor to the University of Arizona: "[Douglass] is a little up a stump about who is to handle the archaeological end of things there, what with his time taken up with cycle studies. Our conversation finally got around to one possibility: [Gordon] Baldwin [then with the Arizona State Museum] can do the dating at Flagstaff (if you will have him), Douglass would like to have Getty [then at the Department of Archaeology, University of Arizona], and this vacancy in the department could be filled by you. This was idle talk of course, but I think something may come of it." Douglass had in the meantime also appealed to the president of the University of Arizona to have Baldwin transferred from the Arizona State Museum to work on tree rings full-time. McGregor, however, never returned to work at the University of Arizona.

On May 1, 1935, a sparsely recorded, if not sparsely attended, symposium entitled "Trees: Recorders of History and Climate" was held as part of the Southwest Division Meeting of the American Association for the Advancement of Science in Santa Fe, New Mexico. It was at this meeting, and apparently not at the First Tree-Ring Conference, that the Tree-Ring Society was formally established. The society included Douglass, Glock, Gladwin, Hawley, Stallings, and Edmund Schulman, Douglass's assistant for climatology, as members, but it is unclear who actually attended the meeting in Santa Fe. Haury was certainly there, and almost certainly became a member, for correspondence reveals plans for his paper as well as the enthusiasm with which he received the meetings as a whole. Haury had initially planned to present a paper on the Mogollon culture (Haury to McGregor, February 26, 1935), but on March 20, 1935, he shifted to a broader consideration of dendrochronology: "I would like to sum up the gross results, i.e. the number of ruins dated, the span in years, and the area covered. Of how many sites will you have released dates by conference time? Such problems as your 200-year pit house, culture lags, etc., etc., are some of the points that should be taken up." This was a daunting task, and Haury's revised plans were less ambitious: "[I am] trying to restrict myself to interpretive questions, rather than to try to review the whole archaeological situation in light of the tree-ring data. [I] talked the matter over with [Douglass] in Tucson Monday and he seems to feel that the method is OK" (Haury to McGregor, April 18, 1935). Haury's paper was apparently well received and was subsequently published as "Tree-Rings: The Archaeologist's

Time Piece" (Haury 1935a), which laid the foundation for archaeological tree-ring dating theory and remains a classic in the literature.

In 1935, Hargrave was once more ensconced in research in Tsegi Canyon and Dogoszhi Biko, while Colton and McGregor again engaged the Sunset Crater problem. This time, however, McGregor sought to date the eruption indirectly by crossdating artifact assemblages from sites under the ash with securely tree-ring-dated archaeological sites along the Little Colorado River (Downum 1988:128). The latter half of 1935 was spent by all parties in the analysis of previously gathered materials. McGregor, as assistant managing editor of the *Tree-Ring Bulletin*, was beginning to feel pressure because the last issue of the *Bulletin* had been "skimpy." He felt that there were disturbingly few papers in the pipeline and that subscribers would react negatively to the paucity of articles and associated delays in publication. He asked Douglass for a contribution on the early extension of the chronology, but Douglass was already overcommitted and any such contribution would be some time off. By November, the *Tree-Ring Bulletin* was five weeks late, and Colton appealed to Haury for help: "Can't you stir up Dr. Douglass about TRB? We have no manuscripts and the volume is financed for the year. He does not answer our letters. I wonder if you could see him some time and get him to delegate the procuring of manuscripts to other younger men. I hate to see the thing fail. Glock ought to get out some climate papers. It is five weeks late now" (November 6, 1935).

One month later, Haury reported the disappointing results of his attempt to "stir up" Douglass: "I saw Douglass in Tucson the other day and got nowhere fast as usual. As far as the Bulletin is concerned, there is no doubt about his intention to hang on to it, and to proposals on my part to help, one gets a reply 'that would be fine' etc., and the matter ends there. So, I don't feel that it is up to me to keep hammering. I told him frankly that the thing would have to come out on time or fold up" (December 16, 1935).

The *Tree-Ring Bulletin* did not fold, however, and in May 1936, McGregor informed his former department head at the University of Chicago, Fay-Cooper Cole, that Douglass was finally ready to publish dates for Basketmaker sites. McGregor considered the implications of that dating:

> Our whole concepts of archaeology are changing so rapidly and violently that we are almost literally going "round and round." Just today I received the manuscript from Dr. Douglass which will release the dates on all of the early cultures here in the southwest and for the first time

date the Basketmaker stages. Morris has agreed to give a paper on the culture associations to accompany it in the *Tree-Ring Bulletin*. This is the greatest contribution to the history of southwestern archaeology to date. I am sure for now we can make all our comparisons on the basis of time, and it is not too much to expect that we shall soon be writing histories of the prehistory here. Add to this the Mogollon culture and its influences in various directions at a very early date and you can see why we are all working so feverishly now. . . . The rate at which information is accumulating is almost overwhelming. . . . I cannot help laughing when I look back a few years to the time when we felt everything, at least in general, was pretty well understood. (May 24, 1936)

Archaeological investigations by the Museum of Northern Arizona in 1936 were restricted to Twin Caves Pueblo in Tsegi Canyon and Winona Ruin east of Flagstaff, though some additional testing was conducted at the Citadel at Wupatki National Monument. This concentration of effort reflects a shift in research emphasis away from dating Sunset Crater toward more detailed definition of local culture units in the Flagstaff area (Downum 1988:129). Only 172 tree-ring specimens were collected during the 1936 season (Colton 1937).

The correspondence record from 1937 to 1940 indicates that the Museum of Northern Arizona continued to direct efforts at the definition of local culture units. Colton, McGregor, and Hargrave were each engaged in their own projects, and though tree-ring dating continued to be conducted by McGregor, MNA received only six specimens in all of 1937 (Colton 1938). Laboratory research was conducted and published, but no great changes or controversies in archaeological tree-ring dating or interpretation are evident. Richard van Valkenburg of the Bureau of Indian Affairs sought information on droughts "of any consequence" between A.D. 1200 and 1900 on the Navajo Reservation (February 27, 1937). Watson Smith, who had been working at Awatovi Pueblo with J. O. Brew, asked McGregor to date wood from that site and others investigated by the Rainbow Bridge–Monument Valley Expedition (October 21, 1937; see Crotty 1983). McGregor was the obvious choice for this task because of his familiarity with the ring sequences in the area, but for reasons that are not stated in the correspondence, he refused the job (November 13, 1937). Brew subsequently tried to get Haury to date the specimens, but he too was busy; Brew then solicited Getty, who also declined. The Awatovi specimens ultimately went to the Laboratory of Anthropology for analysis by Edward Twitchell Hall, Jr. (see Chapter 6).

The *Tree-Ring Bulletin* crisis continued unabated, though Haury assumed the editorship in mid-1937, just as he was preparing to become department head at the University of Arizona. McGregor submitted to Haury for publication a list of ruins dated by the Museum of Northern Arizona over the previous six years (McGregor 1938a). Haury's comments on McGregor's date list are interesting from the perspective of archaeological tree-ring date interpretation, as Haury tried to understand the relationship between tree-ring date ranges and actual site occupation dates:

> In most cases the date range covers a relatively short span of years which, in general, can be taken as the construction period. In a sense the range also gives the duration dates, as in most structures—late ones at any rate—there was probably some building as long as there was occupation. Where the range of dates is long, I can see that construction cycles might fall within the range—and it would be very valuable to show this. . . . My [date] list [for Gila Pueblo (Haury 1938)] is also completed . . . this list will be worth its weight in gold because it should serve as a basis for some interesting discussions by ourselves. . . . It's high time, I feel, that we get into more interpretation. (July 10, 1937)

It had been nearly two years since Haury's first treatment of archaeological dating (Haury 1935a), and theory clearly was still on his mind. In this emphasis on tree-ring dating theory, however, Haury was still at least two decades ahead of his time (cf. Ahlstrom 1985; Bannister 1962; Dean 1978a; Nash 1997a; Smiley 1955). Most archaeologists simplistically equated tree-ring dates with dates of occupation, and though some archaeologists considered the problems caused by beam reuse, most acted as if the derivation of a tree-ring date and the assignment of a site to a period in the Pecos Classification was both the means and the end of chronometric analysis.

In 1938, Hargrave's field research focused on "ethnic" problems in the area west of the San Francisco Peaks (Downum 1988), where tree-ring dating could not be applied because of the lack of datable tree species. Colton and Hargrave had recently published their *Handbook of Northern Arizona Pottery Wares* (1937). McGregor's research focused on dating the prehistoric ceramic types listed in the handbook (McGregor 1938b). Colton and Hargrave (1937:26) described McGregor's effort as "one of the greatest advances in Southwestern archaeology in the last ten years" because it provided archaeologists who were not trained in dendrochronology the ability to obtain date ranges for their sites on the basis of identified ceramic assemblages.

McGregor (1938b) differentiated three kinds of dating for the ceramic types on the basis of interpretive reliability: primary dating is based on the tree-ring dates themselves, secondary dating is derived from the direct association of tree-ring dates and pottery types, and tertiary dating is obtained from the association of pottery types identified at undated sites. Stallings was appreciative of McGregor's effort, for "too many of the dates referred to pottery types have been by guess and or by God, without any analysis of the factors underlying the dating" (Stallings to McGregor, April 13, 1939).

In 1939, MNA excavations were again in full swing. McGregor and Benjamin Wetherill excavated or tested some thirteen sites in and around Ridge Ruin and continued excavations at Winona Ruin, which McGregor had been excavating for MNA and the Arizona State Teacher's College since 1936 (McGregor 1941; Colton 1941). The dating of these sites assumed greater importance as the excavation neared completion. Douglass reminded McGregor that there was still a weak point in the Flagstaff chronology ca. A.D. 1250–1350 and suggested that he target his sample-collection activities accordingly. On June 17, McGregor sent Douglass some specimens from Winona and nearby sites for date verification. When he had not heard anything by late December, he again appealed to Douglass for help, citing the interpretive significance of Winona and Ridge ruins: "The entire report [on Winona and Ridge ruins] should hinge about the dates from the tree ring material, so I am more or less at a standstill until I can get some dates which are releasable. Hence this note to find the status of the material I sent you. [I am] particularly interested in specimens from NA 2133A [a component of Winona Ruin]. This would give us the beginning of Hohokam culture in this section of the north, and is of utmost importance" (December 28, 1939).

In 1939, McGregor published an article entitled "Archaeological Problems," in which he argued that the goal of archaeology is interpretation, not just chronicle. Harvard anthropologist Clyde Kluckhohn concurred (Kluckhohn 1939) and wrote to congratulate McGregor on his effort, adding that it was nice to see that "a respectable number of archaeologists are beginning to think and express themselves articulately about these questions" (February 29, 1940). McGregor was in good company, for articles by Julian Steward (1937) and Alfred Kroeber (1935) are now often considered with Kluckhohn's (1939) as breaking new ground in the interpretation of North American prehistory.

In late winter 1941, McGregor received correspondence from C. T. Hurst of Western State College in Gunnison, Colorado, who was excavating

Tabegauche Cave in the west-central part of the state (Hurst 1940, 1941). Hurst was interested in doing his own tree-ring dating and hoped that McGregor's Flagstaff chronology, or a chronology based on the Mesa Verde sites alone, might be more appropriate for his purpose than Douglass's Central Pueblo Chronology. Despite a valiant effort, Hurst and his colleagues met with little success:

> Sixteen cross-sections were made for the various [pinyon and juniper] timbers found in the cave. . . . In the laboratory, two well-trained assistants spent from one to three hours daily on the Tabeguache wood for 5 months and have succeeded in definitely cross-dating only three of the pieces. Great difficulties were encountered in incomplete rings, missing rings, irregular rings, double rings, lenses, and other irregularities that necessitated cross checking from piece to piece. However, on the basis of this study, we confidently state that the completely determined logs were felled in the 4th Century (348, 361, and 372 A.D.). (Hurst 1941:11)

THE GLADWIN DEBATE

Gladwin's attack on MNA archaeology and dendrochronology is rooted in the 1931 dating of sites in the Medicine Valley northeast of Flagstaff, especially Medicine Fort (NA 862) and Medicine Pithouse (NA 1680), for Gladwin firmly believed the tree-ring dating of these sites to be in error. His attack is important not because he was correct on methodological or technical points but because his critique of Flagstaff-area archaeology (Gladwin 1943) prompted Colton to reevaluate MNA's archaeological and tree-ring research of the previous decade. This reevaluation ultimately led to the correct dating of the eruption of Sunset Crater (Colton 1945, 1946), nearly 15 years after that event had become a focal point of MNA's research.

On February 12, 1931, Douglass wrote to Colton to inquire whether the tree-ring dates he had tentatively arrived at for Medicine Pithouse made sense in light of the archaeological evidence from that site: "The group of specimens from the pit near Medicine Fort all cross date, four or five of them I think. I find a strong resemblance in their series of rings to one hundred years preceding 888. Please tell me at your leisure if the specimens taken from Medicine Fort pit house could be taken as of the century suggested." Colton replied less than a week later in a partly illegible handwritten letter that the century preceding A.D. 888 was reasonable for the Medicine Pithouse, given MNA's understanding of the archaeological evidence, but noted that they had previously expected the site to date even earlier, somewhere between A.D. 600 and 800 (February 18, 1931). Hargrave originally thought the site might be even older, guessing at a date between A.D. 500 and 700 (Hargrave 1930:3).

The important correspondence regarding the debate between Gladwin and the staff of the Museum of Northern Arizona began in 1940, even though several letters had been exchanged between Gladwin and McGregor in 1938 that discussed preliminary results of Gladwin's tree-ring studies. As discussed in Chapter 4, by mid-1940 Gladwin was beginning to feel that significant change was in the wind for interpretations of southwestern prehistory. Using curiously informative mixed metaphors, Gladwin confided to McGregor that "things are beginning to make a little sense, but I am afraid that many of the accepted ideas will have to be revised. In climate, as in finance, it is a mistake to put all of your eggs in one basket (i.e. droughts in the SW)." He then began to undermine Douglass's authority and build a case for his own credibility by citing Douglass's critics from other sciences:

> I think that Dr. Douglass is preeminent in many ways, but this does not mean that [Douglass's critics] [Forrest] Shreve, [D. T.] McDougal, [I. W.] Bailey, and [Ernst] Antevs are all wrong because they do not agree with him. Since we are not trying to prove that some are right and others are wrong, we have now extended our investigations to include the Sierras and such stations as Monterey, Santa Barbara, Mt. Wilson, and San Jacinto, in California. . . . It is obviously too soon to make any specific statements, but I am willing to go so far as to say that there is *a* dominant climatic factor which affects tree-growth but that this factor varies with the environment and sometimes with the local climate. To put this more specifically, I think it can now be demonstrated that high temperatures and deficient precipitation have sometimes been responsible for minimum growth in the SW. . . . It is also true that a narrow ring is not infrequently the result of a cold, wet summer with low temperatures and excess precipitation. Much the same thing can be said of conditions in California, although it looks to me, at present, as if temperature played a greater part along the Pacific Coast. . . . The essential thing to remember is that, in tree-rings as in archaeology, it is a great mistake to start with a theory and twist one's facts to prove the theory. . . . The only way we can ever hope to make any progress is by establishing our facts and then build our hypotheses on the basis of such facts. (May 21, 1940; emphasis in original)

Comments in this letter identify points that would later be taken up in earnest (Gladwin 1947), particularly those pertaining to the relationship between ring width and precipitation. Gladwin's somewhat unorthodox use of the terms "fact," "theory," and "hypothesis" is evident, along with his incipient belief that he was not trying to prove anybody wrong. In view of his subsequent publications (Gladwin 1943, 1944, 1945, 1946, 1947), this statement is curious at best. Finally, he used inductive reasoning, which was in the philosophical mainstream of North American archaeology of that era.

In 1942, Gladwin expressed his hope that he and McGregor might work together on their common problems: "I say you [McGregor] and I because I hope and believe that your attitude towards my work is more open minded than some other members of the Douglass school and I am certain that we can best help one another by sympathetic cooperation" (July 6, 1942). Gladwin's next move was not especially conducive to "sympathetic cooperation," however, for he sent McGregor a draft copy of his review and analysis of the Flagstaff culture (Gladwin 1943). In this manuscript he argued that, among other things, McGregor's tree-ring dates were incorrect. He also implied that tree-ring dates are not facts: "[I am] sending you under separate cover my review and analysis of the Flagstaff culture. I hope you will be able to look it over and tell me of any mistakes of fact which I may have made. By facts I mean architecture, pottery, distances, and quotations—such things as my interpretations or differences of opinion as to tree-ring dates cannot be regarded as facts, but, again, I shall be glad to have you correct me if I have been guilty of any misrepresentation" (October 29, 1942).

On November 7, 1942, McGregor wrote to Gladwin regarding this manuscript. In so doing he outlined many of the salient points in MNA's response to Gladwin's attack, which focused on Gladwin's exclusive use of decorated instead of both decorated and undecorated pottery in his analysis and critique; his failure to examine personally the bulk of the Flagstaff tree-ring specimens; and the apparently poor surface preparation of the Gila Pueblo tree-ring samples:

> From my discussions with you a year or so ago in Santa Barbara you know my interest in and appreciation of the work you have done along this line. However, I do not believe you have examined enough of the tree ring material from Flagstaff to reach the generalized conclusions you attempt to present in this paper. In fairness to yourself, and everyone else in this entire problem, I would suggest you really should go over most or all of these specimens, checking them by your method, before you strike so directly and with such a critical evaluation of the entire situation on the relatively few specimens you have reviewed.

McGregor added that Gladwin was free to examine the MNA specimens should he come to northern Arizona: "Just before I left Flagstaff I outlined and got together all of the dated tree ring material in our collections. Dr. Colton has written me that this has been placed in a separate case, or cases, and is now available for ready study. . . . If you could go over them all, or most of them, I believe any such criticism as you contemplate, if it can be demonstrated, would be more sound and convincing." He then expanded on his concerns regarding Gladwin's scholarship and generalized conclusions in a letter to Colton:

> I suspect the wire I sent you last night may have been quite disturbing, but Alma [Mrs. McGregor] urged me to send it after reading the paper Gladwin sent on to me for examination and comment. She felt it was better to upset you now than later. . . . The paper Gladwin submitted to me is a critical review of the cultures and archaeological work the MNA has done in the Flagstaff area. I admit we have done many jobs which were not as good as I would like to have seen them done, but many others have too. As I was very much afraid he would do sometime sooner or later he has gone off the deep end with this. . . . He simply says the tree-ring dates are wrong . . . . I suppose Gladwin has sent this to me more or less in confidence, so you had best not write him too directly what I have written you. . . . I surely wish I could be back there [in Flagstaff] now to see this entire matter through to a conclusion personally. (November 7, 1942)

Douglass's reply to a similar letter from McGregor is interesting for its measured tone and its succinct but diplomatic analysis. It also indicates how Douglass, as the established authority, could dismiss Gladwin's critique on technical issues that he felt invalidated Gladwin's results and therefore precluded comparison of their respective dates:

> I am interested in what you say about the proposed attack on the Flagstaff dating. We have had other attacks from that source of which I don't think there are now any important ripples. . . . The author of the attack to which you refer hasn't yet reached first base—in fact, let us say he has two strikes against him! The first one is that he is making a basic and vital mistake that invalidates almost all that he does, including all specimens in his averages, because he does not choose those which have been growing in highly selective localities where they isolate and put on record certain climate effects. His second strike is that he does not produce reliable dates in his specimens, partly because he does not insist on proper surfaces for seeing the rings accurately, and second because he therefore does not use cross-

dating character as a preliminary condition which shows climatic influence.

The specimens from Forestdale which had been treated in his laboratory and which I had seen previously in 1939 were badly broken and cut into slices, their surfaces so marred that the delicate rings were in most cases wholly obliterated. I did in one or two cases pick out a faint resemblance to the date he proposed in what was left of the rings. Such a date, however, was evidently of no value whatsoever.

This is not a controversy, and it is not a subject on which I want to be quoted, nor do I write these details for the purpose of being quoted, but perhaps as much to put them on record in my own files as in yours. The fact is, I feel that the man referred to does not know what this is all about. (November 10, 1942)

Douglass, and to a lesser degree Colton, had the authority and professional standing to declare Gladwin's technique, and thus the resulting data, invalid. On those grounds, Douglass could publicly ignore his nemesis's critique. Less senior scientists, especially McGregor and Haury, did not enjoy such privileged, and well-earned, positions and therefore felt the need to engage Gladwin more directly.

Haury's response to McGregor's concerns offers insight into one of the basic tenets of Haury's career: arguments are solved with the shovel, not with the pen (Thompson 1995). Haury wrote: "I am rather perturbed about what you say of Gladwin's new report. Of course we all know that he isn't happy unless he can stir up trouble but it seems to me that he is rapidly earning the name of 'that madman Gladwin.' I would not object to his tearing anybody to pieces, me included, if he could provide new data which was the result of his own work. He reminds me of a lot of the armchair strategists" (November 17, 1942).

Haury also gave a preliminary indication of the importance of the early tree-ring date (A.D. 310) recently obtained for the Bluff Site in the Forestdale Valley, both for his own arguments regarding the origins and development of the Mogollon culture and for Gladwin's arguments about Mogollon and Hohokam chronology:

These [Bluff Site] dates are more or less confidential but this should answer Earl Morris when he demands proof that Mogollon sites with pottery are older than [Basketmaker] and it will put Gladwin behind the eight ball in his revision of Snaketown dates. Hohokam pottery was present in the Bluff site in the fourth century when it was not supposed to have been in existence until the seventh or eighth centuries. He doesn't know about this yet but knowing his feeling about

Douglass I can predict his answer—the tree-ring dates are no good—
and so it goes. (November 17, 1942)

On November 27, 1942, Gladwin wrote to Colton for the first time
regarding his critical paper, stating that his interest in the Flagstaff culture was due principally to its bearing on the Snaketown chronology.
That same day, Gladwin defensively replied to McGregor's comments,
curiously suggesting that tree-ring dates are matters of opinion, not fact.
Gladwin again tried to discredit the dendrochronological authority figure and, by association, all archaeological tree-ring research to date:

> As I understand your penciled notes, there are no instances in
> which you question my listing of facts—such as architectural features,
> pottery, locations or distances—and I am very grateful that there are so
> many items on which we appear to be in agreement. How far you are
> willing to go in agreeing with some of my opinions, I do not know, and
> I do not propose to try to pin you down as I realize the difficulty of
> your position. . . . As I see the problem, Dr. Douglass was responsible
> for the initial mistake back in 1930 [sic—1931], when adequate com-
> parative dating material was scanty. He was riding the crest of the
> wave, due to the acclaim with which he was being hailed, and it did
> not seem possible that he could ever be wrong. Nevertheless, I am now
> convinced that he not only did make a mistake but that this was the
> cause of the present confusion as to the archaeology of Flagstaff.

Gladwin never specified what, exactly, "the mistake" was, and he
continued to refer to it only vaguely. This vacuity placed the burden of
proof on Douglass and made it much more difficult for Douglass, or
McGregor, to counter Gladwin's criticism. Gladwin erroneously argued
that Douglass derived the controversial Medicine Valley tree-ring dates
"when comparative material was scanty." In so doing, he demonstrated
conclusively that he misunderstood the basics of Douglass's dendrochronology. As discussed in Chapter 2, Douglass's comparative material was, to some degree, "scanty" in the late 1920s, but it is clear that
Douglass had a reasonably good idea of where the gap existed in his
chronology as early as 1927 and that he collected "comparative material" during beam expeditions in 1927, 1928, and 1929. By the time
Douglass (1929) published dates on the basis of that chronology, he was
sure he understood the vagaries of growth in each year covered by the
chronology. Indeed, Douglass's conservatism with regard to date publication is well known, and it was this conservatism, not a cavalier willingness to publish dates on "scanty" bases, that frustrated so many
archaeologists and dendrochronologists.

Gladwin continued his rebuttal of McGregor's comments. In so doing, he refused to do more work himself and dismissed the idea that his own scholarship was lacking and therefore was the basis of the controversy he was trying to create and define to his advantage:

You suggest that I should go over all or most of the material at Flagstaff before publishing my paper, but I am afraid that this will be impossible. As you know, my measuring equipment is bulky and it is also rather delicate to haul around. There is also the problem of the preparation of the specimens and, while several improvements have been made in our handling of charcoal, I doubt if Colton or Douglass will ever approve of my methods. . . . It will interest you to know, however, that I have already taken steps to check my belief that mistakes have been made in the building of the Central Pueblo Chronology. I have recently completed the revision of Haury's and Douglass's dating of White Mound, Forestdale, and the Tusayan Ruin [Gladwin 1945, 1946], and there is not a single date upon which we agree, except 786 at White Mound. In some instances the differences run up to as much as 200 years and there cannot be any doubt that one of us is very wrong. (November 27, 1942)

Finally, Gladwin tried to control the agenda to solve the controversy: "Under the circumstances, it seems to me that the next step will be to submit the problem to a few archies [archaeologists] and be guided by their advice." He did not name who these "archies" were, but they almost certainly would not have been archaeologists such as Morris, whom Gladwin saw as sympathetic to the Douglass "school."

In a letter on December 8, 1942, McGregor argued that Gladwin should refrain from publishing his revision of the Flagstaff culture for procedural, as well as personal, reasons. In so doing, McGregor examined the impending effects of the Gladwin "controversy" from a much broader perspective and considered the consequences for the individuals involved:

Anyone should be prepared for and welcome honest criticism, and in younger men it is a stimulant to better work. Even with men whose vocations are not at stake, such as you and Dr. Colton, it can never be the serious matter it is to an older man whose life work is questioned and criticized. I can appreciate this situation more than most for I saw at first hand what Paul Martin's [1941b] review [of Cummings's 1940 Kinishba Ruin report] did to Dean Cummings. It is difficult for people like us to conceive but it pretty well discouraged him in attempting to write any more, and I should say about killed any spirit of contribution he had. . . . Dr. Douglass is of course much better equipped to defend his work, but I cannot see any necessity for precipitating a violent round of arguments just at this stage of his work. As it is now outlined in this report, you have made a blunt challenge to the entire Douglass method. As an individual with interests and some understanding on both sides, I can see that if such an open and deep reaching argument is launched just now, little may be accomplished beyond the creation of the most violent and bitter personal feelings. It is, of course, not your intention to precipitate an hysterical and pointless argument, but rather to encourage a calm and honest re-evaluation of the status of the study. I feel that by throwing down such a blunt challenge today [you] might defeat your aim and achieve less than a modified questioning of the validity of the results. It is my honest opinion that more would be accomplished in the end in this way, and would actually result in no serious unpleasantness. If dates in error have been published, I cannot see that it will seriously affect the overall picture of the Southwest beyond eventual correction.

McGregor thus warned Gladwin about the consequences of the controversy for Gladwin's reputation and career. Gladwin was, however, independently wealthy and concerned only about the possible professional repercussions if the controversy was resolved in his favor. He therefore ignored McGregor's plea for restraint, perhaps because, as he wrote Colton, "the older I get, the less I feel like taking things seriously" (December 7, 1942). Gladwin again explained his perspective to McGregor on January 22, 1943, and showed that he was now entrenched in his crusade. He implied that the undefined "mistake" was spreading like a virus to archaeological research beyond the Flagstaff region:

I have no desire whatever to indulge in futile argument or to make personal attacks. I am confident that Dr. Douglass has made some mistakes and I will go so far as to say that, in my opinion, there are several features of Dr. Douglass's methods which are conducive to such mistakes. I do not agree with you that such errors will eventually correct themselves, as a prerequisite to such correcting is [a] need of pointing out that a mistake has been made. . . . I also believe that the effects of the initial errors in the Flagstaff dating can be seen to have spread, and that such a compounded dating error has been directly responsible for Haury's predicament at Forestdale [with early dates for the Bluff and Bear ruins].

Even Haury, once Gladwin's assistant director at Gila Pueblo, is "infected," though it is unlikely that Haury would concur that he was in a "predicament" because he obtained dates that supported his and others' contention that the Mogollon culture was earlier than, and therefore separate from, the Anasazi and Hohokam cultures.

In a letter to Colton, Gladwin justified his attack on the basis of unspecified endorsements of "other men," a common tactic that makes it difficult to evaluate directly the work of these supposed authorities. He notified Colton that Haury's work was subject to question as well. At the same time, Gladwin suggested that he was making a move to interpret the dates he derived at Gila Pueblo:

> After reading this Medallion, McGregor thinks it will be a mistake to precipitate the issue and that mistakes will be corrected. Other men have expressed the opinion that the sooner the problem gets threshed out the better. Personally, I incline to the latter point of view as it seems to me that a mistake must be pointed out before it is likely to be corrected, and it is also undoubtedly true that the longer we have our conclusions on false premises, the more difficult it becomes to undo the damage. A good example of this can be seen in the situation at Forestdale where Haury has been trying to reconcile the irreconcilable— due, I believe, to the initial mistakes in the Flagstaff dating which have become incorporated into the Central Pueblo Chronology. . . . It has been suggested that I should deal more thoroughly with the dating problems which are raised by my analysis, and I have already made a beginning in this direction. (January 22, 1943; see also Gladwin 1944, 1946)

Colton replied that Gladwin failed to consider MNA's own revisions of its work in the early 1930s (e.g., Colton and Hargrave 1937; Colton 1941). In essence, he pointed out that Gladwin was out-of-date, if not out-of-touch, and implied, as Douglass had the previous year, that Gladwin was working on a nonexistent problem: "I have now read your paper in detail. Your conclusions are about those of ours in 1934, before we studied the undecorated storage and cooking wares of our area. The architecture is taken into account, although there are a few unexplained discrepancies, most of the sites fall into definite patterns, or, if abnormal, the deviations from the mode can be explained" (February 12, 1943).

Colton noted also that Gladwin failed to recognize that the sites in question are located on a cultural frontier and, therefore, contain culturally mixed artifact assemblages. He suggested that Gladwin do more basic analysis before publishing his critique and defended the work of his institution, which had already refined earlier analyses: "All the discussion about [NA] 2002A depends on dates by McGregor from several pieces of charcoal and a Citadel polychrome sherd found by Hargrave on the floor, which seemed to confirm his dates. [The sherds] place the site early so the true date lies probably in the 1000s. . . . Some of my conceptions have changed since [the Museum of Northern Arizona] Bulletin 17 [Colton 1939] was published." Colton concluded: "Thank you for letting me see your paper. However, I think you are about ten years behind the times. It is partly our fault for not getting the results of our work quicker into print, but I feel that until more of our work is published you are in no position to make a synthesis of the archaeology of the Flagstaff area without making serious errors, for you have not seen our collection of type sherds, our files of sherd statistics, the unpublished notes on our excavations, and the results of our surface surveys. Without the sherd analysis, the discussion of many sites are futile." Gladwin, however, ignored Colton's suggestions: "As you say, I shall undoubtedly be guilty of errors, but it would be a very dull world if we all agreed and no one ever made a mistake" (February 23, 1943). He later told McGregor that Colton "had nothing constructive to suggest" (April 22, 1943) in his letter of February 12.

One clear and important effect of Gladwin's critique is that it provided Colton and the MNA with the impetus to undertake a needed and thorough review of Flagstaff-area archaeology. This work was published three years later as Colton's *The Sinagua* (1946) and ultimately led to the accurate dating of Sunset Crater (Colton 1945). Colton explained the situation to Haury, noting that the only solution to the Gladwin problem required complete reanalysis of original data:

> [Gladwin] is unable to understand the discrepancy in cultures recorded, as we have never published the details of the ceramic analysis which makes the picture perfectly clear to us. He is puzzled in the same way which we were in 1933 before we undertook the recognition of pottery types and sherd analysis. . . . The sites, which troubled him, are on the frontier where three branches come together, Cohonina, Kayenta, and Sinagua. These sites are frightfully mixed up, as all three branches occupied them for short intervals. It is impossible to define culture complexes from a frontier of this sort. . . . It is going to take a lot of work on our part to present all the ceramic data on which our conclusions were based, and, at the present time, it will be a long time before I can get at it so as to present it in a satisfactory form. Our method of synthesis has changed over a period of ten years, so this means that I shall have to go back to the original data and recompute the percentages. I intend to do this when I have an opportunity. (April 1, 1943)

Haury agreed that reanalysis was necessary, but his scope was not limited to sherd assemblages. As he told Gladwin, "resolution of all this will require a lot of time [and] a re-examination of a lot of wood" (May 28, 1943). He told McGregor: "Gladwin asked me to come over to California this summer to help settle the Gladwin-Douglass [and, by extension, the Gladwin-MNA] controversy. The only way that can be done is by going back to source material and H.S.G. [Gladwin] won't have it that way. I don't care much to get mixed up with it now even if I did have the time. I haven't had any recent indications of his intention to publish" (August 11, 1943).

Predictably, Gladwin disagreed with Haury's call for large-scale reanalysis. Not only did Gladwin dispute the idea that reanalysis would solve the problem, he rejected Douglass's role in the debate because of the latter's supposed bias:

> I think the problem can be dealt with without all the work you mention. I think the problem is well defined and the solution compara-
> tively simple. . . . As I see the situation, I have run foul of Dr. Douglass
> in regard to certain features of the Douglass system. Dr. Douglass has
> made it very clear that he does not wish to have any dealings with me
> and I doubt if he would consider my objections, even if a meeting
> could be arranged. In my opinion, there are only two men who are
> capable of weighing the evidence impartially, yourself and Earl Morris.
> (June 8, 1943)

By the time "A Review and Analysis of the Flagstaff Culture" was published as Medallion Paper 31 in October 1943, the general feeling among the "Douglass school" was that Gladwin had wasted a great deal of time and money producing a document that largely amounted to a critique of typographical errors and already-revised interpretations. McGregor thought it "was a masterpiece of most sarcastic and deliberate confusion" (October 26, 1943). Colton agreed, though with the restraint characteristic of a senior scientist: "With respect to Gladwin's paper, as yet I have not opened my copy, knowing if I did it would make me mad. Also I am not in a position to answer it until I reorganize the statistics on the sherd analysis which represents nearly all the sites we have recorded in the Flagstaff area. . . . My answer to Gladwin's Medallion Paper 31 will come when I publish a paper with final [sherd] statistics" (November 8, 1943). Colton subsequently wrote to Haury (November 23, 1943) and, like Douglass before, noted that further debate with Gladwin was probably futile: "Our differences of opinion are so fundamental that argument is useless, as they hinge on what pottery is indigenous and that which is not. I think I have a good criterion and he thinks I have not, so that is that."

During late 1943 and early 1944, Colton engaged himself in the Gladwin-induced reanalysis of MNA's work and collections from the previous 16 years, a task that required the reexamination of data from more than 200 sites in the Flagstaff region. His work replicated McGregor's conclusions regarding calendar dates for the various ceramic types (Colton to Haury, February 15, 1944; McGregor 1938b), but it also led to the startling discovery that McGregor's (1936) dating of the eruption of Sunset Crater between A.D. 875 and 910 was incorrect. By August 1944, Colton had finished a draft of his reanalysis, which he sent to McGregor for review:

> I do not want you to be too shocked by my chapter on the Dating of Sunset Crater, for last winter I arrived at a date different from yours. I want you to show me where I err. I also arrived at a few modifications of your pottery dates but not seriously. The old pottery dates seem to stand up remarkably well and are confirmed by the new material that is now available. . . . I think I have shown that the discrepancies between the archaeological dates and the tree ring dates in every case that Gladwin thought were in error, could be explained by the hypothesis of reused beams. (August 17, 1944)

Colton was still working on the eruption date one year later, but by that time he could report to Douglass that he had narrowed the date down to between A.D. 1046 and 1071 (July 17, 1945). He was quick to point out, however, that this new dating was the result not of the analysis of new tree-ring data but rather of an intensive reanalysis of published tree-ring data and the MNA archaeological data (Colton to Douglass, September 10, 1945).

On September 14, 1945, Douglass provided, apparently from memory, the supportive dendrochronological analysis Colton needed. This ultimately fixed the eruption date or dates at between A.D. 1064 and 1066:

> I suddenly understood your dating of Sunset eruption at 1046 to 1071 by the well-remembered rings and by the puzzles I had at one time in the Wupatki rings. I would put the date of that eruption affect [sic] at 1066–7. It appears strong in the ring of 1067. The ring made in 1062 was small. Then in most beams '63, '64, '65, and '66 were especially large; then 1067 was often absent and always minute, '68 very small or absent, then '81 smaller than larger rings, but '85 small, '86 very small, and 1087 large. That 1087 was my RD 500 in that floating chronology. . . . This series was strong in Pueblo Bonito . . . and in some fine Douglas fir from Black Mesa. . . . I should check up on the

Wupatki pieces but I remember that about there somewhere the rings grew smaller and smaller and formed what I called "starvation" rings until the tree died or was cut.

The "puzzles" in the Wupatki rings to which Douglass referred have to do with the fact that the specimens from Wupatki that yielded early dates (ca. A.D. 1070–1080) came from stressed and young trees that appeared to have died naturally (i.e., slowly) rather than abruptly, as one would expect if they had been harvested with stone axes for use in construction. Douglass recognized, but could not explain, this phenomenon in 1927, when he wrote Judd that "it is possible that the earlier dates come from trees which died before cutting" (May 6, 1927). He inferred from this evidence that colonists who came to reinhabit the ash-fall area used for construction purposes trees that had died slowly rather than had been killed catastrophically by the eruption of Sunset Crater.

Thus it would not stretch the bounds of credulity to suggest that a positive result of Gladwin's critique of the Flagstaff culture (Gladwin 1943) was the correct dating of Sunset Crater (Colton 1945), which would not have happened without Colton's thorough reanalysis of MNA's archaeological research.

In the fall of 1944, Gladwin released his Medallion Paper 32 on the tree-ring dating of the Medicine Valley sites northeast of Flagstaff (Gladwin 1944). Over the next four years, he published one highly critical Medallion Paper per year (Gladwin 1945, 1946, 1947, 1948), after which time his interest in archaeological problems waned dramatically (Haury 1988). The correspondence regarding these Medallion Papers is unfortunately meager, evidence that Haury, Colton, Douglass, McGregor, and others had grown weary of Gladwin's tirades.

Some of the most direct treatments of Gladwin's later work come from Haury's pen in letters to Antevs, who in 1946 wrote favorable reviews of two of Gladwin's articles, "Tree-Ring Analysis: Methods of Correlation" (Gladwin 1940b) and "Tree-Ring Analysis: Problems of Dating I: The Medicine Valley Sites" (Gladwin 1944). Not only did Antevs (1946a, 1946b) approve of Gladwin's use of quantitative methods, he was also emotionally supportive of Gladwin, apparently endorsing the latter's vendetta against Douglass and the "Douglass school."

On November 23, 1945, Antevs wrote Haury, with copies to Sayles, Colton, and Gladwin. The letter appears to be a draft of Antevs's second review of Gladwin's work:

> During an analysis of the archaeology near Flagstaff, Arizona, Mr.
> Gladwin found that tree-ring dates determined by Professor A. E.

Douglass and Dr. J. C. McGregor by the Douglass method were in conflict with the evidence of the pottery and architecture (*Medallion* 31,
1943). Now he has applied his new method of correlating tree-rings to
several charcoal specimens from this field and has found that they
show the best agreement with the master chart where the archaeological evidence seemed to suggest they should date. . . . In Gladwin's mind
it is highly improbable that pithouses were used so late (p. 8), that one
of them, NA 2002, was continuously occupied for 200 years, or 912–
1115, that pit-houses and Black Mesa Black-on-white pottery
remained unchanged for over 300 years, and that the pit houses were
contemporaneous with Medicine Fort, which may [instead] be a
pueblo. . . . Gladwin believes NA 2002 dates to ca. 835, arguing that
due to recurrence of natural cycles which suggest several good dating
locations, therefore the archaeological evidence should be used to date
the material. Tree-rings may then give the exact date within the limits
of the period. . . . Construction of pit-house NA 2002 about 835 agrees
nicely with the building of NA 2001 in 825 A.D. Finally, the probability
that the five charcoal specimens came from planks of only three trees,
and the unlikelihood that the plank or beam dated 914 A.D. could have
lasted for 200 years in contact with earth to be burnt in 1120 A.D. support Gladwin's dating. . . . The main points in Gladwin's study are consequently: For rough, general dating archaeological evidence carries
more weight than do tree-rings, for, on account of periodicity or recurrence of patterns, suggestive tree-ring correlations may be made at
more than one place on a long master chart, even by Gladwin's objective method. But, within archaeologically fixed limits, tree-rings are
usually competent to determine exact dates. These opinions are confirmed, for Gladwin obtains the best ring correlations with the master
chart within the time limits indicated by archaeological traits, or, otherwise expressed, he finds contemporanaeity of cultural progress in
Medicine Valley and other parts of the Southwest. Two pit-houses, NA
2001 and 2002, have been dated at 825 and about 835 A.D., respectively, and the masonry structure NA 862 at about 1060 A.D. An inter-
vening cultural/local gap of about 200 years is attributed to the
eruption of Sunset Crater about 885 A.D.

Antevs thus uncritically accepted the very points that Douglass, Haury,
Colton, and McGregor disputed: the independence of the archaeological
record, failure to appreciate beam reuse or structural repair in date distri-
butions, and the assumption that quantitative data are necessarily objec-
tively acquired. Antevs was not a dendrochronologist or an archaeologist

and therefore was not well qualified to get to the root of the problem. In a letter to Colton one week later, Antevs explained the emotional nature of his support for Gladwin. He simultaneously acknowledged Gladwin's personal vendetta and the ad hominem nature of his attacks:

> I have an opinion and perhaps some knowledge of the reasons and purposes of Gladwin's recent studies. First and last he is firmly convinced that Douglass' method of tree-ring dating is fallible and is determined to prove it, for he is incensed by the pious pretense of infallibility which Douglass and his pupils wrap around Douglass' ideas and work. He has probably been personally insulted by Douglass and/or by some of his pupils (not McGregor or Haury) who can be peculiarly obnoxious. He transfers his scorn for Douglass' method, caused by Douglass' failure freely to admit its occasional incompetence, to those who have fallen flat on their faces before Douglass (e.g. to Hooten for recanting the time estimates on the number of skeletons at Pecos) and to some extent even to those who have been mildly critical. He began with his revision of Snaketown. Flagstaff was naturally next on the list. Now he has revisions of other areas in [manuscript], under work, or under plan. You at the MNA are essentially innocent bystanders getting hit in his attack on Douglass' methods. Though McGregor receives heavy blows, these probably are not intended for him personally; I believe that Gladwin has friendly feelings for McGregor. (November 30, 1945)

Antevs noted that Gladwin felt that Douglass never acknowledged his method's "occasional incompetence," but Douglass never argued for his method's perpetual competence or, for that matter, its universal applicability. If any ring sequence was found to be inadequate, for any reason, Douglass simply did not publish a date for the specimen. His methods, techniques, and biases were well published by that time (e.g., Douglass 1934b, 1935b, 1937, 1941a, 1941c), and he often refused to publish dates if he was not "infernally sure" of their veracity. Antevs tried to galvanize Colton's support by impugning Douglass's scholarship. He used a tactic similar to Gladwin's by emphasizing unidentified "mistakes." Indeed, he maintained that these mistakes were "psychological," not methodological, as Gladwin had argued: "Douglass' (and some of his pupils') actions and attitudes seem to have been an unbroken series of psychological mistakes. As far as I can judge, Douglass' method is all right in most cases; but it is obviously incompetent and misleading at times. Why has this not been openly admitted? I do not expect that Douglass can be influenced and changed, but someone among his better

pupils should have shown a little foresight and independence"
(November 30, 1945).

Antevs apologized for the petulant Gladwin and interestingly
directed blame away from Gladwin's scholarship and toward the archaeological community, which he felt had effectively created the crisis by
ignoring Gladwin's work: "We can scarcely blame Gladwin for taking it
so seriously, for the lid has been pressed down on the kettle much too
long, tree-ring work is exceptionally irritating, and he has slaved at it
from morning to night for years. We can't just ignore the matter. One
way to ease the tension is to air the problems. Therefore, and because to
my knowledge nobody has paid attention to Gladwin's method now
years old, I am writing these reviews, though I do not know any archaeology" (November 30, 1945). Antevs thus absolved himself of responsibility and authority by removing himself from the archaeological
community. He concluded his explanation by mitigating the criticism
that Colton might feel from these passages and admonished Gladwin for
his failure to consult MNA's collections in detail: "But, of course,
Gladwin should have visited your Museum to study your material and
discuss mutual problems in a friendly way with you."

Haury's reply to Antevs's letter and review offers insight into the situation from the only dendrochronologist and archaeologist to have
worked for both Douglass and Gladwin. Haury tried to be dispassion-
ate and neutral while still opposing Gladwin's logical flaws and scientific errors:

> My whole quarrel with H.S.G. is not necessarily that his system is
> no good, because I think you can get correlations as you have shown
> by his system using the different running averages. Furthermore, on
> wood that is easily read Douglass and Gladwin will both come out
> with the same answer. It is on difficult wood where the trouble arises
> and it is definitely my impression that this is where the Gladwin tech-
> nique breaks down. In other words my question hinges upon the basic
> step of evaluating a given ring as being a true one. Gladwin, of course,
> would not like to be reminded of my feeling about this, and I am
> telling you this for your own benefit. . . . Another matter that bothers
> me is the way Mr. Gladwin tends to date tree-rings by the archaeology,
> a procedure which in my mental makeup is not permissible, at least if
> we wish to use tree-rings as a dating tool in an honest sense. There is,
> after all, some divergence of opinion as to archaeological interpreta-
> tions, so how can one justify the assigning of dates to trees on the basis
> of that archaeology? However, all of this aside, I am glad you have

reviewed the *Medallions* as you have. I only wish that Gladwin would see the desirability of writing in a truly scientific sense rather than in his pseudo-facetious vein. This last statement is for your eyes only. (February 11, 1946)

On March 30, 1946, an impromptu meeting of dendrochronologists was held at the University of Arizona in an attempt to determine how to address Gladwin's most recent attack. Douglass reluctantly agreed to write a response, though to do so he needed to examine the specimens, or duplicates thereof, that Gladwin included in his analysis. Only two were found at the University of Arizona; Gladwin had not supplied that institution with duplicates. Over the next two months, Colton acted as arbiter between Douglass and Gladwin in an attempt to secure the relevant specimens for Douglass's reexamination. Gladwin refused to send the specimens because they were the only copies he had and because they had been permanently loaned to Gila Pueblo by MNA. He did, however, graciously offer to allow anyone to examine the specimens at his laboratory in Santa Barbara (Gladwin to K. Bartlett, May 6, 1946, and Gladwin to Colton, May 25, 1946). Douglass (1946) quickly published a response on the basis of his experience with Gladwin's specimens in 1939, when he first realized that Gladwin could not possibly be analyzing ring-width measurements because his surfacing technique obscured rather than revealed the rings.

In late December 1946, Douglass took exception to Colton's (1946:33) seemingly favorable characterization of Gladwin's tree-ring technique as "quantitative" and Douglass's as "qualitative." In the "hard" sciences, quantitative data are often considered more accurate and objective, whereas qualitative are considered impressionistic and subjective. Colton was correct in stating that Douglass's dating technique does not make use of measurements in the establishment of dates, but Douglass felt that Colton should have recognized the systematic and replicable nature of his dating, qualities that were so far lacking in Gladwin's analyses. The ensuing polite exchange of letters between Colton and Douglass properly summarizes the situation with regard to Gladwin's tree-ring analysis. Colton wrote:

> I note that you take exception to my use of the words qualitative and quantitative in discussing the Douglass and Gladwin methods of tree ring analysis in the Sinagua [Colton 1946] and that you feel that my choice of words gives a wrong impression on the relative accuracy of the two methods. John [McGregor] read my manuscript on that chapter and did not criticize my use of the words. [Sid] Stallings,

however, reading a copy of the page proof when it was too late to change, called my attention to it. Because the Gladwin method requires absolute measurements in every stage, I still think it is more quantitative than yours, but this does not mean that I think it a more accurate method. . . . Gladwin has worked out a method which takes skilled judgment in the first two steps—the preparation of the material, which you rightly question, and the recognition and measurement of rings. After that any high school graduate properly trained, can carry through the routine statistical methods and can decide on the best fit of the ring patterns without, necessarily, any particular experience. In your method on the other hand, as I have seen it applied, skilled judgement must govern every step, preparation of material, making skeleton plots, cross-dating, and the compilation of the master plots. In the Gladwin method the last three are purely routine. . . . To an archaeologist tree ring dates are only of value if they are consistent with archaeological data. The dates published by you and your students are remarkably consistent. (January 14, 1947)

Douglass explained his understanding of the shortcomings in Gladwin's method to Colton two months later. To do so, he used devastatingly familiar analogs to explain how he identified individual rings in a chronology, thus effectively refuting the idea that "quantitative" data are necessarily more reliable than "qualitative":

To build a chronology we have to carry dates from tree to tree; (from trees of today to trees of yesterday); that we call crossdating. Mr. Gladwin does it by comparing average ring sizes by correlation coefficients—we do it by comparisons of individual rings by means of ring patterns. Each individual ring has to form its part of a pattern. That pattern is built of individuals, not of averages, and is therefore precise to the individual ring, which is not true of correlation coefficients. . . . When you recognize a friend you don't use mere resemblance (as in correlation coefficients), you see many details that you are acquainted with. So in crossdating we first get well acquainted with ring groups and thus know every individual in the group, like recognizing eyebrows, nose, mouth, in forming a face. So we know and use both group and individual rings, precise and certain in a way that correlation coefficients never can be. . . . Do you identify pottery by correlation coefficients? No, you do it by more and more minute details of form, color, composition, design, etc. So we individualize ring dates in that way. Each ring taking its place in an intricate pattern that cannot be duplicated if we take long enough series of rings. Does Gladwin do this? Not at all, he takes averages of resemblance without the minute and complex details that we use. (March 28, 1947)

Douglass then explained the methodological shortcomings of the Gladwin technique:

> All this refers to the lesser of two parts of Gladwin's process that discredit his results. This lesser part as you see, is the substitution of an old inferior [quantitative] process (of crossdating) for our new discovery of how to use the complex and intricate patterns of individual rings in place of mere averages. . . . The vital and major error that at once cast doubt upon every date Mr. Gladwin has proposed, is his failure to understand that his abraded surfaces on charcoal are not permitting him really to see the smaller and fainter annual rings. It is his failure to understand that he is not recognizing rings by their botanical structures. . . . His abraded surfaces are not giving him annual rings and he doesn't know it.

Finally, Douglass synthesized these arguments as he returned to the distinction between qualitative and quantitative analyses in dendrochronology:

> The word "qualitative" signifies estimation and lack of definite measures. Quantitative means surely a lot of definite measures, but what good are measures if you are measuring the wrong thing? And that is what he is doing. Remember that the introduction of a single error in a specimen may change greatly the correlation coefficient and change the apparent location by a hundred years but by our method we detect that error at once by crossdating and remove it. . . . And as to quantity of measures by perhaps the best measuring instrument we measure all our rings but do it *after* cross-identification of the ring and not before. If you measure first and then try to crossdate you are throwing away the God-given opportunity of working directly on nature's ring in the wood or charcoal. . . . You see we have discovered a process which Gladwin has never understood—pathetic isn't it? . . . This letter shows how I distrust all results from his laboratory. His method and my method are different methods and cannot be compared in statistical terms. (Emphasis in original)

CONCLUSION

Archaeological tree-ring dating enjoyed a prosperous career at the Museum of Northern Arizona during John McGregor's tenure there between 1930 and 1942. Significant accomplishments include the dating of the Flagstaff Type 1 series within the Central Pueblo Chronology in

1931, the secure dating of Pueblo I and Pueblo II period sites in the Medicine Valley in the mid-1930s (McGregor 1938a), and the dating of a number of significant northern Arizona ceramic types (Colton and Hargrave 1937; McGregor 1938b). Dendrochronology at MNA was initially less successful at dating the eruption of Sunset Crater, but after Gladwin provided the incentive, Colton's reanalysis of Flagstaff-area archaeology led to the derivation of a precise date for that important event (Colton 1945).

On January 12, 1950, Colton notified Douglass that the Museum of Northern Arizona hadn't had a curator for its dendrochronological collection in eight years and noted that the future of tree-ring dating at MNA did not look bright for financial reasons. That same day he wrote McGregor and explained that he planned to donate MNA's collection to the University of Arizona. McGregor replied that he was concerned that the collection be placed where it would be used, for he had had firsthand experience with the University of Chicago's dendrochronological collection (see Chapter 7), which was donated to the University of Oklahoma–Norman in 1947, where it languished unused. Formal arrangements were made for a permanent loan of MNA's tree-ring collection to the Laboratory of Tree-Ring Research on the condition that if the latter facility became "inactive" for two years, the entire collection would be returned to the Museum of Northern Arizona. It remains in Tucson.

Lyndon Hargrave became curator of ornithology at the Museum of Northern Arizona in 1934 but continued conducting archaeological fieldwork throughout the 1930s, focusing especially on defining the Patayan culture west of Flagstaff (Hargrave 1938). He resigned all posts at that institution in 1939 and in 1947 could be found running the Oasis Court Motel in Benson, Arizona. In 1956, he returned to scientific and academic pursuits with the National Park Service at the old headquarters of the Gila Pueblo Archaeological Foundation in Globe, Arizona, and later at Prescott College in Prescott, Arizona (Dick and Schroeder 1968). Hargrave died in 1976 (Taylor and Euler 1980).

John McGregor left the Museum of Northern Arizona in 1942 to become director of the Illinois State Museum after Thorne Deuel left to join the army. He spent the remainder of his career in Springfield, though he returned to the Southwest to conduct archaeological fieldwork from time to time. McGregor did not conduct any original tree-ring research after leaving Flagstaff, though he was engaged as a consultant to evaluate Florence Hawley's work at the University of Chicago later in the 1940s (see Chapter 7). He died in 1992.

CHAPTER 6

Santa Fe Style

*Dendrochronology in
the Rio Grande Valley*

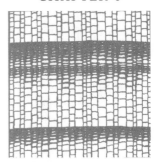

Douglass's (1929) publication announcing the results of his 15-year effort to develop a southwestern tree-ring chronology and date archaeological sites was entitled "The Secret of the Southwest Solved by Talkative Tree-Rings." This title is a misnomer because tree-ring specimens from archaeological sites in a major portion of the American Southwest, the Rio Grande valley, were not datable against Douglass's Central Pueblo Chronology. Douglass recognized as early as June 24, 1927, that Rio Grande Valley trees possessed a climate signal different from those in the Four Corners region. He reported to Judd that he was "at a loss [to explain the ring sequence] on some of the specimens from the Rio Grande Valley for many of them are harder to date than I expected" (June 24, 1927). Douglass's deficiency in this regard was not due to a lack of effort or paucity of specimens, however.

Jeançon and Ricketson collected numerous Rio Grande Valley specimens for the First Beam Expedition in 1923, and Kidder had been submitting specimens to Douglass from his excavations at Pecos Pueblo since that year as well. Though Douglass could identify his Flagstaff sequence in living trees from the Rio Grande valley, he was not at all comfortable with the crossdating in the prehistoric specimens. Given the dendrochronological prerequisites for archaeological tree-ring dating, Douglass would not consider dating archaeological samples until he was certain that the climate signal in both the archaeological and living-tree specimens was the same. Douglass's discomfort with the Rio Grande specimens was severe enough that he (Douglass 1929) withheld publication of prehistoric dates for Pecos Pueblo. In view of the methodological importance of Kidder's work at that site with regard to stratigraphic excavation techniques, it must have been extremely disappointing to both men that they could not obtain reliable tree-ring dates. Douglass explained his decision in late October 1929. He wrote Kidder: "It seems to me on the whole that for inclusion in a final list like that [to be published in *National Geographic*] the Pecos date should have received a careful comparison with other Rio Grande material. I shall not feel satisfied about the Rio Grande area until it receives a complete chronological study from modern trees back as far as one can go. It has I know many points of similarity to the Flagstaff area and I believe the dates I sent you are all correct, but in final statement I hold them subject to checking with other Rio Grande material" (October 28, 1929). The establishment of archaeological tree-ring dating in the Rio Grande Valley thus became a primary goal of the recently incorporated Laboratory of Anthropology in Santa Fe (Elliott 1987; Stocking 1982). See Table 6 for a chronology.

W. Sidney Stallings and Chronology Development, 1930–1933

In the spring of 1930, interested archaeologists understood that there was a good possibility that Haury, under Douglass's close supervision, would attack the Rio Grande tree-ring dating problem. Indeed, Douglass entertained the idea that this work might result in a secure line of funding to pay his able assistant's salary. Jesse Nusbaum, as director of the Laboratory of Anthropology, informed Kidder, chairman of the Board of Trustees, that "we should make a move on Haury" (April 9, 1930). While Kidder examined sources of funding, Nusbaum solicited a detailed proposal and budget from Douglass, though Nusbaum estimated on his own that the entire project, including Haury's salary, would cost about $2,000. Within a month, however, Haury had accepted the assistant directorship of Gila Pueblo and was no longer available. By the end of May, McGregor and W. Sidney Stallings (Figure 27) were considered leading candidates for the position. McGregor, however, was committed to teach at the Arizona State Teachers' College in Flagstaff though mid-August 1930, and Kidder, Nusbaum, and other archaeologists in the area wanted work to begin as soon as possible. Stallings was finally hired in 1931, after Nusbaum had acquired administrative approval and funding from the Laboratory's Board of Directors.

As eager young scholars are wont to do, Stallings helped his case for the laboratory position in 1930 by collecting archaeological tree-ring specimens while working at Chetro Ketl with Hewett and on his own at the Jemez ruins (Douglass to Nusbaum, January 22, 1931). He worked

TABLE 6. Timeline: Archaeological Tree-Ring Research at the Laboratory of Anthropology.

1927 Douglass begins to recognize differences in the Rio Grande Valley tree-ring records.

1931 June: W. Sidney Stallings hired as dendrochronologist.
October: Grand opening, Laboratory of Anthropology.

1932 Nusbaum and Douglass consider the prospect of dating tree-ring materials from Cave du Pont.
August 8: Stallings "bridges the gap," establishes a Rio Grande chronology.

1933 May: Stallings announces the Rio Grande Chronology.
Stallings publishes the Rio Grande Chronology.

1934 Irwin Hayden accuses Rainbow Bridge–Monument Valley Expedition employees of site desecration.

1935 Stallings focuses on archaeological problems.
Morris contacts Nusbaum regarding Cave du Pont specimens, to no avail.
Nusbaum resigns as Laboratory of Anthropology director.

1936 March: Stallings accepts a position at the Taylor Museum in Colorado Springs, Colorado.

1937 Stallings begins graduate studies at Yale University.

1938 Edward Twitchell Hall, Jr., employed as dendrochronologist by the Awatovi Expedition.

1939 Stallings dates specimens from Cave du Pont.
Stallings transfers to Harvard University.

1941 Stallings conducts tree-ring analysis of Spanish *santos* at the laboratory.

1942 Stallings enters the Intelligence Service of the U.S. Army.
Hall enters the U.S. Army.

1944 Hall publishes *Early Stockaded Settlements in the Governador, New Mexico*.

1947 Stallings becomes director of the Taylor Museum.

1950 Laboratory of Anthropology donates tree-ring specimen collection to the University of Arizona.

on the samples in Tucson during the academic year as salary and laboratory arrangements were finalized in Santa Fe. At the end of March 1931, Douglass wrote Nusbaum that he was pleased with Stallings's efforts: "Stallings is industrious and making progress. I believe we have excellent tree records going through the 1500's and to 1650. The others begin

FIGURE 27. The staff of the Laboratory of Tree-Ring Research, 1946. From left, Fred Scantling, Sid Stallings, A. E. Douglass, Edmund Schulman, and James Louis Giddings.

about 1725. Working on the Rio Grande material in hand. Trying to get modern trees that cover 1650 to 1725. Will come up [to Santa Fe] with Stallings for 10 days in June. He will need a car and an assistant. $80 to $100 a month for salary, three months fieldwork and six months analysis" (March 28, 1931). Douglass had also formulated a specific research design that called for sample collection along a north-south transect: "I am confident based on preliminary work on Jemez mission, Jemez ruin, and the modern trees that there is a most important set of dates coming out of our efforts. First work should be [in the] general area [from] Santa Fe to Pecos in order to use consistently beam material. Then to the Jemez mountains, and then to Gran Quivari [sic] and the Mimbres [Valley]" (Douglass to Nusbaum, April 17, 1931; see Figure 28).

Douglass and Stallings motored from Tucson and arrived in Santa Fe on June 10, 1931; Douglass remained there for ten days to help Stallings set up the newly established tree-ring laboratory. He also examined new specimens from the national forests around Santa Fe and finalized research plans with Nusbaum. By late July, Stallings had settled in comfortably and gained the favor of both Kidder, who took a "great shine to Stallings" (Kidder to Douglass, July 6, 1931), and Nusbaum, who commented on his diligent work habits: "Mr. Stallings, in my mind, is one of the finest fellows to work with and to have about an institution that I

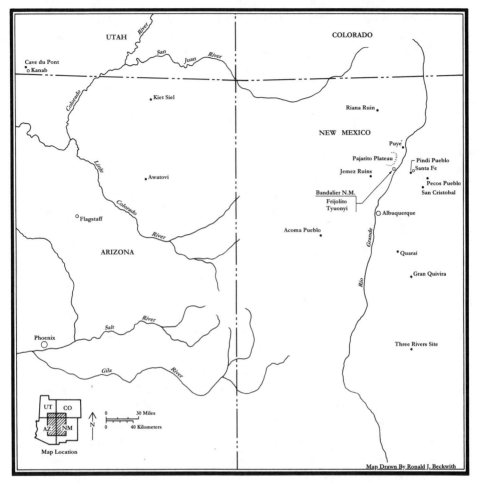

FIGURE 28. Sites sampled by the Laboratory of Anthropology and mentioned in the text.

have known for a long, long while, and he is a hard worker, coming here night after night to check up on the last material recovered in his expeditions" (Nusbaum to Douglass, July 22, 1931). Kidder applauded the faculty at the University of Arizona as well: "[Douglass] and Cummings have been turning out some splendid material these last few years" (Kidder to Douglass, September 7, 1931).

Stallings conducted four months of fieldwork in 1931, collecting samples from living trees, stumps, and archaeological sites on National Forest Service, National Park Service, state, and private land in order to build the Rio Grande tree-ring chronology. He filed detailed progress reports with Douglass on July 7, August 5, August 25, September 7, and September 15. Annual summaries were filed on October 1 with the U.S. Department of Agriculture and Department of the Interior, the state of New Mexico, and the Laboratory of Anthropology. Stallings provided Nusbaum with a comprehensive report that included statements about the strategy behind each phase of the research. Among Stallings's many 1931 accomplishments were the collection of more than 300 living-tree specimens along the Rio Grande, the dating of samples from the Palace of the Governors and several Spanish missions around Santa Fe, and the sampling of a number of archaeological sites in the area, including Tyuonyi in what is now Bandelier National Monument and Puyé and Tsankawi on the Pajarito Plateau (Figure 29). Ironically, Stallings also noted a scientific "benefit" of pothunting: the holes left as a result of illicit excavations often revealed whether or not charcoal was present in a site and therefore saved time for his dendrochronological survey, which, like that of the Museum of Northern Arizona, did not undertake excavations without prior evidence of charcoal at a site.

Stallings hoped that the 256 wood specimens and 127 bags of charcoal collected in prehistoric and protohistoric sites in 1931 would allow him to establish the Rio Grande Chronology back to at least A.D. 1100. Though he did not have much Rio Grande archaeological or tree-ring experience before his arrival in Santa Fe, his research design had obvious parallels to Douglass's effort to develop the Central Pueblo Chronology during the 1920s, and Stallings had the additional benefit of Douglass's dendrochronological experience and expertise to guide him. Stallings used a pottery sequence established by Harry P. Mera, county health officer, retired physician, and curator of archaeology at the laboratory, to target sites for examination. On October 1, Stallings returned to Tucson to further his dendrochronological analyses with Douglass and to earn his master's degree.

The Laboratory of Anthropology enjoyed its formal opening in October 1931 (Elliott 1987; Woodbury 1993). A distinguished group of scientists, including Douglass, traveled to Santa Fe for the gala and associated scientific conference. It is possible that Nusbaum and Douglass at that time discussed the possibility of moving Douglass's entire tree-ring research program to Santa Fe. In January 1932, Nusbaum dropped a not-so-subtle hint to Douglass: "We . . . look forward to the time when you can work at least part of the year with us here at the Laboratory" (January 7, 1932). Nusbaum, as director, was engaged in a struggle to

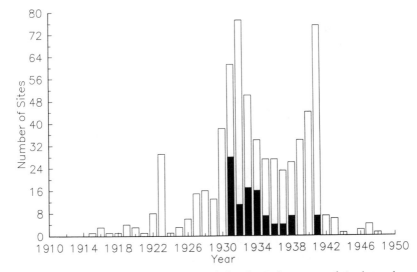

FIGURE 29. Archaeological tree-ring research by the Laboratory of Anthropology 1931–1941. Note the peak in activity in 1931 from Stallings efforts to develop an archaeological dating chronology applicable to sites in the Rio Grande Valley.

build the laboratory's research programs (Stocking 1982), and the addition of Douglass would have been a major accomplishment that would have shifted the center of tree-ring research from Tucson to Santa Fe. For such a move, Douglass would have had to abandon his beloved Steward Observatory at the University of Arizona to focus on tree-ring studies, especially archaeological applications, which, however important they may have been to others, were not the central focus of his scientific career (Webb 1983). Whether tempted by Nusbaum's offers or not, Douglass remained in Tucson.

Stallings recommended that no substantive fieldwork be conducted in 1932 in lieu of continued laboratory analysis of the many specimens already in hand, but he expressed his desire to find living trees greater than 500 years old to add sample depth to the problematic sequence between A.D. 1436 and 1510 in the Rio Grande Chronology. In addition, Stallings delineated his research plan once the chronology was fully established: "After cross-identification [crossdating] is accomplished there remains the further laboratory work of measurement of specimens, plotting of curves, arrangement of data, and the photographing of specimens so as to be able to present proof of dating" (April 1, 1932).

On May 15, 1932, Stallings wrote to Douglass that he had examined some 1,500 pieces of charcoal and 290 pieces of wood "more or less intensely" and that he could now report two significant chronologies. These consisted of a "dated sequence for the Jemez Mountain area back to 1510, with some doubt back to 1436, and a late undated sequence of 340 years from the Pueblos of Pecos, San Cristobal, and Quarai."

Stallings bridged the gap between the two chronologies on August 8 (Stallings to McGregor, September 20, 1932). He explained to Douglass that the Rio Grande Chronology was well established to A.D. 1200 and that the Pecos Pueblo specimens for which Kidder so desired dates ranged from A.D. 1310 to 1695. He noted that an "intensive drought" occurred in the Rio Grande valley during the early A.D. 1400s, thereby accounting, in part, for the difficulty in bridging his two major chronologies (August 17, 1932). He explained his achievement to McGregor one month later:

> The tree-ring situation in New Mexico is looking up just at present. On August 8th I got the chronology back to 1200—it may not be early to you, but after working for over a year on the stuff, it seemed to me that 1200 was really antiquity, and dated a few sites from Rio Grande [Pueblo III period Black-on-White] sites up. Not for publication—the B-on-W site dates 1310, a Glaze III site, Frijolito, dates 1450, and the last big building period at Pecos and San Cristobal dated from about 1430 to 1450. When Kidder gets out his notes on the distribution of the pottery types in the different Pecos rooms we will have a fair idea of the correlation of dates and pottery from there. (September 20, 1932)

In a brief exchange in November 1932, Stallings and McGregor addressed the differences between their respective chronologies. McGregor inquired in particular whether the Rio Grande Chronology indicated a "drought immediately following the Pueblo Indian revolt; that is, during the years 1680–1690," for, according to his studies in Flagstaff, a drought occurred in northern Arizona during that decade (November 14, 1932). Stallings considered the sociopolitical and histori-cal implications of such a drought but replied in the negative:

> There is no good evidence of an extreme drought during this time. A few specimens show a slightly smaller set of rings during this time, but it is not an unusually small set. 1680 and 1689 were flood years; 1685 is small, in many cases absent. The slightly dry spell during this decade appears to have been scattered locally, and even in such spots was not on the whole extreme. All this is contradictory to the testi-mony of the Indians following the Re-conquest, but one must bear in mind that this decade was one of social instability around the [Rio Grande] Pueblo population, which would surely affect to some degree their pursuit of agriculture. Further, such testimony was exactly what

the Spaniards wanted to hear, and whether completely true or not, it would have been the politic thing to say. (November 20, 1932)

In the spring of 1933, Stallings prepared a series of reports and publications. He and Nusbaum made plans formally to announce the Rio Grande archaeological dates at the Southwest Division meeting of the American Association for the Advancement of Science, held in Las Cruces, New Mexico, May 1–4, 1933. Stallings first needed to have Douglass verify the chronology and dating (Stallings to Douglass, January 18, 1933). Douglass and his wife traveled to Santa Fe in April 1933 to achieve this end, and he quickly affirmed Stallings's work. Stallings thus presented the Rio Grande Chronology and dates less than two years after he was hired, a remarkable accomplishment that, like Haury's work at the University of Arizona in 1930, reaffirmed the viability of the Douglass method of tree-ring dating.

A notable corollary accomplishment of this research was that Stallings, in a report submitted to Nusbaum entitled "The Oldest House in Santa Fe," debunked the idea that that structure was of pre-Spanish origin:

> Traditionally, the "Oldest House" is supposed to have been built by Indians before the coming of the Spanish. . . . There is no material evidence to support this view. In the first place, there is no irrefutable evidence, historically or archaeologically, that the site of Santa Fe was occupied by Indians at the time of the founding of the Spanish settlement. The latest historical information, from recently discovered documents in the archives in Mexico City, indicates that Santa Fe was not founded before 1609, and probably in 1610, by the third governor of New Mexico, Pedro de Peralta. The evidences of aboriginal occupation which were found during restoration of and excavation in the Palace of the Governors undoubtedly dates [sic] from the Pueblo Rebellion, when the edifice was occupied by Indians from 1680 to 1694. Black-on-white sherds can be found in various parts of the city today, and such sherds were picked from the walls of the "Oldest House," but villages in which this type of pottery was made had been abandoned and in a state of ruin well over a century before the discovery of America. Positive evidence that the "Oldest House" is of post-Spanish origin is found in that building itself. In the many places where plaster has fallen away and walls are exposed, adobe brick can be seen. The Pueblo Indians did not make adobe brick before being taught by the Spaniards, but used a "puddle" method of construction. . . . The gist of the above evidence is, then, that the "Oldest House" does not date before 1610, and it might well have been built later. If it was first built

in the early 17th century, there is a good chance that the house was at least partially destroyed during the Pueblo Rebellion of 1680. . . . It was thought that a study of roof beams might yield data on the antiquity of the house. [Seven specimens were collected and dated to 1741–1768.] . . . In summary, there is no foundation except tradition that the "Oldest House" was built in pre-Spanish times. The present roof of the old, lower story was probably built in 1764. Further conclusions [are] not possible until plaster coatings are removed. (March 8, 1933)

On September 25, 1933, Stallings filed with Nusbaum his annual report, "The Dendro-Archaeological Project." He noted that in 1932–1933, 284 specimens had been dated as far back as A.D. 1100 for a number of mission churches and prehistoric archaeological sites including Gran Quivira, Pecos Pueblo, and some unnamed Pueblo III period sites designated by Laboratory of Anthropology survey numbers (Figure 27). Stallings achieved some closure in this first phase of research when he published the Rio Grande Chronology later that year (Stallings 1933).

Seeds for a Tree-Ring Conference: Willful Destruction by Dendrochronologists?

Early in the spring of 1934, a little-known yet decidedly unpleasant situation arose when Irwin Hayden, then an engineer doing restoration work at Kiet Siel in Tsegi Canyon for the Civil Works Administration, accused Rainbow Bridge–Monument Valley Expedition employees of desecrating ruins while collecting tree-ring specimens in 1933. Hayden's charges focused primarily on Kiet Siel and other sites at Navajo National Monument but had implications that reached farther than perhaps even he had intended. His accusations struck a nerve in Jesse Nusbaum, director of the Laboratory of Anthropology and former National Park Service superintendent, who a decade earlier had become infuriated when members of the First Beam Expedition blatantly disregarded his orders while collecting samples in Mesa Verde National Park.

As a condition of the permit granted the First Beam Expedition, Jeançon and Ricketson were to use the tubular borers designed by Morris and Douglass to collect tree-ring samples in standing ruins. The manual borers require a great deal of strength and patience to use, and up to two hours of drilling were necessary to collect a single sample. The hole left behind is only about an inch across and can be easily plugged with cork or other materials to obfuscate the scar. Jeançon and Ricketson used the borers to collect samples in Mesa Verde sites such as Cliff Palace that are accessible to the public, but when they strayed off the beaten path, they dropped the borers and used saws, which are vastly more efficient. Because the use of saws often requires the removal of entire beam ends, this method is extremely destructive (Nusbaum to Colton, March 10, 1934). Given Nusbaum's explicit prohibition, the First Beam Expedition's use of saws amounted to illegal site destruction, and Nusbaum informed Douglass and Judd in no uncertain terms about his displeasure. No formal charges were filed as a result, but it is clear that Nusbaum did not forget the episode. Thus, when Hayden's charges came to light, they only rekindled Nusbaum's anger.

Hayden filed a complaint with Frank Pinkley, superintendent of Southwestern Monuments, who passed it on to the director of the National Park Service, Arno B. Cammerer, on February 7, 1934. In excited prose, Hayden cited Douglass as a model of proper sampling technique: "I understand that Douglass plugs his holes. Others do not. The butchery, however, done at Keet Seel, with a saw or saws, in 1933, is just too bad. Standing timbers in kivas, hatchway posts, roof beams, have been cut leaving the sawed ends to spoil the picture. Nothing was gained which could not have been gained by taking cores in a decent, scientific way." He then described the difficult situation that was left for his CWA work crew: "Our party, faced with the duty of cleaning and repairing Keet Seel, is embarrassed with the problem of what to do with the unique corner posts, cut off by saws below the tops of the walls." Hayden was not interested in pointing fingers; he just wanted to ensure that additional damage was not inflicted: "I am not concerned with who did this, but with making certain that permits include requirements that collectors abide by federal guidelines. . . . To go into a National Monument with saws, to cut off timbers which are an integral part of the ruins, is a desecration and a mutilation which is nothing more than vandalism, regardless of the motive, the more so because it is unnecessary." He felt that something had to be done "to regulate and standardize the taking of sections of timbers from National Monuments and from ruins on Federal lands, for tree-ring study" (February 7, 1934).

Pinkley agreed with Hayden's assessment: "Some of these boys hate to use a hollow bit and take cores because it takes a little longer and takes a good deal more man power because boring with a hollow bit is hard work. That, however, is no reason for us letting them spoil the effect of our ruins with a lot of sawn beam ends." He sent a copy of Hayden's letter to Nusbaum, who despite personal frustration and anger, suggested that caution prevail and accusations be muzzled until all the facts were in. He knew that in addition to the Rainbow Bridge–Monument Valley

Expedition, the Museum of Northern Arizona had sent a group to gather specimens in Tsegi Canyon. No matter which was the guilty party, Lyndon Hargrave of the MNA was implicated because he was the field leader of both expeditions. Hayden elaborated his charges in a personal letter to Colton:

> The needless butchering of Keet Seel timbers will, I think, result in the refusal of permits to take tree ring specimens from National Monuments or from ruins on Federal Lands. I have urged Sup't Pinkley to work for such an order, refusing such permits to any and all, except when specimens are to be taken under direct supervision of a custodian or ranger and/or under methods prescribed by the Federal authorities. The conditions at Keet Seel, as I find them, are truly sickening. One room has three ends of roof-beams sawed off; one kiva, the best one now standing, has two standing posts sawed off. Another has a projecting roof beam sawed off close to its wall-surface; a wattle and daub wall has large end-posts from the tops of which great wedges have been cut. . . . The degradation of the art of taking tree-ring specimens is clearly shown here at Keet Seel; Dr. Douglass, the scientist, took cores and plugged the holes. Neil Judd took cores and did not plug the holes.[1] Then came the [1933 Rainbow Bridge–Monument Valley] outfit, with a saw and saws and seems to have indulged in a sort of sophomoric sawing spree.

Colton showed this letter to Hargrave, who immediately became offended by the fact that he had to answer a "blind" accusation and that he and the Museum of Northern Arizona were implicated without being formally charged with any infraction. In a letter to Ansel Hall, director of the Rainbow Bridge–Monument Valley Expedition and also of the National Park Service, Hargrave wrote:

> It is a disappointment to be doubted by officials of the Department [of the Interior] when I, personally, and the Museum, as an Institution, have been so active in the preservation of our natural resources; have cooperated in all instances with the Department to the extent of great expense and loss of time to us; since through us the Department, and science in general, have learned facts that otherwise would not have been available for some time; and since we have always been prompt in conforming to the rules and regulations and have always sent our

---

1. There is no evidence in the archives I examined that Judd ever collected tree-ring samples at Kiet Siel.

reports in on time. It is therefore with a sense of disappointment that I answer a blind charge.

The Museum of Northern Arizona has been active in the dating of our prehistoric ruins since 1928 [sic—1929] and there probably is no one, excepting Dr. Douglass, who has played a greater or more important part in this work than I. McGregor of our lab did the dating for Rainbow Bridge–Monument Valley Expedition free of charge and at Museum expense. . . . I was operating under standing permits to Museum of Northern Arizona from Department of the Interior, explicitly a letter from [Assistant Secretary of the Interior] Mr. [John H.] Edwards of January 16, 1933, and an extension of that permit dated June 27, 1933, that included everything but Canyon de Chelly.

Regarding methods of collecting. The Museum has been forward in developing methods for this branch of science and has considered of prime importance the preservation of a structure. There were many loose timbers at Keet Seel from previous investigators. I recall only one standing timber that had a sawed off end, and [Richard] Wetherill called me on it, but we agreed that the timber would have to be either removed or buried in masonry [during restoration], so I went ahead with the cut. My conscience is clear.

I have now covered three angles of this subject: the matter of permits (authority), field methods and consideration of the site, and reports on work done. When one considers the value of the work done by my institution, the apparent disregard for expense and time in service and the expensive publication of reports which rightly should be borne by the Department, and the willing cooperation always given the Department by us, it is difficult to understand how a sudden lack of confidence can be shown without even the consideration of giving the basis for such action. (March 5, 1934)

Colton defended Hargrave and the museum's work in a letter to Nusbaum:

Lyndon Hargrave showed me a letter that he had from Ansel Hall, in which he was criticized in the matter of collecting beams in the Tsegi. No specific charges were made, so that he is in the dark as to what has been reported. Knowing how careful Lyn is in all matters of conservation, and how he cooperated in every way with Government agencies I cannot but feel that a mistake has been made by someone. I know of no institution which is more punctilious than we are in the matter of permits, living up to the requirements, and making reports upon those permits. I think we should know the nature of the charges and who has made them. (March 6, 1934)

Pinkley subsequently admitted that his goal in submitting Hayden's letter to the Park Service director was not to "cause serious action to be taken against the man who took those particular beams" but rather to "call attention to the looseness with which our permits for taking beams have been worded" and therefore to induce a servicewide "tightening of regulations" (Pinkley to Cammerer, March 8, 1934). Part of the National Park Service's mission is to preserve and protect archaeological sites within park boundaries; if indeed destructive sampling practices were employed under federal permit, the Park Service could have been accused of neglecting its assigned duty.

On March 10, Nusbaum related to Colton the gist of a letter he sent to Pinkley, in which he considered work of the past with an eye toward the future, including a possible conference of dendrochronologists, administrators, and archaeologists interested in tree-ring dating:

I am the first to admit that wasteful methods have been followed in the past and are continued by some in the collecting of beam material. One only has to visit a large group of ruins to ascertain this fact for themselves. I have again and again written statements to the Secretary of the Interior as to the methods which I thought should be followed in taking beam material from ruins in the National Parks and Monuments.

For a period of years [since 1930] Harold Gladwin was considerably upset over the stand that I took with reference to a program of beam collecting that he proposed under which his institution hoped to have available to supply to others on their demand sections from important Southwestern beams. I could not see any justifiable reason for permitting him to build up at Gila Pueblo a large collection of beam material that would duplicate Douglass' collection at a comparatively short distance away, and also place him in a position to supply others. [Gladwin's] permit was the only one issued with my instructions attached as to methods of collecting, and you and Hargrave both know the policy that I have suggested; namely, that I have recommended the essential necessity of taking cores from beams in buildings in National Parks and Monuments in such a way that the value of the beam in the building was not diminished in any manner whatsoever from the public and educational standpoint, nor the beam weakened so as to threaten in any way the feature it might be supporting.

I wrote Ted Kidder that I was disturbed about Hayden's report and suggested at the time that I thought it might be well at an appropriate time in the spring to bring together in conference at the Laboratory or at Flagstaff a group of men who are concerned either in the study of tree ring materials or in the collecting, to the end that they formulate in conference a code to be followed in collecting tree ring materials in structures, exposed in debris, or sub-surface [contexts].

In closing my letter to Pinkley I stated taking a core may mean several hours of arduous work, whereas sawing off the end of the beam may be but a few minutes; but coring it shall be in the future in National Parks and Monuments. In closing let me make very clear to you that I, officially and unofficially, from the commencement of your Museum of Northern Arizona, have deeply appreciated the splendid contributions that you and your institution have made to the spread of knowledge and understanding of archaeological and other scientific features of that area.

By late March, it was apparent to those familiar with the situation that, although some egregious sampling had occurred, at least part of the problem seems to have stemmed from a personality conflict between Hayden and an unnamed member of the expedition (Ansel Hall to Nusbaum, March 23, 1934). On May 5, the impetuous Hayden went off again:

While at Keet Seel Ruins, in January and February, I had daily occasion to curse the fools who sawed off the corner posts of kivas, of roof timbers, and other integral portions of the ruins, in the mad quest for sections of wood for tree ring study. This was also done at Turkey Cave, Turkey House, and the Custodian for Navajo National Monument told me that it was done wherever the MV–RNBE [sic] found timbers on National Monuments or on ruins on federal lands. Not only did these would-be archaeologists saw, but they painted letters and numbers in conspicuous places. . . . The number[s] are meaningless to the public, or to Archaeology, and [have] no place save in a notebook or a museum file, or otherwise we may assume that if the files are lost, where the hell is Keet Seel! . . . What assurance can we have that he will not again turn loose a bunch of Yahoos on priceless ruins? I will take this matter up with everybody to the President if need be.

Three days later, after receiving an explanatory letter from Hall in which Hargrave's response to the charges was summarized, Hayden retreated in a letter to Nusbaum: "Hall has made it clear that everything is all right as far as the future of tree ring collecting is concerned, and I am satisfied. I knew all the time that Mr. Hall probably did not even know that his chief archaeologist, Mr. Hargrave, had been responsible.

Please throw my letter of 5 May [cited above] in the waste-basket. I have been darned sore at the way Keet Seel was butchered and when I did not seem to be getting anywhere I blew up, sorta."

Nusbaum replied to Hayden's letters of May 5 and 8 on May 10. He informed Hayden that plans were being made for a conference of tree-ring workers at Flagstaff in which a primary item on the agenda was the establishment of a tree-ring sample-collection protocol. Shortly after the First Tree-Ring Conference in 1934, a letter outlining the protocol was sent to the director of the Department of the Interior, who was to attach a copy of the protocol to any permit awarded by that office. The protocol required that archaeological tree-ring specimen collection be conducted by a "competent field man," though qualifications for "competence" were not delineated (nor were the ramifications to be expected if a woman collected the specimen). Furthermore, the protocol required that tubular borers be used almost exclusively, that saws be used only on free-lying beams, that cores be taken close to standing walls to avoid weakening beams, that all bore holes be plugged, and that the sampling institution identify itself on the plug.

Dendrochronology at the Laboratory of Anthropology, 1933–1942

From December 1, 1933, through June 1, 1934, Stallings and his colleague Stanley Stubbs excavated Pindi Pueblo, a Rio Grande Pueblo III site on the Santa Fe River. Labor was supplied by the Emergency Relief Administration and Civil Works Administration. Stallings began excavations at two earlier sites near Pindi three weeks later in order to secure tree-ring materials that would help extend the Rio Grande Chronology back before A.D. 1100. During the course of these excavations, he acquired so much tree-ring material that Nusbaum was able to secure Emergency Relief Administration funding for an assistant. He wrote Douglass on August 22 to ask if a qualified individual, perhaps Carl Miller, was available. No one was ever hired for this position, and it is not clear whether the ERA-offered funding disappeared or no qualified assistant was available. Miller subsequently worked for Douglass at the University of Arizona (see Miller 1934, 1935), however, and attempted to apply tree-ring dating at Colonial National Monument in Virginia in 1936–1937 and at sites in Alabama for the Works Progress Administration in 1939. It is likely that the Emergency Relief Administration funding never materialized.

In his annual progress report, Stallings noted that the chronology had not been extended before A.D. 1100. On the positive side, the

twelfth and thirteenth centuries in that chronology had been considerably strengthened by samples collected during his excavations at the two
sites near Pindi Pueblo. Two hundred sixty-one specimens were dated
that year, bringing Stallings's four-year total to 533. He reported that 13
black-on-white sites had been dated, as well as 17 Biscuit Ware sites and
17 historic buildings. He reported in a paper entitled "Pueblos of
Historic Times on the Pajarito Plateau, New Mexico," read by a colleague at the AAAS meetings in Berkeley, that "our present ideas of the
time element involved in the divisions of Rio Grande Pueblo IV culture
must be changed," because tree-ring evidence demonstrated that, like the
"Oldest House," many supposedly prehistoric sites in the Rio Grande
Valley had actually been occupied after European contact (Stallings to
Nusbaum, September 28, 1934). Stallings's revelation had implications
for historians, who had to reconsider Spaniards' accounts of their relationship to Native American populations in the area.

During the fall of 1934, Stallings continued working on the specimens collected the previous year and began a revision of the standardized archaeological tree-ring dating nomenclature published by Glock
(1934b) that he felt contained some ambiguities. He circulated a list of
terms and definitions to other dendrochronologists for comment, but the
list was never published. In reference to this work, Nusbaum wrote
Kidder the following:

> I think, as you read over this statement, you will be very deeply
> impressed with the fact that Stallings is a man of great promise in
> future tree-ring work and, further, that he is destined to be a leader.
> You perhaps noted, as I did with a great measure of satisfaction, that
> his name was added to the list of editors in the second issue of the
> Bulletin. It hurt him a good deal to see every other institution on and
> himself and the Lab off in the first edition, and I thought the same
> about it, particularly in view of the fact that I was the first one to sug-
> gest such a conference, and further in view of Dr. Colton's wish to put
> the whole conference into his lap. (December 29, 1934)

With the Rio Grande Chronology firmly in place, Stallings increasingly turned his attention to the application of tree-ring dates to archaeological problems. In a memo to Nusbaum and Douglass early in 1935,
he related the following approximate dates for the Rio Grande ceramic
periods:

> Glaze I: 1375 ± 75 years
> Glaze II: short or absent
> Glaze III: about 1500

Glaze IV and V: 1500 to 1700, some lag and overlap

Glaze VI: about 1700

Despite a four-year search, Stallings still had difficulty finding tree-ring material to date the Glaze II period because he could not locate any sites that were abandoned while that ceramic ware was in vogue. In a letter to Nusbaum on January 28, Stallings discussed the Glaze Ware phase dating, the interpretive implications of which were not qualitatively different from the ramifications of the Central Pueblo Chronology: "We have at present an approximate chronological outline of Rio Grande Pueblo IV, with lowest probable dates for the sub-periods. This outline is at variance with older concepts, particularly as regards the later periods, the estimated age of which was inferred from historical (documentary) sources; such towns as Puyé and Tshirege are now known to have been occupied well into the historic period, and the whole development of Rio Grande Pueblo culture has been pushed up considerably in time."

In the same letter, Stallings discussed a proposal that Elsie Clews Parsons had made to Alfred Kroeber regarding the use of tree-ring dating in the study of extant and historic pueblo communities. Stallings knew firsthand of the difficulties involved in collecting tree-ring specimens in occupied villages, as well as the difficulties of interpreting the data once specimens were dated, because of extensive beam reuse in the area. He reached the surprising if considered conclusion that additional stylistic (relative) dating be performed *before* intensive beam-by-beam tree-ring analysis was attempted:

> Dates from any (historic) site mean little unless they can be correlated with certain traits which have important chronological values. . . . The difficulties in the way of collecting in the inhabited villages, and the great deal of work entailed [pose problems]. I believe that the proper procedure at the present time is to date the regional chronological horizons as they have been determined by stylistic changes in pottery, and to apply the approximate dates so obtained to any pueblo or group of pueblos, the main features of the ceramic history of which are known. When such an outline has been formulated, and general historical conclusions drawn, beam dates . . . can then be evaluated as to their possible significance. (January 28, 1935)

Stallings concisely stated this strategy in a letter to Benjamin F. Betts of the Housing Research Project at Purdue University, who inquired about tree-ring dating at Acoma Pueblo: "We have been chronology building with an aim to establishing the sequence of prehistoric and historic horizons, with emphasis on dating of stylistic changes rather than the details of individual sites." Stallings was a pioneer in recognizing that dendrochronological data may be too refined for uncritical acceptance within most archaeological analyses (Baillie 1995).

For much of 1935, Stallings was again engaged in laboratory analysis of the many tree-ring specimens collected during the previous year's excavations, though he conducted fieldwork at Pindi Pueblo for three weeks in late August and early September. Nusbaum's annual report to the Board of Trustees notes that Stallings derived 125 new dates from 15 sites, leading to a total of 658 dates from 62 sites (October 31, 1935).

In early 1936, however, the Laboratory of Anthropology was in trouble. Jesse Nusbaum resigned as director in late 1935 to become superintendent again of his beloved Mesa Verde National Park. He was replaced by Kenneth Chapman, who was already in his sixties and suffering from tuberculosis. The laboratory's financial situation was deteriorating, and the $20,000 budget Stallings submitted to the Rockefeller Foundation for his tree-ring program was cut in half. Worse for Stallings from a personal standpoint was that laboratory funding for his doctoral work was now out of the question. He wrote Douglass: "As you know the Laboratory intended to send me back to school for a doctorate. This must now be written off the books, but there is a slight possibility that school can be managed by other means. If it does become possible I want to see some sort of report on the Rio Grande chronology finished before I go if that is at all possible" (January 26, 1936).

For a fleeting moment in February 1936, it appeared that Stallings was going to be employed in Egyptian dendrochronology (Douglass to Stallings, February 29, 1936), but by mid-March he had accepted a job at the Alice B. Taylor Museum in Colorado Springs. Mrs. Taylor had previously funded Laboratory of Anthropology tree-ring research to the tune of $1,000 and, in exchange for Stallings's services in 1936, made another donation to the troubled laboratory. She inquired what salary would be required to bring Stallings to the Taylor Museum permanently. He had other job offers as well. Donald Brand offered him Florence Hawley's position at the University of New Mexico while she was on a one-year leave of absence at the University of Chicago. Roy Lassetter offered him a job with the Tennessee Valley Authority, which Stallings declined because he and Douglass were leery of the uncomfortable political situation that had developed between Hawley and Lassetter at TVA (see Chapter 7).

Kenneth Chapman's 1936 report to the laboratory's Board of Trustees stated that Stallings in 1936 had extended the Rio Grande

Chronology back to A.D. 950, though this extension was still provisional and subject to Douglass's verification. In 1936, Stallings dated material from Pindi Pueblo and the Riana Ruin, excavated by Frank Hibben in 1934, and extended tree-ring dating to south-central New Mexico by dating material from the Three Rivers Site collected by Hattie and Burton Cosgrove of the Peabody Museum. Stallings also gathered 132 living-tree specimens from Tennessee, Georgia, and other southeastern states during a whirlwind tour in the summer, but the specimens proved of little dendrochronological value since they were from secondary-growth forest contexts.

Archival material relating to the research Stallings did at the laboratory in 1937 is meager, though he apparently focused on dating as many specimens as possible before leaving in September to begin graduate studies at Yale University. He dated some 300 specimens from 29 sites, leading Director Chapman to note that "the steady increase in the demands of others for the technical services of [the tree-ring] department will make necessary a reconsideration of [that] program" (Chapman to Board of Trustees, October 31, 1937). Chapman was supportive of tree-ring research at the laboratory but was soon replaced as director by H. Scudder Mekeel, an applied anthropologist who did not share his sentiments for dendrochronology. During Mekeel's tenure, the Dendro-Archaeological Project at the Laboratory of Anthropology was not well supported, and tree-ring research at that institution faded away.

During his six-year tenure as dendrochronologist at the Laboratory of Anthropology, Stallings made a number of significant dendroarchaeological contributions. First and foremost, he established to A.D. 950 the first high-quality tree-ring chronology applicable to tree-ring specimens from prehistoric and historic contexts in the Rio Grande valley (Stallings 1933; Smiley, Stubbs, and Bannister 1953). In so doing, he independently verified Douglass's crossdating and chronology-building techniques, thus strengthening the methodological and theoretical bases of archaeological tree-ring dating. He dated nearly 700 tree-ring specimens from more than 60 sites and produced unpublished manuscripts on the history of archaeological tree-ring dating as well as a glossary of dating terms. He also contributed to the design of tree-ring exhibits at museums across the country.

Stallings was at Yale for an entire year and did not resume his tree-ring studies at the laboratory until September 2, 1938. Chapman noted in his annual report for 1938 that Stallings had succeeded in extending the Rio Grande Chronology back to A.D. 890, with a tentative extension to A.D. 770, and was still working on the publication of that chronology.

In the spring of 1939, Stallings applied to and was accepted by Harvard University, which had a more prestigious archaeology program than Yale. His application was no doubt helped by glowing letters of reference from Douglass and Kidder. In the meantime, he continued to work on the full publication of the Rio Grande Chronology and some shorter articles for the *Tree-Ring Bulletin*, the latter especially because Haury had written that he was "getting ready to ditch the *Bulletin* for lack of material" (April 10, 1939).

Though he was not employed as a dendrochronologist, Stallings continued to publish tree-ring dates (Stallings 1941) and general treatments of dendrochronology (Stallings 1939). Unfortunately, he never published the long-awaited detailed treatment of the Rio Grande Chronology (see Smiley, Stubbs, and Bannister 1953). There is no mention of tree-ring dating in the Laboratory of Anthropology annual report for 1939 or 1940. The report for 1941 states that Stallings used laboratory facilities to conduct some dendrochronological analysis. This work probably related to his study of Spanish Colonial *santos*, or pine-panel paintings, for the Taylor Museum (The Museum of Northern Arizona in 1936–1937; Nash 1997b; Stallings 1940; Wroth 1982). Stallings entered the Intelligence School of the U.S. Army Air Corps in mid-1942 and was discharged in mid-1945, serving as a photo analyzer with the Second Photo Charting Squadron in Mexico. In 1947, he became director of the Taylor Museum in Colorado Springs.

Two additional episodes in the history of the Laboratory of Anthropology's archaeological tree-ring research were important in the greater development of southwestern archaeological tree-ring dating: Stallings's successful dating of a Basketmaker II period specimen from Cave du Pont in Utah, and the work of Edward T. Hall, Jr., on tree-ring specimens from Awatovi.

Basketmaker II Period Dating

In March 1935, Douglass was secure enough in his dating of Basketmaker III material to publish his chronology and the archaeological dates it supplied (Douglass 1936; Morris 1936; see Chapter 3). Douglass felt, however, that the early extension of the Central Pueblo Chronology was reliable for dating purposes only back to the mid-300s. That left Basketmaker II period sites largely undated. Morris contacted Nusbaum regarding Cave du Pont, near Kanab, Utah, excavated by Nusbaum in 1920. Morris knew Cave du Pont was one of the few pure Basketmaker II sites existing in the Southwest, and he hoped it might be dated through the dendrochronological analysis of a number of pinyon specimens excavated and presciently cached there by Nusbaum 15 years earlier. Nusbaum told Morris that he would examine his Cave du Pont correspondence to try to determine who might be available in Kanab to retrieve the specimens. He warned Morris, however, that because of cultural lag, the Basketmaker II dates at Cave du Pont might actually fall later than the Canyon de Chelly–area Basketmaker II sites that Morris was interested in dating.

Nusbaum had actually explored the idea of recovering the Cave du Pont specimens as early as 1932 and in fact had obtained approval to collect the specimens from the local landowner in February (Douglass to Nusbaum, February 23, 1932). Nothing seems to have happened until 1936, when Morris went to Mesa Verde National Park for the "specific purpose of jogging Nusbaum into further effort to secure the Basketmaker II timbers from Kane County, Utah" (Morris to Douglass, May 22, 1936). Morris's prodding seems to have worked, for Bannister, Dean, and Robinson (1969) note that Nusbaum collected samples from Cave du Pont in 1936. Gila Pueblo's specimen cards on file at the Laboratory of Tree-Ring Research indicate that Gila Pueblo acquired specimens from the cave in 1937, but these are likely to have been duplicates of Nusbaum's samples rather than original specimens. Although Morris wanted Douglass, not Stallings, to do the dating, because the former was more familiar with the Central Pueblo Chronology against which the specimen would be compared, Douglass was concentrating on cycle studies and had little time for archaeological dating, so Stallings conducted the analysis.

On June 26, 1939, Stallings told Douglass that he had obtained a date for one specimen from Cave du Pont but needed a copy of Douglass's early chronology to verify it. On September 12, he reported to Douglass a date of A.D. 217, with a center ring dating to A.D. 92, and sent the specimen to Douglass for verification. Nearly two years later, again delayed by Douglass's busy schedule, Stallings obtained Douglass's verification and quickly published the date in the *Tree-Ring Bulletin* (Stallings 1941). With this publication, dendrochronologists finally dated each of the major Pecos Classification periods.

The Dating of Awatovi

After Stallings's departure for graduate school in the fall of 1937, a University of Arizona graduate student and occasional employee of the Laboratory of Anthropology, Edward T. Hall, Jr., made a major contribution to dendroarchaeology by dating tree-ring material from J. O. Brew's excavations at Awatovi, on the Hopi Mesas in northeastern

Arizona. Brew had begun a five-year project at Awatovi in 1935. He and his crew engaged in an intensive survey of the region that year, and in 1936 they began excavating the historic component of Awatovi, recovering a sizable quantity of tree-ring specimens. Brew and Haury had been classmates at Harvard, and it was to Haury that Brew turned when he wanted the Awatovi specimens dated in 1936. Brew's specimens from Alkali Ridge in southeastern Utah had not dated well, but Haury reassured him that, since Awatovi was culturally similar to the well-dated sites of Kawaiku and Kokopnyama and was located in a similar environment, he stood "a good chance of getting dates from Awatovi" (January 29, 1936). That was an understatement. What is interesting about the Awatovi dating, aside from the sheer number of dates, is that it led to changes in procedural aspects of archaeological tree-ring dating.

When Brew received Haury's dates for specimens collected in 1936, he wrote in his acknowledgment: "Your very welcome letter containing dates from the 1936 dig is at hand. I am very grateful for these and they arrived at quite the best time for them to be useful. I was very anxious indeed to have them as a help in continuing tests this year in the western part of the site" (July 28, 1937). This marks the first explicit use of tree-ring data in the development of an archaeological research design by an archaeologist who was not also a dendrochronologist. There are plenty of examples in which archaeologists from the Museum of Northern Arizona, the Laboratory of Anthropology, the University of Arizona, or the University of New Mexico used tree-ring dates and dating to modify their research plans. Aside from Earl Morris, who often decided where to excavate on the basis of the likelihood that he would recover good beam material, however, no archaeologists other than Brew before World War II used tree-ring dates to do anything but "date" their sites in the most general sense of the term. That is, most archaeologists used the accurate, precise, and highly resolved tree-ring dates essentially as one would use relative dates—simply to place sites in a chronological sequence. Brew used the tree-ring dates to target his coming field research, a practice that had not been conducted before.

In October and November 1937, Brew shipped to Haury tree-ring specimens collected that summer. In May 1938, Haury reported that progress was being made on the 1937 collection, and he made an interesting recommendation: that the 1938 Awatovi excavations be conducted with a dendrochronologist on site. He told Brew: "We are working very hard on your wood collection from Awatovi and one student in particular, Mr. Hall, is doing very good work. In talking the matter over with Douglass and Getty it seems wholly advisable that you should have a man of Hall's ability on your party to take care of the wood on the spot. I believe this would not only be a very satisfactory arrangement for you but it would also lessen the laboratory work here. I am sure you appreciate what a time-consuming job tree-ring analysis is. Hall gets his M.A. this year. [He] has enough experience to require [compensation]" (March 2, 1938).

In April, Brew offered Hall $75.00 per month plus board to work on the Awatovi expedition. It was the first time a dendrochronologist was specifically employed on a contract basis by an excavation or institution that did not otherwise have a tree-ring professional available to do the dating. Previously, samples submitted to the Museum of Northern Arizona, the Laboratory of Anthropology, Gila Pueblo, or the University of Arizona were dated and verified by dendrochronologists when they could take time away from their own research, which was supported by funding from other sources.

The immediate advantage to having a dendrochronologist in the field was in the area of sample selection and collection. Up to this time, Douglass and others had advocated the collection of all wood and charcoal specimens to ensure that no potentially datable specimens were discarded, but it quickly became apparent to Hall that archaeologists, in this case Paul Martin at Lowry Ruin and Brew at Awatovi, did not always heed this dictum. In a letter to Haury, Hall wrote:

> [I have] been working in Santa Fe for the last three weeks, on the wood and charcoal that we brought out. It was fortunate that a Dendrochronologist was on the expedition, as the wood (charcoal) was at least 90% juniper, all nice specimens, which could be ignored, [but] it was from the scattered bits of pinyon that dating was possible. . . . Pinyon in that area (and all others I suppose) is extremely sensitive, and crowds a lot of years in a very small piece. Even these pieces were not any too simple, a series of photographs published in the [Tree-Ring Bulletin] of typical records from Chaco finally gave me the dope. . . . The material from [the Awatovi] area apparently shows a number of Rio Grande characteristics. It is possible that the few pieces of pinyon that Paul Martin sent us [from Lowry Ruin] might be worked out in the light of what we got from our pit. You might have Harry [Getty] send up the plots, so that I could see if there was at least a superficial resemblance.

> I am sure that Dr. Martin could have gotten a date out of that ruin, if he had had one of us with him. . . . Think of the trouble they [Martin and Brew] go to, to excavate a nice juicy piece of juniper, and then pass

up that little hunk of pinyon that fell out beside it because it looked too small and unimportant. . . . Brew is the same way—sends juniper all wrapped up in cotton, and then tosses pine into a box. I told him I could save him a lot of time by [identifying] the material on the spot, his reply was that you could date juniper. He doesn't seem to think much about tree-rings or the work, perhaps it is because he has gotten his dating gratis. (July 21, 1938)

Hall's letter suggests that, despite several tree-ring conferences and the *Tree-Ring Bulletin*, archaeological tree-ring dating was characterized by poor communication between archaeologists and dendrochronologists regarding advances in the field. Pinyon samples had been known to be datable since Haury's work at the University of Arizona in 1930. Archaeologists seem to have assumed that juniper was datable because the preserved pieces were large, but conclusive crossdating in juniper had not yet been demonstrated in 1938.

Another procedural issue came to light in the fall of 1938, when Brew suggested that dendrochronologists should remain ignorant of the archaeological context of specimens they wished to date. Brew argued that a date determined in the absence of contextualizing archaeological knowledge was more valid than one for which the archaeologist knew the cultural context:

> In the course of my conversations during the last ten years with numerous men working with tree rings, I have very often heard them express the desire to know the cultural association of the specimens in order to speed up their handling of the material. Both Mr. [Donald] Scott and I feel that we cannot agree to this. In order for this [tree-ring] work to provide maximum value as a check on the archaeology, it seems to us that the dating must be done completely without reference to cultural association. In other words, we like to feel that the man doing the dating has placed the specimen in position on the master chart without knowing at the beginning whether it is ten years old or fifteen hundred years old. Naturally, this is not a reflection on anyone's professional honesty, but, since the high value of tree-ring evidence lies in its objectivity, we feel that every possible subjective element be removed. Please let me know if you agree to this. (Brew to Haury, October 29, 1938)

Haury convincingly countered their claim on both theoretical and practical grounds:

> Concerning the matter you bring up regarding the desire on the part of the tree ring analyst to know the cultural association of the wood, I would like to make these comments. Theoretically I agree with

you and Scott that the analyzer is working only on wood and needs to
know nothing of the associations. In the case of Hall and the Awatovi
wood it would be perfectly logical procedure and will maintain his
work on as purely an objective level as possible. But I would like to
point out that heretofore the wood that was analyzed by Stallings or
McGregor or myself was handled at no expense to the institution
which sent in the wood yet someone had to stand the costs and in this
case it was Colton or the Laboratory or Gila Pueblo. Since this work
was being done gratis and since we were sacrificing our own researches
in favor of someone else's this request to know the cultural association
of the wood seemed not only logical but as a courtesy to our members,
inasmuch as it definitely is a labor-saving step. I have often felt, and I
am not alone in this conviction, that the people who are on the fringe
of basic tree ring researches are still quite unappreciative of the
painstaking and trying labor involved, and I dare say that you yourself
after working with wood intensively for a period would come to feel
the advisability of knowing something about the physical conditions
under which the wood was found. After all, when I go out to dig I am
quite aware of the cultural association of my own material. That this
might influence some experts in attaining a date is quite within the
bounds of possibility and that, of course, is the danger. But it seems to
me that those who are actually producing today are maintaining the
scientific integrity in the matter. However, as I said before, where you
are *employing* a person as in the case of Hall, it is perfectly logical to
demand that he work at the wood more or less sight unseen. (Haury to
Brew, November 7, 1938; emphasis added)

Haury and Brew agreed on a price of $.30 per specimen up to a max-
imum of $600 for Hall's examination and possible dating of some two
thousand Awatovi specimens. After spending one season attempting to
date tree-ring specimens in the field, Hall decided that although a staff
dendrochronologist might collect, sort, pack, and catalog tree-ring specimens in the field, the dating itself was best left to the laboratory, where
light and other conditions were better controlled. Thus, with remunera-
tion, the relationship between dendrochronologist and archaeologist
changed. Although there may not necessarily have been a formal contractual agreement, there was nevertheless an understanding that Brew
could expect certain services in a reasonable amount of time.

Initial results of Hall's analysis indicated that the interpretation of
tree-ring dates from early components at Awatovi would be much easier
than those from later components:

[I am] pleased that the work is going forward so rapidly and was particularly pleased with the dates you sent last. They demonstrate, it seems to me, that the tree-ring work will be very valuable in our study of earlier sites where the re-use of timbers did not occur to the unfortunate extent to which it does in the large Pueblo IV and Pueblo V sites. The dates which you sent recently are all from the D-shaped kiva at Site 4, which we have assigned to middle or late Pueblo III, and which is now placed rather conclusively by this group of thirty-six dates as being built between 1255–1260. (Brew to Haury, February 21, 1939)

Over the next two months, Hall finished his analysis of the Awatovi specimens while Brew and Haury tried to digest the dates and their implications. They discussed the possibility of a *Tree-Ring Bulletin* article on the dating of a room in the Pueblo III portion of the site, the group of specimens from which presents "one of the most conclusive bits of tree-ring dating I have encountered" (Brew to Haury, March 22, 1939). Haury approved of Brew's idea, though he was quick to point out that "Ned Hall has worked like a dog on your material and I hope you will be able to give him some credit" (April 10, 1939). The article never materialized, however.

One of the most interesting aspects of the Awatovi dating was the tremendous range of dates obtained from any given room in the main site area. One of the rooms had tree-ring dates from the eleventh through eighteenth centuries. Brew suggested a meeting: "We have got to get together for a rather lengthy session on these dates from the big site. With such a tremendous range in the dates in any room from which we have a large number of specimens we have got to work out how much value if any can be placed on the date when a given room has only one or two dated specimens" (Brew to Haury, April 12, 1939). Scott was nevertheless excited by the results: "Practically every specimen shows that it is a timber which has been used more than once and we therefore have not the original dating of the various rooms directly from the timbers employed. On the other hand, by correlating this mass of material with our archaeological findings we should be able to get a great deal of valuable information" (April 26, 1939).

No contribution specific to the Awatovi material was prepared for the *Tree-Ring Bulletin*, though Hall kept working sporadically on the materials until mid-1942, when he entered the army. Just before enlisting, however, he supplied Douglass with 17 additional pieces of charcoal forming the early sequence at Awatovi, spanning A.D. 580 to 810. This was soon followed by a manuscript summarizing his work for Awatovi and in the Gobernador area of New Mexico. Hall derived approximately 1,000 dates from 159 structures on 68 sites. His "Early Stockaded Settlements in the Governador, New Mexico" (Hall 1944) included an extensive treatment of tree-ring dates from these sites, but the Awatovi dating has never been published in full.

The Awatovi and Gobernador dating performed by Hall marks the end of dendrochronology at the Laboratory of Anthropology. The laboratory's tree-ring collections were transferred to the University of Arizona in 1950, where they remain fully integrated in the research collection.

CONCLUSION

Tree-ring research at the Laboratory of Anthropology benefited from talented personnel, strong if temporary financial backing, and an interested and supportive Board of Trustees. Stallings was considered one of Douglass's top students, second only to Haury, when he was hired by the laboratory in 1930. The fact that he completed the Rio Grande Chronology in less than two years is testimony not only to his abilities and diligence but to the cooperation of Douglass, Mera, Nusbaum, and others who facilitated his fieldwork and analysis. The laboratory's contributions go beyond the Rio Grande Chronology, however. Nusbaum was instrumental in securing specimens for the extension of the Central Pueblo Chronology to date Basketmaker II sites and also played an important role in developing a tree-ring sampling protocol after the Hayden complaint regarding the Rainbow Bridge–Monument Valley Expedition work at Kiet Siel. With financial difficulties came a slow decline in dendrochronological research at the laboratory, though Hall's research in conjunction with Dorothy Keur's work in the Gobernador and J. O. Brew's work at Awatovi brought the laboratory's tree-ring program one last taste of success. The Laboratory of Anthropology Dendro-Archaeology Program's poor publication record stands as the only serious shortcoming of a decade's research. Ten years after the last dendroarchaeological work at the Laboratory of Anthropology, Smiley, Stubbs, and Bannister (1953) reanalyzed the laboratory's samples and finally made them available to the public.

Sid Stallings became director of the Taylor Museum in Colorado Springs in 1947 and never again conducted archaeological tree-ring research. Ned Hall became a specialist in visual anthropology and in 1997 received the Anthropology in Media Award from the American Anthropological Association; he, too, removed himself from dendrochronological research after the late 1940s.

CHAPTER 7

News Leaks,
Gender Politics,
Spies, and
Historic Deforestation

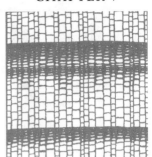

*Tree-Ring Dating
in the American Midwest*

Florence Hawley (Figure 30) obtained her master's degree from the University of Arizona in 1929 and spent the following academic year teaching there with classmates Emil Haury and Clara Lee Tanner. In the summer of 1929, she worked for Hewett at Chetro Ketl in Chaco Canyon, where he had been leading a joint University of New Mexico and School of American Research field school. Hawley concentrated on ceramic analysis; her initial research combined "stratigraphic analysis, cross-finds of pottery, and the study and comparison of pigments used in decoration . . . to establish [a relative] chronology" for Chetro Ketl and other sites in the area (Hawley 1930:523). The validity of her interpretations was demonstrated by Douglass's tree-ring dates (Douglass 1929), which entirely confirmed her independent and ceramically derived chronology.

Hawley was a member of the inaugural tree-ring class of spring 1930. She collected 174 tree-ring specimens at Chetro Ketl in 1930 and 29 in 1931. During academic year 1931–1932, she concentrated on the dendrochronological analysis of charcoal from the midden at that site, though she analyzed samples from other sites in Chaco Canyon as well. One specimen she collected at Una Vida in Chaco Canyon proved crucial to Douglass's effort to extend the Central Pueblo Chronology, for it added 90 years to the early portion of that chronology. Also in 1931, she examined 286 specimens from Kinishba (Fort Apache Ruin), the site of the University of Arizona Field School under the direction of Byron Cummings (Cummings 1940). On the basis of 78 dates she demonstrated that Kinishba was occupied in the late thirteenth and early fourteenth centuries and was one of the few sites known to have

FIGURE 30. Florence Hawley, Gladys Phate, Emil Haury, and Clara Lee Tanner at the University of Arizona field school in 1926. Courtesy of the Arizona Historical Society, Tucson.

been occupied throughout the Great Drought. Dates for six of these specimens were ultimately published by Baldwin (1935).

In 1932, Hawley continued her research along the lines of the previous two years, though she began to turn her attention to a synthetic analysis of masonry types, architecture styles, pottery, and tree-ring dating. She collected 107 tree-ring specimens from Chetro Ketl, Pueblo Bonito, Kin Klizhin, Kin Bineola, Una Vida, Penasco Blanco, Tsin Kletsin, and Kin Ya-a. Her work on charcoal specimens from the Chetro Ketl dump was designed to "date the strata of accumulation" (Hawley 1932a, 1932b).

At the May 1–4, 1933, meetings of the Southwest Division of the American Association for the Advancement of Science in Las Cruces, Hawley presented a paper entitled "New Developments in Application of Tree-Ring Study to Archaeology." There she summarized her analysis of charcoal from the Chetro Ketl dump, noting that the dating of these often small pieces of hearth charcoal was especially difficult. Nevertheless, she informed her colleagues that she had achieved some success with a "mathematical comparison of mean [ring] sensitivity," the calculation of which she unfortunately did not put into print. A brief treatment of her 1933 Chaco Canyon tree-ring dating work was published in *El Palacio* (Hawley 1933).

Hawley applied for and received a $300 scholarship from the University of Chicago in 1933, no doubt in part because of a glowing endorsement from Kidder (Cole to Kidder, February 4, 1933). She enrolled at Chicago in the fall to earn a doctorate in anthropology, using her Chetro Ketl research as a dissertation topic. In June, she presented the results of her Chetro Ketl midden charcoal analysis to the American Anthropological Association in Berkeley, noting that her effort was "perhaps the most intensive application of tree-ring study yet undertaken on a single ruin" (Hawley 1934a). Hawley saw her Chetro Ketl analysis through to publication as her Ph.D. dissertation at Chicago (Hawley 1934a), a task she felt had purgatorial implications: "I have earned a front seat in heaven for that [research] if never for everything else—unless I get a front seat in Hell for swearing at all the little [charcoal] pieces" (Hawley to Paul Reiter, June 10, 1933).

Publication of Hawley's dissertation was nearly delayed because Neil Judd argued that it would be "unethical" for Hawley to publish an original analysis of Chetro Ketl dates before Douglass issued his detailed treatment of the dating of Pueblo Bonito (Douglass 1935a), which Judd had awaited for five years (Judd to Douglass, April 27, 1934). It is not clear, however, how the National Geographic Society could claim priority over original research funded by the School of American Research and the University of New Mexico, except for the fact that Hawley used Douglass's as-yet-unpublished tree-ring chronology to date the specimens. In addition, Douglass had already obtained written permission from Judd, on June 6, 1930, for Hawley to work on the Chaco Canyon tree-ring material. Perhaps the long-standing feud between Judd and Hewett finally became manifest (Judd to William Webb, August 29, 1934). Publication of Hawley's dissertation was ultimately delayed for a much more mundane reason caused by the Great Depression: the University of New Mexico Press ran out of paper (Hawley to Douglass, May 28, 1934). Although Hawley offered courses in archaeological tree-ring dating at the University of New Mexico over the next decade, she never again published on southwestern archaeological dendrochronology. Table 7 provides a chronology of the dendrochronological work of Hawley and others in the Midwest.

DENDROCHRONOLOGY IN THE AMERICAN MIDWEST

Serious consideration of archaeological tree-ring dating east of the Rockies goes back at least to 1931, when Waldo Wedel, a student in Douglass's first tree-ring class, attempted to date tree-ring samples collected during excavations along the Republican River in Nebraska. It is interesting that less than one year after taking the class, Wedel submitted

TABLE 7. Timeline: Archaeological Tree-Ring Research in the American Midwest.

1933 Hawley enrolls for graduate study at the University of Chicago.

1934 January: Hawley examines Moundbuilder wood from Kincaid Site.

     May: Hawley presents "The Adaptation of Oak and Cedar for Tree-Ring Dating of Prehistoric Mounds in the Mississippi Valley" to the American Anthropological Association.

     Late spring: Cole distributes circular entitled "Dendrochronology in the Mississippi Drainage."

     June: Hawley and Lassetter hired by Tennessee Valley Authority.

     December: Unverified tree-ring "dates" released by Science News Service.

1935 August: Lassetter stages a coup; Hawley is released as head dendrochronologist and retained as "consultant."

1936 Fall: Cole obtains a four-year commitment to funding for tree-ring research at the University of Chicago from Eli Lily.

1940 William Mulloy taken hostage by suspicious landowners.

1941 Hawley publishes *Dendrochronology in the Mississippi Valley*.

     Hawley returns to teach full-time at the University of New Mexico.

1942 Robert Bell assumes leadership of midwestern dendrochronology at the University of Chicago.

     July: McGregor becomes director of the Illinois State Museum.

1943 Mississippi Valley dendrochronology ceases until the end of the war.

1946 Bell discharged from the army, returns to Chicago and tree-ring dating.

1951 Bell publishes tree-ring dates for the Kincaid Site (Bell 1951).

---

his samples to Haury for dating rather than attempting to date them himself. Haury's reputation as the leader in archaeological tree-ring dating may have already been so well established that Wedel deemed it necessary to get help from his old classmate.

In 1932, several scientists and philanthropists wrote Douglass about initiating tree-ring dating in the Mississippi Valley. H. T. Stetson, of the Perkins Observatory in Delaware, Ohio, and Eli Lily, a philanthropist from Indianapolis, both contacted Douglass in the first six months of 1932. Fain W. King, owner of Wickliffe Mounds, Museum, and Burials in Wickliffe, Kentucky, contacted Douglass in June 1933. Though Douglass was interested in tree-ring dating in the Midwest, he was already too busy to engage new projects. It is likely, however, that he discussed these contacts with Hawley when he learned she was to enroll at the University of Chicago.

The exact start date of Hawley's tree-ring research in the Midwest is difficult to determine, but it occurred early in the 1933–1934 academic year. On arriving at the University of Chicago, she probably collected tree-ring specimens or examined samples of archaeological wood from the university's excavations in southern Illinois and elsewhere. In January 1934, she visited the Kincaid mounds to "see what they have to offer in ancient charcoal, and look for stumps in the area which may yield modern specimens" (Hawley to Cole, January 25, 1934). By March, formal plans for University of Chicago sponsorship of her work were being considered, with the idea that Hawley would attempt to crossdate Kincaid and other sites in Illinois after crossdating wood from mounds in western Kentucky, where wood and charcoal samples were much better preserved. Douglass expressed his interest in this work, though he suggested that Hawley first search for crossdating in mound wood housed in museum collections before sampling any living trees. Such a strategy ensured that Hawley would not waste time collecting living-tree specimens in areas where crossdating had not already been identified in archaeological specimens.

Douglass later supplemented this plan with three conditions that he felt must be met before Hawley could consider announcing dates. First, he argued that she must establish a quantitative as well as qualitative understanding of crossdating in modern trees, for he knew that ring-width variability in temperate tree species was less extreme than that found in coniferous species living in semiarid regions. Second, he argued that she must identify all potential false rings in the chronology to ensure that the crossdating was correct. Third, he warned her of the political implications of her work for all of dendrochronology: "What you do about the question of mentioning dates at this time, even though [the dates may] prove entirely correct, is very important to the fortune of all tree-ring work" (Douglass to Hawley, 1934, month and day unknown). Douglass knew that the worst thing that could happen to the young discipline of dendrochronology in North America was the publication of tree-ring dates before they had been absolutely established and verified. His admonition proved prescient.

Late in the spring of 1934, Hawley prepared a proposal entitled "The Adaptation of Oak and Cedar for Tree-Ring Dating of Prehistoric Mounds in the Mississippi Valley" (Hawley 1934b). She presented it as a paper at the Central Division meetings of the American Anthropological

Association to an enthusiastic reception (Hawley to Douglass, May 28, 1934). She had already determined that oak ring growth in the region was well correlated with March–June precipitation. She was optimistic but not overconfident about the future, stating that the "establishment of dating in the Mississippi is a large problem and will require time." She explained, however, that the potential benefits of tree-ring research in the Mississippi Valley far outweighed the costs: "If this project for dating in a new area with new varieties of wood is successful, as there is every reason to believe it will be, it will not only solve numerous problems in this district where even reliable chronologies were difficult to obtain, but it will provide considerable basis [for] extension of tree-ring dating into still other archaeological areas of the world" (Hawley 1934b).

Archaeological interests were piqued by Hawley's presentation. The project received a boost when Hawley's department head at the University of Chicago, Fay-Cooper Cole, wrote a circular entitled "Dendrochronology in the Mississippi Valley" (Cole 1934). The circular was distributed by Carl Guthe, chairman of the Committee on State Archaeological Surveys, to approximately 100 archaeologists east of the Rocky Mountains, and it announced the University of Chicago's sponsorship of an effort to date the Mississippi mound-building cultures. Cole implored archaeologists working in the Midwest to submit preserved wood specimens because they were so difficult to recover from any one site.

In response to Cole's appeal, William S. Webb, director of the Department of Physics and Anthropology at the University of Kentucky, contacted Cole to inquire about the possibility of cooperative tree-ring work between the University of Chicago and the Tennessee Valley Authority, whose excavations he was directing (see Fagette 1996). Webb had high hopes for the project because of the extensive tree cutting and archaeological excavation being conducted in preparation for the creation of Norris Lake in Tennessee. He wanted tree-ring work to begin immediately, and by June 1934 arrangements had been made to have Tennessee Valley Authority workers collect tree-ring samples during their excavations. Later that month, Hawley was in the field with her assistant, Roy Lassetter, and a TVA crew. They collected oak, cedar, and other types of wood samples, including a spectacular oak specimen with a 392-year ring record. Hawley was encouraged by the results and excited about prospects for the future. She wrote Douglass: "The cooperation, the type of trees and the plans of the archaeologists of this area for future work in tree-rings is encouraging beyond all expectations. I wish we could have had such backing in Arizona. . . . It appears that Roy and I will have several weeks of work ahead of us for the Mississippi Valley, and we are counting on your advice and aid" (June 20, 1934).

By mid-July, Hawley and Lassetter had moved to Wickliffe, Kentucky, to work on the mounds owned by Fain King. Hawley reported to Cole that she had established a chronology back to the A.D. 1600s, that Lassetter was an excellent assistant, and that crossdating was demonstrable within and between trees in Tennessee and Kentucky. Douglass reminded her that the "urgent thing to do is demonstrate crossdating" and informed her of the results of the First Tree-Ring Conference, which she had missed in June (Douglass to Hawley, August 2, 1934).

Tree-ring sample collections during summer 1934 were impressive. Hawley and her crew collected 150 living-tree specimens from western Kentucky as well as charcoal from the Wickliffe mounds and 200 modern specimens from the Norris Basin in Tennessee. In a letter to Cole, Hawley stated that the Norris Basin pine chronology went back to A.D. 1520, whereas the oak chronology was established to A.D. 1580. She added the caveat that Douglass must check everything before any results were published. In this, she followed the 1934 tree-ring conference protocol, as relayed to her by Douglass.

Webb was so impressed with Hawley's work that he began an intensive administrative effort to arrange for her to take a year-long leave of absence from the University of New Mexico so that she might focus exclusively on midwestern tree-rings. Judd was quick to remind Webb not to expect results too quickly: "Judging from Dr. Douglass's experience in the Southwest, little progress can be made with the dating of your Indian structures until the growth characteristics of Southwestern [*sic*—midwestern] trees are better known. Much more is involved than the mere counting of growth rings" (Judd to Webb, August 29, 1934). He then added his perspective on the possibilities for Hawley's leave of absence and alternate courses of action:

> I have every confidence in Miss Hawley's ability and sincerely trust both that the TVA can provide for her temporary employment and that the UNM will release her for a year from her present contract. While my interest in the problem before you is very real, circumstances are such that I cannot assist you directly in the present instance. Mention of my name in your communications with Dr.

Hewett might prove a hindrance rather than otherwise.[1] Knowing this, it has occurred to me that, in the present emergency and provided Miss Hawley is not available, arrangements might be made with the Laboratory of Anthropology, in Santa Fe, to borrow the services of Mr. W. S. Stallings, Jr., one of Douglass's most brilliant students of Dendrochronology.

Judd had passed his correspondence with Webb on to Kidder, who in response gave Webb his endorsement of the proposed research and offered to help influence Hewett, with whom Kidder had no quarrel: "Neil Judd has sent me copies of your letter to him of 23 August and his reply of 29 August. I am extremely interested to learn of the very bright possibilities for the dendro-chronological determinations in the TVA. I most sincerely hope that your project for having Miss Hawley continue her work will be approved and that it may be possible for her to secure leave from the UNM. I should only be too glad to wire or write Dr. Hewett if you think it would do any good. Please command me" (August 30, 1934). Kidder, as a board member of the Laboratory of Anthropology, Stallings's current employer, did not agree with Judd's backup plan: "I trust that Miss Hawley's services may be obtained, for although Stallings is equally as good a dendrochronologist, he has had no experience with eastern trees. Miss Hawley is obviously the person to carry on this research."

For reasons that remain unclear, Hawley's leave of absence did not materialize. She taught four classes at the University of New Mexico during the fall of 1934, which obviously left no time for fieldwork or analysis. On the bright side, however, Webb secured a budget of $10,000 for a 1935 TVA tree-ring program to be directed by Hawley and assisted by Lassetter. Cole assured Hawley and Lassetter of University of Chicago backing should the TVA funding disappear. In reviewing these developments for Douglass, Hawley informed him that Lassetter would remain in Tennessee collecting samples full-time when she went back to

---

1. Hewett and the School of American Research had "raised objections" regarding the National Geographic Society Pueblo Bonito Expedition as early as 1920. Relations between Hewett and Judd deteriorated to the point that Hewett sent Lansing Bloom and Wesley Bradfield to Chaco Canyon to guard the waterhole and cabin from Judd and NGS (Judd to Kidder, May 5, 1921). The dispute was resolved when the parties agreed not to excavate in Chaco Canyon concurrently. The Pueblo Bonito expedition agreed to leave Chaco Canyon by August 31 each year; the Chetro Ketl expedition agreed to enter the field September 1 (see Judd to Coville, October 24, 1922).

New Mexico to teach during the fall. She also noted that TVA hydrologists and administrators had grossly underestimated the difficulties associated with the development of reliable tree-ring chronologies. After learning that the tree-ring research would be delayed by Hawley's commitment to the University of New Mexico, TVA administrators wanted to send a hydraulic engineer to learn tree-ring dating in "a day or two" (Hawley to Douglass, September 2, 1934).

In a progress report to the TVA, Hawley identified the problems that would continue to plague midwestern tree-ring dating over the next decade: poor sample preservation and, more important, the difficulty of finding old-growth forests that contain long-lived specimens capable of bridging the gap between the living-tree chronology and the one derived from archaeological specimens.

Hawley was in a difficult position because, as archaeologist, dendrochronologist, and project supervisor, she had to manage the needs of a depression-era funding agency staffed by bureaucrats who wanted to demonstrate quick results for the investment (Fagette 1996), scientists who were unfamiliar with dendrochronology, and eager if not jealous archaeologists who knew that sites had already been dated by tree-ring analysis in the Southwest. None of these groups, however, was familiar with the time-consuming nature of tree-ring research, the cumulative aspect of its results, and the long period of intensive analysis needed to establish tree-ring dating in the Southwest, where crossdating and preservation are of much higher quality than in the Midwest. Hawley may have stretched the truth when she tried to placate the TVA, stating that "there is no question as to the datability of these specimens. Probable dates have been obtained for the small group studied thus far; these dates are to be released as soon as checked by Dr. Douglass according to the code of dendrochronologists" (November 30, 1934).

After learning of Hawley's plan to release dates in December at the annual meeting of the Society for American Archaeology in Pittsburgh, Douglass quickly reminded her that the dates she obtained must be considered provisional until checked by him, as stipulated by the First Tree-Ring Conference: "It would be a mistake to publish any dates until several fundamental items are fully checked." He was nevertheless careful to provide encouragement as well: "The one thing of tremendous importance you have done is to show that crossdating exists in those modern trees. . . . I feel that the actual dating is not proved by the pieces I have seen but, [by] crossdating these, the sure dating will be reached eventually. . . . While urging you not to embarrass yourself and [your] work by giving dates at this time, I congratulate you on laying the foundation of crossdating for eastern Tennessee" (December 15, 1934).

Hawley respected Douglass's judgment but had already written the paper containing the provisional archaeological tree-ring dates. Because Douglass suggested that she refrain from announcing them, she "blotted out" the two sentences containing dates in her text (Hawley to Douglass, January 5, 1934). Unfortunately, she was not able to attend the SAA meetings; Lassetter was designated to read the paper for her (Hawley to Douglass, December 22, 1934). For some reason, he did not read the paper either, but Robert Lowie of the University of Chicago did (Hawley to Webb, January 24, 1934). Regardless of who read the paper, the provisional tree-ring dates were leaked to the press. According to Hawley, the Science News Service acquired a copy of the paper from the press office at the meetings. Because she had only "blotted" dates out of the text, they were not completely obliterated. Reporters who obtained copies of the paper were thus able to read the dates, perhaps by illuminating the typewritten sheets from the back. As a result, tree-ring dates were printed in the *Chicago Tribune*, the *New York Times*, and the *St. Louis Tribune* as direct quotations from Hawley, who, needless to say, was greatly distressed (Hawley to Douglass, January 5, 1934). Cole reassured her that "if this is the worst mistake the newspapers ever make concerning your work, you may consider yourself very lucky" (Cole to Hawley, January 29, 1935).

By late February 1935, Hawley again wanted to publish dates, but the dendrochronological data had not improved. She wrote Douglass that "the idea of tree-rings is taking the country by storm. . . . Apart from the newspapers and magazines there are a number of eastern institutions waiting almost with drawn breath for publication of these promised results. . . . I think the psychological moment [is now] for the release of these dates in view of the support upon which we can then count." Since her "probable" dates had already been published in various newspapers, she felt that the publication of the 48 dates she now thought reliable would simply correct information in the public domain: "I think we should release our dates as preliminary evidence of the feasibility of the project and as bait for its further support, especially since the newspapers have distributed our general date [*sic*] all over the country already" (February 19, 1935).

Over the next two weeks, Hawley and Douglass exchanged a series of letters and telegrams. Douglass continued to argue that the dates were still provisional and warned of the damage that would occur to the credibility of all dendrochronology if she published dates that proved to be incorrect. In a telegram on February 26, 1935, Douglass wrote: "I can't OK dates until fully assured by personal study. [I] believe [it would be] unwise [to] publish . . . unconfirmed dates in [*American Anthropologist*] as against resolutions of Tree-Ring Conference but Webb might accept provisional results in [his report] recommending work next summer. I will wire him if you wish."

Hawley lamented the fact that TVA funding for midwestern tree-ring dating was contingent on her providing publishable dates, but she understood the needs of the funding agency. As she wrote Douglass, "it looks to me as if the Moundbuilder dating is sunk. . . . Major Webb has plenty of trouble convincing those engineers of the importance of archaeological projects and of archaeological methods which proceed slowly and consequently with cost" (February 27, 1935). Douglass was not so pessimistic. Though he never experienced the degree of administrative and professional pressure that Hawley was under, he was able to provide some perspective on her situation: "The publicity you are having is magnificent if your results are correct. If they are incorrect, then it is the worst possible thing for you and for all of us. . . . You have no reason to gamble on results. . . . You have in all this a great responsibility. You must act with all the wisdom you have . . . I urge you to go slow at the crossroads" (February 27, 1935).

Hawley was in a classic Catch-22. She had been hired by the archaeology division of the Tennessee Valley Authority to produce tree-ring dates for sites that were to be inundated by the construction of a series of dams on the Tennessee River. TVA administrators, hydrologists, and archaeologists who did not understand dendrochronology expected her research to be applied, not "pure" or exploratory. Dendrochronological methods had been devised in the Southwest; TVA administrators thought all she had to do was apply these techniques to specimens gathered in the Midwest. They did not understand that midwestern tree species respond to different climatic variables and that the nature of crossdating and specimen preservation in the two areas is therefore radically different.

After another season's fieldwork in 1935, Hawley reported to Douglass that she felt the Tennessee sequence was extended to A.D. 1295 on the basis of 125 prehistoric and 255 modern specimens and that the Kentucky sequence went back to the A.D. 1600s on the basis 150 modern specimens (August 11, 1935). In spite of these achievements, new problems arose. Some of the local landowners did not approve of her work, probably because of simple gender bias—many Americans during the Great Depression felt that working women, especially those paid by government relief efforts, were taking money out of the hands of male breadwinners (McElvaine 1993). In this opinion, they ignored the specialized nature of the research that required a highly trained and qualified individual. Hawley wrote Cole: "These farmers are of the variety who think that the Bible is an encyclopedia of natural science, and [that] all scientists are lunatics" (August 11, 1935).

By the end of August, Hawley's attempt to develop archaeological tree-ring dating in the Mississippi drainage came to a halt, for Lassetter, whose official position was assistant dendrochronologist and who had remained in Tennessee for academic year 1934–1935, used his position within the TVA's "old boy network" to stage a coup. He arranged to have Hawley dismissed as chief dendrochronologist. Up to that time, Lassetter had been focusing on the climatological and hydrological aspects of Tennessee Valley dendrochronology. In the minds of the TVA hydrologists, he had produced results (stream-flow reconstructions) where Hawley had produced nothing (i.e., publishable dates) during the same time span. Regardless of the analytical validity of Lassetter's reconstructions, which lacked statistical rigor, he was allowed to assume control of the archaeological aspect of TVA dendrochronology. Hawley was officially retained as a consultant, though she knew full well that the TVA would not come calling. She was understandably upset by this incident for many reasons, not the least of which was that she had introduced Lassetter to archaeology and tree-ring dating while he was a student at the University of Arizona and had loaned him $500 (equivalent to $4,500 in 1995) to help him stay in school (Hawley to Douglass, August 21, 1935). Hawley related the story to Haury the next month:

> When Roy was out here [in New Mexico] last spring, he told Sid [Stallings] that he wanted to make a place for himself alone in this work, and in a high-handed manner while I was here (UNM) last year [1935] and during last summer, he managed to do just that. With self-confidential reports on his own ability to handle things, with many private conferences which he persuaded his bosses to give him, and with some comments on the place of a woman in this field, he arranged that he be left in charge of the department with me as consultant only, and I think that there is plenty of reason to doubt that the consultant will never be consulted. (September 27, 1935)

Major Webb supported Hawley and her work throughout this crisis and stated that he would do everything in his power to keep Lassetter from continuing the archaeological work in Kentucky. Further, Webb promised to do what he could to support her work in the future. Hawley again tried to get Douglass to allow her to release dates, for "with dates, Webb can put through an archaeological-dendrochronological program. . . . This project is being held up until I produce a few dates" (September 30, 1935). Hawley thus attempted to pressure Douglass, just as TVA administrators had pressured her, to release dates not on the basis of their dendrochronological veracity but because the project depended on it. Douglass's persistence in refusing to allow her to publish even provisional dates, though within his right under the provisions of the First Tree-Ring Conference, exacerbated the difficulty of her situation. Her funding was dependent on the production of dates, yet verifiable dates could not be produced without additional time, effort, and therefore money. Following the law of unintended consequences, Douglass's refusal may have strengthened Lassetter's position at the TVA by suggesting to TVA administrators that Hawley's failure to publish was a result of her incompetence rather than the difficult nature of the dendrochronology.

Douglass did not give in, however, feeling that dendrochronology was more important than the needs of a single individual or project. In a detailed letter to Webb, he outlined the rules regarding date publication and the cumulative nature of tree-ring research and warned that the release of unconfirmed dates would hurt dendrochronology everywhere: "We have specific rules about the publication of dates—they must be checked by a qualified dendrochronologist. It took 25 years [sic—15] to develop the chronology here [in the Southwest]; I would be very surprised if reliable results could be verified/reliable after only two years work. . . . There is much value in seeing this effort to completion. . . . It is unbelievable that the door is closed to dendrochronology in that area simply because the dating in the difficult region is not concluded in two years" (January 21, 1936).

To verify his own conclusions regarding Hawley's samples, Douglass asked Haury to examine her material: "Both of us [Douglass and Haury] agree dates are not yet convincing. . . . We suggest and hope that you can secure some financial support for Dr. Hawley for another year or two. . . . The work which has been done is by no means wasted. It is fundamental ground work and Dr. Hawley has done an extremely good job of it" (Douglass to Webb, January 21, 1936).

In light of Douglass's assurances, Webb's support for archaeological tree-ring dating remained steadfast. Hawley did not undertake fieldwork in 1936, but Webb enlisted the cooperation of TVA fieldworkers for specimen acquisition and submittal. T. M. N. Lewis of the Department of American Archaeology at the University of Tennessee remained skeptical that Webb's overture to TVA fieldworkers would lead to productive cooperation, largely because of the well-known dispute between Hawley and Lassetter (Lewis to Cole, January 8, 1936). Nevertheless, some specimens were collected and submitted. In the meantime, Cole sought funding for Hawley's research from philanthropist Eli Lily of Indianapolis (Cole to Lily, January 4, 1936).

Hawley remained pessimistic because she could not publish the 48 archaeological dates she felt were secure, and she was concerned that Lassetter might preempt her goals for archaeological dating: "I will write Major Webb that there are to be no dates for his paper. That is the end of any more tree-ring work in that area, I expect, except for whatever Roy may do. I wouldn't be surprised to see [Lassetter] popping up with a set of mound dates someday. . . . This is a bad situation, as the easterners are considering the project all a failure and won't go ahead with more money for work or for collections" (January 22, 1936).

Douglass reminded Hawley that the dendrochronological situation remained essentially unchanged and tried to help her keep things in perspective:

> I feel that the situation is the same as it was a year ago, and the various letters which I wrote at that time against giving out dates apply equally well at the present time. . . . About the whole matter, you need have no fear that there will be an end to the application of dendrochronology in that area, depending on whether Dr. Webb gets appropriations or not. The only thing that will exclude dendrochronology from that area is the publishing of dates that are not satisfactory. . . . If an error is made at this time the consequences will be on me and on all of us. In the long run, you will be greatly honored for being conservative. (January 22, 1936)

Lewis still wanted an archaeological dating program for the Tennessee river valleys, and because Hawley was out of contention, he instigated a search for other qualified individuals. First and foremost, he thought of Stallings. Lassetter, whose research still focused on climatological and hydrological problems, wrote to Stallings to offer him a job. Lassetter provided some telling comments on the impossible situation Hawley faced at TVA, exposing his own biases in the process: "You will probably wonder why Hawley was not included in this work—and that my friend is a long story which perhaps is [best] untold unless Lewis sees fit to tell you after you get here. I will tell you this much however—

Lewis wants and needs a *man* for the job. Please, if you decide not to come keep all this under your hat. No one but a few know of the situation that Hawley was involved in here last year and it would only hurt her for it to get out so I am asking you to depend on me that everything is O.K." (March 5, 1936; emphasis in original). This is an excellent example of how gender bias and gossip operate in science (Parezo 1993). We may never know if in fact Lewis "wanted" a man for the job, nor was it self-evident that the TVA "needed" a man for the job, whether or not popular sentiment preferred that men be employed before women. In asking Stallings to "keep all this under [his] hat," it is clear that Lassetter was dealing in the realm of gossip. It is interesting too that Lassetter feigned protectionism over Hawley when he had been the primary cause of her problems at the TVA.

Stallings refused the job offer, and Lassetter and Lewis next considered Harry T. Getty, who had obtained his master's degree at the University of Arizona in 1932 and who served as Douglass's assistant for several years, most notably undertaking a large-scale dating program at Mesa Verde National Park in 1932 and 1933 (Getty 1935a, 1935b, 1935c). Douglass endorsed Getty's abilities as a dendrochronologist, but he advised Getty not to take the TVA job unless two conditions were met: first, that he be put in full charge of the dating program, and second, that he be under no pressure to produce and publish dates prematurely (Douglass to Lewis, April 23, 1936). Getty did not take the position, and on April 29, 1936, Lewis reported to Douglass that he had "found a man" for the job, though his identity remains a mystery. It almost certainly was not a student trained in the Douglass tradition. One of those students was Gordon Willey of the University of Arizona, who collected specimens for the Laboratory of Anthropology during its 1936 summer field program at Moundbuilder sites near Macon, Georgia (Willey to Douglass, August 20, 1936; Willey 1937).[2]

2. Willey stayed in Georgia to analyze his tree-ring samples under A. R. Kelly of the Smithsonian Institution (Willey to Douglass, August 20, 1936). On March 16, 1937, he sent a shipment of 52 specimens for Douglass to examine. Douglass was pleased with what he saw: "There is no question at all about the existence of crossdating. . . . I consider you have done a very important piece of work in a fine manner showing originality and good sense and thoroughness" (Douglass to Willey, April 5, 1937). Douglass thus verified the dating Willey had done, and he published a chronology back to A.D. 1900 (Willey 1937) before applying dendrochronology analysis at Fort Marion in St. Augustine National Monument in Florida (Willey to Haury, November 26, 1937).

There is no evidence that Hawley conducted any dendrochronological fieldwork in 1936, for her funding was in limbo. She fulfilled her obligation to the University of New Mexico field school and spoke of extending her midwestern research into the pine forests of Wisconsin during 1936 (Hawley to Cole, January 13, 1936).

In the fall of 1936, Hawley entertained the notion of obtaining a National Research Council Post-Doctoral Fellowship to study at Harvard under E. A. Hooten and Kidder, to "carry over statistical methods developed in physical anthropology to the analysis and integration of the data of dendrochronology" (Hawley to Cole, November 24, 1936). Nothing materialized from this proposal, apparently because Cole worked out a better deal for her at Chicago. He convinced Eli Lily to finance a four-year archaeological tree-ring research project at the University of Chicago. The agreement was that Hawley would obtain a one-year leave of absence from UNM for the first year, followed by split semesters in Albuquerque and Chicago for the next three years.

After considering her first effort at midwestern dendrochronology a failure, Hawley was again optimistic about the chances for success: "The archaeologists at the [American Anthropological Association] meeting [in Washington in 1936] were all enthusiastic to see [midwestern tree-ring dating] under way again and hope that next time we could be more successful in really working out some dates" (Hawley to Douglass, January 9, 1937). Douglass, however, again reminded her of the need for conservatism and outlined a research design that would lead to eventual success: "If you go into this I don't want you to get caught in a trap as before where complete results seem compulsory in a given time. . . . The objective the first year should not be dating of the mounds; it should be a study of the extent of crossdating in modern trees of the species used by the Moundbuilders. . . . During the first year you should forget the dating proposition completely. . . . Then spend 2 or 3 years on modern wood, then go to archaeological materials. Crossdate the prehistoric pieces first, then try to date them" (January 29, 1937).

In 1937, Hawley's midwestern dendrochronological fieldwork once again began in earnest, starting with a massive sample collection effort that summer. Hawley and her assistant and soon-to-be husband Donovan Senter collected 1,000 living-tree specimens in Wisconsin, Minnesota, Illinois, Missouri, Tennessee, Kentucky, Ohio, and Michigan, in an effort to identify the climate signal recorded by trees across the Midwest (Hawley-Senter 1938). Archaeological wood samples were collected that year only at Fort Crawford in Prairie du Chien, Wisconsin, and the

Dickson Mounds in Lewiston, Illinois, where excavations were already being conducted.

Hawley spent the 1937–1938 academic year at the University of Chicago analyzing the 1937 samples. No record exists of her research from late July 1937 until New Year's Day 1938, when she wrote to Douglass reminding him to check the wood specimens she had left during a Christmas visit to Tucson. Again, she hoped he would be able to verify the dating and allow her to publish midwestern archaeological tree-ring dates.

Hawley reported her progress to Haury, noting that she now had two separate chronologies back to ca. A.D. 1600. One consisted of specimens from Missouri, Illinois, Tennessee, and Kentucky, and the other consisted of specimens from eastern Minnesota and northern and central Wisconsin.

On February 24, 1938, she reported to Douglass the "first date to be obtained by using the tree-ring method with oaks," a date of A.D. 1880 for a beam in a historic log cabin. In a handwritten note on that letter, Douglass reminded himself to ask whether this date was checked by historic information. By late spring, Douglass had examined Hawley's specimens from southern Missouri and Illinois and was pleased to report that he had found good crossdating in them. He explained crossdating and its importance to Cole: "You understand that crossdating is the criterion I use in judging whether a chronology can be built or not. If it is present in good form in modern trees, then conditions are favorable for carrying the chronology back into prehistoric times. Oak crossdating is usable but not as strong as pines and hemlocks. The demonstration of good crossdating in trees of the Middle West is not accidental and has raised greatly my expectation of worthwhile results, and justifies your past and future interest in the project" (Douglass to Cole, May 4, 1938). Needless to say, Cole was delighted, and he assured Douglass they would "press forward as rapidly as possible toward the dating of some of our Indian cultures" (May 11, 1938). The results of this research were published in the *Tree-Ring Bulletin* (Hawley-Senter 1938) and the *Indiana History Bulletin* (Hawley 1938b).

The 1938 field season found Hawley-Senter and Senter on another large-scale collecting trip in Kentucky, Indiana, Missouri, Illinois, Arkansas, and Oklahoma. Her recently changed marital status caused some difficulty regarding her nom de plume; she decided to publish professional contributions under "Hawley" but her popular contributions would be signed with her hyphenated name, "because the farmers know we live together and . . . might worry over whether we were married or not" (Hawley to Douglass, July 27, 1938).

By late November, Hawley reported to Cole that the hemlock chronology from Minnesota and Wisconsin had been extended to ca. A.D. 1550 and the Illinois, Indiana, Kentucky, Missouri, and Tennessee oak chronology had been extended to ca. A.D. 1570. She noted that a pine chronology was established back to ca. A.D. 1680 for the same area. She reported that five log cabins had now been dated, "a feat which proves that dating is entirely possible in the area providing the unknown specimens were cut in the period largely covered by the master chart for the area" (Hawley 1938c). These dates had not, however, been independently verified.

At about time she made this report, Hawley wrote to Cole and mentioned that Senter had suggested that they investigate proxy environmental records and historic documents to substantiate evidence they had found in the tree-ring record for a serious drought in the late 1600s and early 1700s. She felt that such supporting evidence was "decidedly important for archaeologists and would give them something more to think about in tree-ring results." In the same letter, she announced that a baby was on the way. This caused her some concern about her career, given societal views on working women during this period:

> I well realize that one of the prejudices against hiring women for professional jobs is that they are likely to marry and drop the job or, if married, they are likely to produce families and either lose time or drop their jobs. I do not intend to do any of these things, now any more than in the past. It seems to me that having a family is a good idea for a normal life and that there is no need of devoting all one's time to raising it. The arrangement of laboratory and apartment combined in Chicago makes the situation easier than it could possibly be in any other arrangement, for the little one can sleep while I count my tree rings and yet be heard if anything should go wrong.

Despite Hawley's confidence and optimism in the five log cabin dates, Douglass reported on January 16, 1939, that he still could not verify crossdating in her Moundbuilder specimens or in the dates she offered. She found Douglass's reticence inexplicable and five days later sent Cole a note that put a slightly different spin on the situation: "A few days ago [Douglass] sent back my [samples] and a letter saying that he found the mound specimens definitely cross date (which is a big admission from him) but he is not ready to commit himself on the crossdating of these specimens and the log cabin pieces. He is still working on the material and says he thinks the material is datable" (January 24, 1939).

The problem seems to have been one of sample depth. At the time, Hawley was working with fewer than a dozen specimens for the entire chronology, a number that in Douglass's mind was far too small to establish reliable crossdating. Typically, a minimum of five or six climatically sensitive specimens is required to establish each portion of a reliable southwestern chronology, but the midwestern specimens were not so sensitive, and therefore additional specimens were needed. Hawley reported to Douglass that "Dr. Cole writes that it is necessary that we do get some dates published, if at all possible, this spring, for further support, and we must have support or give up the project" (January 25, 1939). Two months later, Douglass again told Cole that more work was necessary before he could verify Hawley's archaeological dating.

In the meantime, Hawley proceeded with her work. She again hoped to be able to announce dates for the Moundbuilder specimens at the American Anthropological Association meetings in Ann Arbor on May 4–6, 1939. She therefore sent Douglass, on April 26, 1939, her four best-dated mound specimens. Douglass sent Hawley a telegram in Ann Arbor telling her again not to announce the dates (see Hawley to Douglass, May 18, 1939). He wrote to her on May 6 and explained that although the current batch of specimens was better than the last, he still needed more to confirm her dating. He also asked her politely to send specimens at least one month before she needed results, not one week.

There is no dendrochronologically substantive archived record of research carried out by Hawley in the Midwest for the last six months of 1939, probably because she was teaching at the University of New Mexico. The correspondence record for spring 1940, however, reads like a broken record: Hawley was under intense pressure to produce dates. Douglass, and in this case also his assistant in climatology Edmund Schulman, Getty, and Stallings, could not verify her dates. Cole continued to minimize the bad news to Lily, who had just supplied the project with another $3,000 (Cole to Lily, February 10, 1940).

On February 13, Douglass again produced a plan of action for the midwestern tree-ring work. First, he advised Hawley to revise her report on work completed to date because he had not verified her dates. Second, he suggested that Senter collect log cabin material that could also be dated by historic documents. Third and fourth, he recommended that Getty and Stallings review her log cabin dating and the crossdating in modern specimens. Fifth, he suggested that Hawley acquire, by whatever means, good prehistoric specimens. Finally, he proposed that either he or Schulman attempt to identify what produces the crossdating in the midwestern specimens. Douglass added the following caveat to this plan: "We understand that your chief desire is for dates, but unless we really know that they are correct, and just how secure we do not have them" (Douglass to Cole, February 13, 1940).

As far as fieldwork was concerned, Hawley added Robert Bell and William Mulloy to her staff in the spring. Global politics and prewar paranoia affected midwestern tree-ring dating in 1940, with an episode that would be funny were it not for its life-threatening implications. About August 5, 1940, a group of local landowners saw Mulloy coring trees and immediately became suspicious of his actions. An ad hoc posse of "patriots" formed, went to the field, and questioned Mulloy, who tried to explain his specific task and the goals of the project. The mob did not believe his explanation and insisted on searching his car. In the trunk, on top of the gas can, spare tire, dirty rags, and sample-collection equipment, was an English-German textbook that he was studying for preliminary graduate examinations. This evidence sealed his fate in the minds of the mob: he was a Nazi spy who had infiltrated the very heartland of America and was planting nefarious espionage devices in trees. Fortunately, he persuaded his persecutors to allow him to contact a local lumberman with whom he had been working. Mulloy narrowly escaped being lynched (Hawley to Cole, August 5, 1940). One suspects that Mulloy avoided western Kentucky for some time thereafter.

Despite periodic hopeful assurances to the contrary (Cole to Lily, June 5, 1940; Hawley to Cole, August 5, 1940), dates were not forthcoming in 1940. In mid-September, Stallings worked on the Moundbuilder specimens and substantiated Getty's finding of "no good crossdating" (Hawley to Cole, September 18, 1940). Cole's tendency to whitewash project findings continued in a September 18, 1940, letter to Lily, though it is probable that he wrote this letter before he read Hawley's note to him of the same date. On the other hand, there is no evidence that Cole retracted or substantiated the following statement to Lily: "I have not heard a final report from him (Stallings) as yet, but if his findings agree with those of Dr. Hawley and Dr. Getty, I think we are in a position to release some dates in the immediate future" (September 18, 1940).

Hawley expressed her frustration with Getty's and Stallings's findings in a letter to Schulman responding to his request for a contribution on midwestern tree rings for the *Tree-Ring Bulletin*: "We had hoped to be able to announce mound dates this fall but we are temporarily stymied again by some material which came in at the end of the summer season.

At the moment all I can do is talk about the difficulty of dating the damned mounds and such a report might be rather hot reading for some of your subscribers. Sorry" (September 20, 1940).

The correspondence and research record for the fall of 1940 is again meager because Hawley was teaching at the University of New Mexico. Nevertheless, she and Bell continued working on the tree-ring specimens throughout that season. They reported in December that the specimens collected by Mulloy the previous summer allowed them to create a master chart extending into the A.D. 1500s (Hawley to Cole, December 14, 1940).

The correspondence for 1941 nearly duplicates that of 1940. In early January 1941, Hawley told Schulman of the new master chart and asked him to verify the dating (January 7, 1941). By April, he had "spent time with the material with not too satisfactory results" (Schulman to Hawley, April 19, 1941). Hawley thanked Schulman with one of the understatements of the century: "The problem of tree-ring dating is anything but easy for this part of the country" (April 29, 1941). In a February 10, 1941, progress report to Lily, Hawley offered a possible reason why Douglass, Getty, Stallings, and Schulman had not been able to verify her work: "It is very hard for these southwesterners to understand that we spend months trying to get every old tree possible in a country where so much timber has been cut off that old trees are terribly scarce. . . . We are going to have trouble persuading the Southwestern dendrochronologists to check cedar records because they so detest the tree."

Dates or no dates, Hawley published *Tree-Ring Analysis and Dating in the Mississippi Drainage* in 1941. Here she summarized the development of archaeological tree-ring dating in the Midwest over the previous eight years and identified the four major causes of difficulty she and her team had encountered: (1) they were working with new species, (2) they were working across a huge area, (3) there was a scarcity of virgin timber due to extensive tree cutting over the previous two centuries, and (4) the wood was very poorly preserved in the damp mound sediments (Hawley 1941; see also McGregor 1942). Cole was, of course, enthusiastic about her book and wrote Lily that "if soon we can add to this a series of dates, I shall feel well satisfied with the progress up to date" (May 6, 1941). The publication was apparently what Lily wanted to see, for he sent another $3,000 on June 12.

Though archaeological interest was stirred by Hawley's book, professional dendrochronologists were less enthusiastic. Schulman, in his official capacity as editor of the *Tree-Ring Bulletin*, wrote to Haury at the end of the summer: "The less said about that paper (which was apparently written up originally as a laboratory progress report for the sponsors) the better. That is particularly true with respect to myself, though I will talk to *American Antiquity* if necessary" (August 4, 1941). McGregor published a neutral review in *American Anthropologist* the following year (McGregor 1942), concluding that the midwestern work should be continued. Afterward he queried his old friend Stallings about the book. Stallings's reply was not nearly as generous as McGregor's review: "You ask what I think of Hawley's paper on the Mississippi Valley. I think the situation is too complicated to attempt to discuss in a letter, but my opinion can be summed in one word—it stinks. I fear that the paper may do [tree-ring dating] a great harm, but all we can do for the moment, in my opinion, is sit tight" (March 25, 1942). In a brief exchange of letters in December 1943, Haury told Douglas Byers of Harvard University that everyone he had asked to review the paper "shie[d] away from it" (December 8, 1943); Byers replied, "I have understood unofficially that it was so full of errors that no one considered it really worthwhile" (December 15, 1943). Glock, no longer part of the Douglass "school," panned the book (Glock 1942a, 1942b).

Tree-ring work proceeded apace at the University of Chicago in the fall of 1941. Hawley and her tree-ring class analyzed living-tree and a few archaeological specimens collected by Mulloy in Montana and by F. P. Keen of the U.S. Department of Agriculture in Oregon. Bell collected archaeological specimens at the Kincaid site in southern Illinois. He also tried to apply Gladwin's quantitative method (Gladwin 1940a, 1940b; see Chapter 4) to Mississippi Valley tree-ring specimens, with very interesting results. Bell found Gladwin's method impractical because of "unequal width of rings and standardization of growth records" (today referred to as "circuit uniformity"; see Stokes and Smiley 1968). Bell conducted "lengthy mathematical experiments" to modify the Gladwin method for midwestern trees. These experiments were also unsuccessful, but he managed to achieve a statistically significant correspondence at the 67 percent level between one prehistoric specimen and a known historic specimen, the ring series of which he knew could not possibly crossdate. This was a serious indictment of the Gladwin technique, at least as far as midwestern trees are concerned.

When the United States entered World War II on December 7, 1941, midwestern archaeological fieldwork and research essentially ceased. Administrators at the University of New Mexico decided they wanted Hawley to commit to a full-time position there. Cole could not yet guess what would happen to his department at Chicago, though it was clear that many students, staff, and faculty would leave to enter war-related occupations. Hawley returned to New Mexico full-time and remained there for the rest of her career.

Archaeological tree-ring work continued at the University of Chicago in 1942 under Robert Bell's aegis. Bell worked on the Kincaid specimens and allowed Cole to "whisper" tree-ring dates to Lily. The tentative dates suggested that the previously estimated chronology for sites in the Mississippi Valley needed to be greatly compressed, just as relative chronologies in the Southwest were compressed by tree-ring dating thirteen years before (Cole to Lily, March 23, 1942). Cole used this development to appeal to Lily for an additional $2,000 to keep Hawley on staff for the summer, Bell in the field, and the laboratory operating for a few more months while they tried to get McGregor to verify the Kincaid dating (April 17, 1942). Though Lily initially balked at the request, Cole persuaded him once again that the money would be well spent. Lily awarded the full amount on May 11, 1942.

That same day, Cole informed McGregor that Thorne Deuel, director of the Illinois State Museum in Springfield, was leaving his job to enter military service. He suggested that McGregor apply for the position, thereby putting him closer to Chicago and the fledgling dating program. Two weeks later, Cole informed McGregor that the directorship was his for the taking (May 22, 1942), and by July, McGregor had accepted the job. Cole reported that Hawley and Robert and Virginia Bell were preparing their tree-ring materials for McGregor's perusal during a brief visit to Chicago on his way to Springfield.

Once McGregor decided to move to Springfield, he wired Douglass to ask for an audience in Phoenix regarding Mississippi Valley dendrochronology (July 5, 1942). The two met at the San Carlos Hotel in Phoenix on August 11. Douglass recommended a thorough reanalysis, by McGregor, of all work that had been done thus far, with an emphasis on determining the nature of the climate signal in the Midwest. Douglass's detailed notes of their meeting show his reservations regarding the midwestern tree-ring work to date:

> Don't try to review or express opinion on Hawley's work till a solid foundation is laid, which can be begun by getting Schulman to go out in the field for a week or two with you and someone who can specialize in climatic aspects. Schulman's visit should cover Ohio, Indiana, Illinois and other near states (perhaps Wisconsin) as he selects. . . . Any work Schulman can do will be that much gained. . . . The Hawley

work should be dropped at present. . . . Don't try to get too much of Schulman's time. . . . I don't believe that any crossdating is so good that it doesn't need a keen scientific investigation as to why it takes place and I believe that such investigation will strengthen and improve crossdating and enlarge its sphere of use. Much more of this basic study is needed in areas like the Midwest (Miss. Valley) where the origin of crossdating is more complex or where, as in the Southeast, the crossdating is in the latewood. (August 11, 1942)

Douglass thus placed McGregor in a very difficult position. Hawley and the Bells were waiting for McGregor in Chicago; Cole and the others thought they would finally get the verification they needed to publish the dates. Douglass told McGregor essentially to forget Hawley's work until the basis for crossdating could be more accurately determined. To make matters worse, when McGregor arrived in Chicago, Hawley was enmeshed in another controversy, this time regarding accusations that she had used departmental secretaries to type her husband's master's thesis, which was not related to her work on midwestern tree-rings. This episode is largely irrelevant to archaeological tree-ring dating except that it involved staff members of the Department of Anthropology who vented their frustrations to Cole in print, and the implications of one set of comments are especially damning with regard to dendrochronological research in the Midwest:

The Hawley situation gets worse and worse. Virginia Bell told me on Monday that what Hawley had been doing all summer was writing Donovan's [Senter's] manuscript on the Spanish-American town for him. He sent up the notes and she wrote up the chapters. That's why she didn't write anything [on tree-ring dating] for us. . . . [Robert] Redfield's comment was that we were all suckers and that he was sick of it. . . . I asked Virginia [Bell] about it today and she said she and Bob [Bell] had been very unhappy about it all summer. . . . The whole thing stinks to high heaven. . . . It will take months of work on Bell's part to get other materials together so that the publication when it comes out will be accepted. If it is published under Hawley's name it won't be accepted anyway, according to McGregor, because nobody—including and especially Douglass—trusts her work. . . . It seems to me that since she has milked the department out of $1000 this summer for no work at all, and the results she got are unpublishable, and since her reputation is so bad anyway, and since she is a cheater into the bargain—we ought to write her a letter and tell her so. And let Bell do the real work on the publication and let it come out under his name and not even mention her. I don't think she deserves an iota of consideration from us—but I don't suppose you will agree with me. (Bob Prentice to Cole, August 25, 1942)

McGregor examined Hawley's cedar specimens in late August and found at least three "outstanding" specimens from the Norris Basin in Tennessee. He concluded that the crossdating evident in them demonstrated the feasibility of dating in that region and recommended a renewed focus on specimens from southern Illinois, Kentucky, Tennessee, and Missouri (McGregor to Cole, August 28, 1942). McGregor relayed his findings of some "unbelievably good" specimens to Douglass, though he argued that Hawley did not yet have enough material truly to substantiate the crossdating (September 1, 1942). McGregor asked Cole where additional specimens had been stored, for he assumed that more specimens must be present if Hawley felt ready to publish reliable results. The Bells told him that no more specimens were available. McGregor conveyed his surprise to Cole, who turned to Hawley for an explanation. To that time, Cole had downplayed any charges leveled against Hawley, but when he realized that the implication of McGregor's query was that Hawley had let dendrochronological research slide for the sake of her husband's thesis, he realized that, if such were the case, "we have let him [Lily] down, we have let the Department down, and have done a great injury to the cause of archaeology in the Middle West" (Cole to Hawley, September 28, 1942).

Hawley admitted to Cole that she had a total of only five cedar specimens and argued that although departmental secretaries had typed Senter's paper, that was compensation for all the typing she had done of her own official correspondence while working at home. She offered to pay for the typing if necessary, though she argued that "going back and forth [between Albuquerque and Chicago] had loosened the tongues of gossip in both" places, despite the fact that she had worked hard for both schools (October 2, 1942). A day later, she wrote a more measured response:

> Yesterday I was horribly upset about this whole thing but today I feel somewhat better because I cannot believe that you will credit the accusations as anything more than gossip founded on a lack of knowledge of facts. . . . If I had set out to swindle the department I would certainly have made some move to cover my tracks. I believe that is proper criminal procedure. . . . Moreover, if I wanted to sabotage a project in which my reputation was involved and had been involved for six years it could only mean the loss of any common sense at all,

and I don't think that has happened to me yet. Donovan and I both count on recommendations from you. . . . Besides, I have been working in tree-rings longer than anyone else except Dr. Douglass and Emil Haury and if I lose my reputation in it it will be from poor work on something I can not manage, certainly not from lack of work. I have never published incorrect dates nor fallen into some of the other pitfalls that have damaged other dendrochronological reputations and if the Chicago tree-ring project falls through it will be because of impossibility of obtaining adequate material, not because of neglecting material nor of not working sufficiently on what we had.

In a handwritten postscript, Hawley added: "I have just received McGregor's report. I shall give you my full comments tomorrow. But this I reiterate: We have gone over everything we had of possible use, mound or modern."

On October 6, Hawley commented formally to Cole on McGregor's report. In her opinion, she and McGregor were not in significant disagreement, although she tried to shift some of the responsibility for any discrepancies to McGregor:

A person not present [i.e., McGregor] when all the work is done can not know some of the issues, difficulties, and methods used. . . . We know better than anyone else how badly we need supporting old wood but only long perseverance and occasional good luck is going to produce it for us. This was my complaint last spring when at first I so hesitated about publishing dates. But—this should be an underlined statement: We have covered everything which seemed in the least useful in all mound and modern wood which has ever come into the laboratory. We cataloged it if we thought we would have any present use at all for it—and that covered all but a small amount of what was brought or sent in.

I gather that McGregor must have had some trouble finding something he wanted and probably did not understand our catalog system. . . . McGregor's suggestion that we go over all mound collections for more wood was carried out last year and the year before: There is nothing else that can possibly be used. I wish to goodness there were. . . . I am beginning to expect people to think I never made charts—or reports—or had specimens cataloged—or carefully chose areas for field parties to explore. . . . I am sorry McGregor felt he could not be sure enough about the dates to check them. But I am not surprised. We have been told repeatedly that no work of comparable difficulty has been done by anyone but Stallings because he had the variable Rio Grande area to deal

with. Dr. Douglass himself does not want to check Missouri wood.
Stallings is in the war. . . . I think there is no question but that you will
have checked dates for the Mississippi Drainage eventually and I regret
as much as you do that the time is not the present.

In spite of numerous good intentions, and from a strictly dendrochronological standpoint, the Chicago archaeological tree-ring dating program should not have been speaking in terms of master charts
and chronologies on the basis of only a handful of specimens, no matter
how good the ring sequences therein actually were. Cole was diplomatic
but no longer optimistic in his reply to Hawley's report:

> It seemed beyond belief that even a part of the charges could be
> correct and so I welcome your explanations. Again in fairness to you,
> but with the friendliest intent, I offer the following: Perhaps your
> greatest source of trouble is laxness in your business accountings; lack
> of receipts, inadequate accounting and the like have several times
> caused us considerable difficulties in the financial line. A second weak-
> ness is in allowing situations to develop which foster talk. We certainly
> did not own twenty-four hours of your day, and it would have been a
> simple matter for us to have made arrangements so that your work on
> [Senter's] paper would have caused no comment.
>
> Within the past year I have twice been questioned by persons out-
> side the department concerning our work in Dendrochronology. They
> felt we were letting Mr. Lily down and that we were endangering his
> interest in Anthropology. . . . Now this should not be serious if we can
> show a real record of progress. . . . The blunt facts of the case are that
> we are on the spot and it is up to all of us to do all we can to produce
> what Mr. Lily expects. (October 12, 1942)

The crisis in Mississippi Valley tree-ring dating did not abate in
1943. Robert and Virginia Bell continued working on specimens in
Chicago while Hawley was at the University of New Mexico. The war
had reduced student and faculty ranks so much that Cole suggested they
try merely to keep Lily interested in dendrochronology without asking
for more money. McGregor continued his review of the Chicago tree-
ring work and in a letter to Douglass on March 6, 1943, listed the problems with the research conducted to date:

(1) [Hawley] wasted time working on wood that was not in the
    mounds. Mounds have juniper (cedar) and she worked with
    pines, ash, and others.
(2) Work she did on juniper was based on too little material. Three
    pieces from Norris Basin, TN compose most of her long chronology.

(3) Other problems—
    (a) Inconsistent ring variations for single years
    (b) Stated similarity of records over a wide area is not apparent
    (c) Lack of correlation of different species in one area, etc.
(4) Juniper collected was not from the area where most recent mound work was done. [I] remain unconvinced that Hawley had dates.

A handwritten note, presumably by Hawley, on the copy of this letter on file at the Florence Hawley Ellis Archives in Albuquerque appears to be a draft of a letter to Douglass, though a typed version is not present in the Douglass collection at the University of Arizona. The author wrote of her frustrations and tried to persuade Douglass to take some active interest in the crises:

> John MacGregor's [*sic*] letter to Douglass: He had been trying for some years to get my job at Chicago. This letter was written after I returned to Southwest, with wide survey made. Bell then, of course, could settle [in] to make detailed areas [analysis?] on the basis of our [illegible] surveys. Douglass did not go to Chicago, in spite of MacGregor [*sic*]. . . . I believe you could do nothing of more real value with tree-rings and archaeology than to give this particular problem some time and effort. . . . I can assure you this work will be well worth your own time and effort, as a contribution to the science of tree-rings and also for you personally. . . . I think you should make every effort to get back here [Albuquerque] well before Bell leaves.

On April 13, 1943, McGregor appealed to Douglass to come to Chicago:

> As I have written you, I believe the whole project has gotten off on the wrong foot and can probably proceed only with reorganization and confident direction. . . . The future of the Chicago TRL is hanging precariously in the balance. You could direct this lab easily, and Cole has put so much into it, we can't let it die. . . . I believe this second laboratory would in effect be under your indirect direction. If the project is ignored at this time it will probably never be reborn. . . . Will write Cole to write to you. If you can make it, I would be very glad to meet with you, Cole, and Bell to work on plans. I am convinced that your little time in Chicago will eventually pay big dividends.

Douglass responded that he could not make the trip for he was working on war-related research in climate forecasting. Though he recommended that Cole not let "any except the most experienced persons try this study," he nevertheless felt there might be some hope for the future: "I still believe that results will be obtained in the middle west but it will require a real piece of research and some one to guide it who is a creative genius and has a strong flare [*sic*] for field work and perhaps a knowledge of Botany and Meteorology" (June 30, 1943). With that, Mississippi Valley archaeological tree-ring dating came to a halt for the duration of the war.

Midwestern Dendrochronology after World War II

The next relevant record comes in the form of a letter from Cole to Hawley on January 20, 1945, regarding archaeological wood specimens that were collected at Kincaid in the summer of 1944, though full-scale excavations were not conducted that year. Cole noted that the specimens were briefly examined by McGregor, who, perhaps wisely, decided he did not want to analyze the pieces until a dating program was once again in place. On March 24, 1945, Cole informed Lily:

> McGregor is our ranking dendrochronologist and is so interested in the problem that he has agreed to devote two or three months to the problem. . . . I believe we have dates. I am willing to do anything within reason to satisfy the tree ring fraternity, but up until now we haven't had much luck in getting the proper checking of our materials. If we date the various levels of the Kincaid component from which we have wood, then we will have dated Cahokia and several other key sites, for we have trade materials sufficient to make this convincing. . . . I still think it promises significant contributions to Midwestern and southeastern prehistory.

McGregor reported to his old boss Colton that it looked as though they had crossdating "within one [prehistoric] site . . . in this area" and that Colton would hear more if the dating program at Chicago was started once again (November 8, 1945).

Bell was discharged from the army in February 1946 and returned to Chicago to continue archaeological tree-ring dating there. McGregor was still director of the Illinois State Museum and could not devote much time to the project. Nevertheless, he reported to Douglass that he had worked on the midwestern cedars during all his spare time over the past four years and now felt he had "secure dates" for seven or eight specimens, all derived using a new "short plot" technique he had developed. This method used histograms based on ring-width measurements and, ironically, might have come in useful during the early days of the Gladwin-Douglass debate: "I am writing because much of the trouble Gladwin caused could have been obviated if we had used some system

like the histograms. Raw ring-widths are included, and all rings are represented. . . . Had we followed such a system I cannot see how he could
have gone off the deep end with his own work as he has done" (July 26,
1946). McGregor added that the Chicago tree-ring work "must now be
presented to the archaeologists" but that "it will be presented simply as
evidence of correlation and dating, without any claim that it is
absolutely correct; that is contains no errors. Histograms will be presented for their use and evaluation."

This was the technique used to date the archaeological tree-ring
samples from Kincaid that were ultimately published by Bell (1951) in
the Kincaid site report (Cole 1951). In 1946, Bell became head of the
Department of Anthropology at the University of Oklahoma, which
offered to assume at least partial sponsorship of the tree-ring dating program when Lily canceled support after seeing the program through to
publication of a few prehistoric dates (Cole to McGregor, August 26,
1946). After Cole retired in 1947, the Chicago Tree-Ring Laboratory
collections were sent to the University of Oklahoma with the Bells, but a
formal tree-ring dating program was never launched there. The specimens and records are now curated by the University of Arizona
Laboratory of Tree-Ring Research.

Conclusion

Hawley faced an uphill battle in her attempt to establish tree-ring dating
in the Mississippi Valley. Dendrochronologically, she had to extend
analysis to many new species,[3] she had to use poorly preserved archaeological wood specimens, and she was burdened by living-tree cores from
second-growth timber stands that did not offer, because of early historic
deforestation in the area, many climatically sensitive trees with ring
sequences long enough to bridge the gap between modern and archaeological chronologies.

Professionally, Hawley was under continuous and unprecedented
pressure from Webb, Cole, Lily, and others to produce and publish tree-
ring dates, but she never succeeded in proving to Douglass or her fellow

---

3. If Hawley had tried working with baldcypress, she might have been able
to develop a sufficiently long chronology (Stahle, Cook, and White 1985; see
also Stahle and Wolfman 1985 and Stahle 1979). This species is not commonly
found in Moundbuilder sites, however, so even if she had recognized its crossdating potential, she would have deemed the species irrelevant to the goals of her
research.

dendrochronologists that the dates she arrived at were reliable. She simply did not have enough specimens with sensitive enough ring records to
produce good crossdating. Her research also suffered from a series of
events that were largely beyond her control, whether press leaks in
Pittsburgh in 1934, gender discrimination at TVA in 1935, patriotic mobs
in western Kentucky in 1940, or perhaps ill-considered financial man-
agement at Chicago in 1942. Nevertheless, Mississippi Valley archaeological tree-ring research was under her direction from 1934 through
1943, and there is evidence that she did not rigorously adhere to the
basic, if somewhat ill-defined, principles of the Douglass method of tree-
ring dating, whether in regard to required sample depth, date verification protocols, or the complete understanding of crossdating in the area
in question. Perhaps the split-semester arrangement between
Albuquerque and Chicago was distracting. Perhaps she faced professional and personal circumstances that would have made weaker souls
flee. Although it is clear that archaeological dendrochronology in the
Mississippi Valley is extremely difficult even under ideal conditions, one
gets the feeling that midwestern archaeological tree-ring dating might be
further along if circumstances had been different. Hawley spent the
remainder of her career at the University of New Mexico and died in
1991 (Frisbie 1991).

CHAPTER 8

A Compass, a Raft, and a .22

James Louis Giddings's Dendrochronology in Alaska

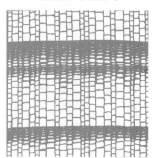

The pioneering Arctic tree-ring research of James Louis Giddings (Figure 31) addressed questions in fields ranging from archaeology to geomorphology, oceanography, paleontology, and forest ecology. Giddings demonstrated the basic principles of crossdating and replication in the analysis of Alaskan spruce cores, and he produced the first accurately dated, long-term, terrestrial paleotemperature record in the world. He also trained graduate students in the early 1950s, some of whom conducted tree-ring research for several years after teaching and administrative duties kept Giddings from continuing his tree-ring studies. Table 8 provides a chronology of the dendrochronological work done in Alaska.

Giddings earned his bachelor of science degree in general science from the University of Alaska–Fairbanks in 1931, after spending three years at Rice University in Houston (Rainey 1965). During the summer of 1936, in his fifth year of placer gold mining for the Fairbanks Exploration Company, he concentrated on the hydraulic removal of massive frozen silt, or "black muck," deposits prior to the dredging of gold-bearing creek gravels along Engineer Creek, ten miles north of Fairbanks (Figure 32). Buried at various levels within these muck deposits were ancient spruce forests, thin layers of volcanic ash, and the bones of extinct megafauna as well as extant animal species (Giddings 1938a). In an attempt to determine the age of the buried forests, thereby providing dates and rates of deposition for the black muck deposits, Giddings began a self-directed study of tree rings in the buried wood samples. Although his methods proved impractical, his interest in tree-

FIGURE 31. James Louis Giddings (1909–1964) in the field in Alaska in the 1950s. Courtesy of Laboratory of Tree-Ring Research, University of Arizona.

ring analysis had been piqued, and at the behest of Ralph Chaney of the Carnegie Institution, Giddings wrote to Douglass on November 24, 1936, to ask for guidance in the analysis of Alaskan tree rings. Douglass replied to Giddings's request six weeks later and sent explicit instructions on how to identify climatically sensitive trees and how to sample them once identified (January 11, 1937). This exchange of letters marks the modest beginning of a significant professional dendrochronological career for Giddings and a close working relationship between the two natural scientists which lasted for the next quarter of a century.[1]

1. Douglass's interest in Arctic tree-ring research can be traced back to 1921, when W. S. Cooper of the Department of Botany at the University of Minnesota sent Douglass a series of wood specimens from Alaska (April 28, 1921). Childs Frick of the American Museum of Natural History, who would later fund much of Giddings's research, sent Alaskan wood samples to Douglass in 1930 (Douglass to Frick, January 28, 1930). Douglass collected living-tree cores himself above the Arctic Circle in Sweden in 1930.

TABLE 8. Timeline: Archaeological Tree-Ring Dating in Alaska.

1936	Giddings begins unsupervised tree-ring research at Engineer Creek.
1937	Giddings demonstrates good crossdating in specimens from the "black muck" deposits.
	Otto William Geist suggests Giddings try to date archaeological sites on St. Lawrence Island.
1938	Spring: Giddings begins graduate study at the University of Arizona.
	Extensively samples sites on the Alaska Range south of Fairbanks.
	Identifies temperature as climatic variable to which Alaskan trees respond.
1939	Conducts first archaeological fieldwork, with Rainey at Jabbertown and Geist at Kukulik.
1940	Samples trees along the Yukon and Tanana Rivers.
	Hikes north, then west, to reach the Kobuk River; builds driftwood raft; samples archaeological and tree-ring sites along the Kobuk.
	Returns to Tucson for continued graduate study.
1941	Receives master's degree from the University of Arizona.
	Returns to the Kobuk River to excavate sites found in 1940.
1942	Journeys down the Yukon River to explore differences between "Series A" and "Series B" dating.
	Returns to Tucson to assist Douglass in dendroclimatic analysis.
1943–1946	Serves in U.S. Navy.
1946	Samples tree stands along the MacKenzie River with Ruth Warner Giddings.
1947	Returns to Kobuk River sites for additional excavation to bridge the gap and date the 350-year floating archaeological chronology.
	Establishes Kobuk River chronology to A.D. 978.

By October 1937, Giddings was able to demonstrate that the tree-ring series found in logs buried in the "muck" were sensitive enough to show good crossdating, so much so that he was able to establish floating chronologies for four distinct levels of buried spruce trees (Giddings 1938a). Giddings felt comfortable enough with the results of his pilot study to write to Frick and Charles Bunnell of the University of

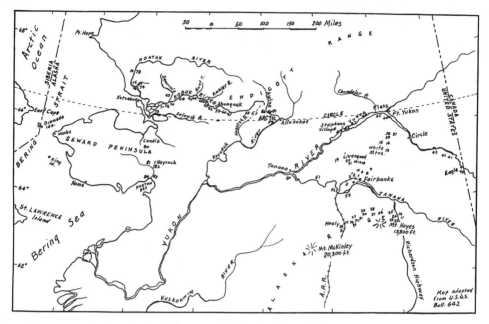

FIGURE 32. Archaeological sites sampled by Giddings in the 1940s. Numbers indicate living-tree and archaeological sites sampled by Giddings while establishing tree-ring dating in Alaska between 1936 and 1940. Courtesy of the
Laboratory of Tree-Ring Research, University of Arizona.

Alaska–Fairbanks to ask for research support (December 22, 1937), in
the hope that they would fund graduate research with Douglass during
the spring of 1938.

Giddings was a naturalist and a field scientist in the best sense of
these terms, but he was not a trained archaeologist, and his early tree-
ring research bears this out. There is no indication that he was interested
in archaeological tree-ring dating until 1938, after he began course work
in Tucson. Archaeological fieldwork and tree-ring dating in the
American Southwest were in full swing in 1938, and Giddings must have
participated in, or at least been exposed to, the excited attempts to date
tree-ring samples collected and submitted by archaeologists ranging
from Brew at Awatovi to Nesbitt at Starkweather Ruin and Cummings
at Kinishba. In the spring of 1937, Otto William Geist of the University
of Alaska suggested that Giddings try to date wood excavated on St.
Lawrence Island in the Bering Sea (Figure 30), where Geist had been
working for more than a decade. Though his interests were still primarily geological and paleontological, Giddings in the spring of 1938 was

cautiously optimistic about the possibility of archaeological tree-ring studies in Alaska. He wrote Geist: "I have thought a good deal about the suggestion you made last spring of dating some of the Eskimo ruins from their construction timbers. If the driftwood [the Eskimos used in construction] came consistently from one watershed, either the Yukon or Mackenzie [River], the chances are greatly in favor of crossdating" (April 14, 1938).

In the 1938 field season, Giddings shifted the emphasis of his tree-ring efforts. He had already established a series of "floating" tree-ring chronologies in the Fairbanks area, and he knew from his work with Douglass that this meant that some common climatic variable was affecting tree growth in central Alaska. Douglass had found as early as 1930 that Arctic trees in Sweden responded primarily to temperature variability, but Giddings would have to explore the climate–tree growth relationship in Alaska on his own to determine what variable the chronologies recorded. As of June 1938, he had not yet ruled out precipitation: "I haven't looked up temperature or rainfall records yet, but the old timers remember 1910, 1912, 1919, and 1928 as years of poor crops. . . . They have had no rain up here this summer. The miners are crying for rain. Perhaps the trees will have something to say about this state of affairs" (letter to Douglass, June 30, 1938).

His sample collecting in June 1938 was thus aimed at determining how variation in topographic setting affects tree sensitivity, and he sampled trees in transects from river bottom to elevational timberline, which occurs in central Alaska between 2,800 and 3,400 feet above sea level (Giddings 1938b). He conclusively demonstrated that the timberline trees were more sensitive, and therefore showed better crossdating, than those in river bottoms, which is analogous to Douglass's finding better crossdating at the lower forest border than in trees at the forest interiors of the arid Southwest. Douglass was pleased, if not surprised, by these results: "I congratulate you on getting crossdating at timberline. I ought to have guessed it. I did think in terms of the inversion of temperatures in the valley bottoms, but of course the logic of good crossdating at timberline or the upper forest border where the cold is so exaggerated that the forest ceases is just as evident as our good crossdating at the lower forest border where the moisture that the forest needs ceases on contact with the desert" (Douglass to Giddings, July 14, 1938).

Douglass was not a man generous in praise, and the immediate foci of his critique of any attempt to establish tree-ring dating in a new area were the successful demonstration of crossdating and the development of a clear understanding of the relationship between tree sensitivity and the appropriate climatic variable. On seeing Giddings's work, Douglass could barely contain his glee: "I am tremendously pleased that you are without a doubt on the right track not only for a better understanding of the meaning of the rings at Fairbanks but for reaching tangible terms on which you can build a chronology" (Douglass to Giddings, July 14, 1938).

Giddings now knew that the trees he examined were more sensitive at timberline and were therefore probably responding to temperature fluctuations, but he did not know the areal extent of the climate signal that made crossdating feasible in the trees of the Fairbanks region. In late August 1938, he set out on one of his many epic and awe-inspiring trips into the Alaska wilderness. His destination was the north slope of the rugged Alaska Range, fifty miles south of Fairbanks. Equipped with an increment borer and a .22-caliber rifle, he hiked 120 miles over the next 16 days, during which time, as he described it in a letter to Douglass, he "climbed many high ridges, waded and swam glacier streams, scrambled over glaciers, and, although my camera and films were ruined in the water, I came out with borings from all the timberline points along the way" (October 4, 1938). By late October 1938, he had completed a rudimentary correlation analysis of the available climate and tree-ring data, which clearly indicated that climatically sensitive trees in central Alaska and the Yukon watershed responded primarily to variations in average June temperatures (Giddings to Douglass, October 21, 1938).

Giddings's tree-ring research in 1938 satisfied Douglass's basic requirements; central Alaska crossdating was established and explained. This work set the stage for more sophisticated tree-ring analyses and the application of dendrochronological techniques to serious questions regarding the natural and cultural history of Alaska. Giddings suggested to Douglass that dendrochronology be applied to the study of polar drift and Arctic sea currents, pointing out relevant economic and safety concerns: "In driftwood, which will have been preserved in constantly accumulating masses on practically all Arctic shores, we have data waiting to be gathered and translated which are just as conclusive as if notes in thousands of bottles have been dropped into the sea at the mouths of all the important north-flowing rivers of the world. . . . As to the value of this subject to science it is necessary only to consider the amount of money already spent in the tracing of sea currents in the Arctic. That is to say nothing of the lives lost" (October 16, 1938).

Geist, on the other hand, wanted Giddings to try to date archaeological samples from his excavations at Kukulik, Gambell, and other sites on St. Lawrence Island. Since the monetary "powers-that-be" prohibited Giddings from returning to Tucson for more course work in the spring of 1939 (Giddings to Douglass, December 30, 1938), arrangements were made with Froelich Rainey of the University of Alaska Museum for Giddings to examine several thousand wooden implements recovered from Kukulik (Giddings 1940). Douglass was enthusiastic about this attempt to date prehistoric artifacts and cultures in Alaska, but he was also cautious, for he knew from his own experience, and that of Florence Hawley in the Midwest (Chapter 7), that the pressure applied by project directors, financiers, and the press to release tree-ring dates before they are certain can be nearly unbearable:

> I am tremendously interested in your report of dating specimens from the St. Lawrence Island. . . . [But] be sure to develop an absolutely unmistakable cross-dating in your prehistoric material. It is safer to do this before making any attempt to date the individual pieces in terms of a chronology . . . [and] it may be very helpful to use small V-cuts in contact with each other and carry the ring patterns from one to the other almost without movement of the eye. This amounts to saying: Do not trust [dating] to skeleton plots; they are only a guide and are not decisive. . . . Since you have the situation in your own hands, don't let anybody hasten you into results that you are not infernally sure of. (May 22, 1939)

Giddings spent the first half of 1939 examining archaeological wood in Fairbanks, refining his tree-ring chronologies for St. Lawrence Island and the Fairbanks region and dating wood from early historic sites on St. Lawrence Island. Later that summer, he joined Rainey and Helge Larsen of the Danish National Museum in excavations at the Jabbertown site on Point Hope, and then he joined Geist in the field at Kukulik and Gambell on St. Lawrence Island. By the end of 1939, Giddings was converted: "I have turned into an archaeologist of sorts" (Giddings to Douglass, December 13, 1939). By May 1940, he stated that he could accurately date Eskimo house logs on St. Lawrence Island back to A.D. 1500, though he did so on the basis of a newly developed chronology that did not crossdate with his timberline chronology (Giddings 1940). He knew that most, if not all, of the wood on St. Lawrence Island was driftwood and, feeling satisfied with the results so far, believed it was time to examine further the relationship between his driftwood chronology, named "Series B," and the timberline chronology, which he called "Series A."

In late May 1940, Giddings boarded a trading boat at Circle City and journeyed up the Yukon River to Eagle, back down to Tanana

Village, and up the Tanana River to Fairbanks. This brief expedition allowed him to find and sample old and stressed trees located at river margin sites, which logically constituted the source of driftwood on St. Lawrence Island and elsewhere. Given the difficulty of finding such specimens, the resulting collection of dendrochronologically useful samples was meager at best. The results of this brief reconnaissance were published as part of his master's thesis (Giddings 1941) and in the *Tree-Ring Bulletin* (Giddings 1942) and formed the basis of a much more extensive trip down the Yukon two years later (Giddings 1943).

After a five-week hiatus at Fairbanks through June 1940, Giddings flew to Allakakeet on the Koyukuk River (Giddings 1967). On July 15, he set his bearings and left Allakakeet on foot, against the vehement protestations of the local missionaries and to the chagrin of University of Alaska president Charles Bunnell, whose terse objection to the trip suggested only that Giddings keep a good accounting of his finances (Giddings 1967:293). Giddings's self-appointed task was to explore the archaeological and dendrochronological possibilities of the uncharted Kobuk River drainage: "[Equipped] with only a forty-pound pack, most of which consisted of a waterproof tent with a sewn-in mosquito net, a featherweight down sleeping bag, rain gear, a change of heavy underclothes one must wear as mosquito protection, and my .22 semiautomatic rifle, I felt more than adequately prepared to stay out the remainder of the summer if necessary. I carried little food as I planned to live off the land" (Giddings 1967:294).

Giddings eschewed offers of accompaniment because of the additional cost required for an assistant and because he wanted to proceed unencumbered and accountable to no one. He trekked due north for four days, crossed the Alatna Divide, and descended into the Kobuk River drainage. He then set a compass bearing due west and headed to where his calculations said he would find the headwaters of the Kobuk. On reaching the river, he built a driftwood raft and floated down the 300-mile length of the Kobuk, collecting tree-ring samples and testing archaeological sites as he went. After arriving at the mouth of the Kobuk, he turned north again, sampling sites along south-flowing portions of the Noatak River, after which he reversed course, crossed the Seward Peninsula, and concluded his monumental journey at Haycock (Giddings 1941).

The purpose of the 1940 trip down the Kobuk was threefold and at least partly archaeological (Giddings 1942). First, Giddings wanted to determine if crossdating was present in northern Alaska trees. If it was present, he wanted to develop a living-tree chronology for the Kobuk drainage. Second, he wanted to conduct an archaeological survey to determine if old sites were present and if ancient wood was preserved in the Kobuk sites. Third, he hoped to determine whether archaeological specimens exhibited crossdating on a consistent basis. This research design was a direct result of Giddings's experience in trying to date archaeological specimens on St. Lawrence Island.

Giddings's 1940 trip fulfilled each of the stated goals: modern and archaeological crossdating along the Kobuk was demonstrated, a preliminary chronology was developed, and a series of archaeological sites of varying age was discovered. In the fall of 1940, he returned to Tucson to complete his master's thesis. The degree was awarded in the spring of 1941 by the Department of Anthropology, even though the thesis contains no archaeological analysis per se and little in the way of dendroarchaeological analysis; the document does list dates Giddings obtained for historic sites at Point Hope, King Island in the Bering Sea, Little Diomede Island in the Bering Strait, Kukulik on St. Lawrence Island, and Ekseavik along the Kobuk River (Giddings 1941). Published jointly by the University of Alaska and the University of Arizona, *Dendrochronology of Northern Alaska* (Giddings 1941) summarized Giddings's dendrochronological research of the previous five years and was immediately hailed as a significant contribution to the archaeology of North America and the climatology of Alaska (Douglass to University of Arizona president Atkinson, April 26, 1941). Reprints were sent to more than 200 scientists around the world, including archaeologists Brew, Gladwin, Hall, Hawley, Judd, Kidder, McGregor, Mera, Morris, Nesbitt, Nusbaum, Stallings, Willey, and Wissler.

In 1941, Giddings returned to the Kobuk with equipment, money, and Eskimo Civilian Conservation Corps assistants systematically to excavate and recover tree-ring samples from the five most important sites found the previous summer. He excavated 18 houses at five sites: Old and Intermediate Kotzebue on Kotzebue Sound, Ekseavik and Ahteut along the middle Kobuk River, and Ambler Island along the upper Kobuk, the last-named of which he was able to date absolutely that summer (Giddings 1942, 1948). He wrote to his parents that he was able to use Kobuk tree rings to date sites back to about A.D. 1600 but that he still had an undated, 350-year "floating" chronology based on specimens from the Ekseavik, Ahteut, and Kotzebue sites. On completion of the summer's excavation, he returned to the University of Alaska as an instructor in anthropology at a starting salary of $3,600 per year.

By mid-1942, Giddings found time to conduct a more systematic examination of Yukon River spruce stands, the purpose of which was, at least in part, to delineate further the boundaries between his two central Alaska chronologies: the "Series A" chronology, which dated timberline and latitudinal tree-line trees sensitive to temperature, and the Yukon Flats river-edge and driftwood "Series B" chronology, which probably responded to temperature as well as some other climatic variable (Giddings 1943). The trip down the Yukon would be his last dendrochronological field trip until after the war, and on completing the trip he began seriously to consider military service. In a desperate attempt to keep Giddings from enlisting, Douglass persuaded him to move to Tucson to assist in the Tree-Ring Laboratory's efforts at long-range climatic and hydrologic forecasting for Boulder Dam on the Colorado River, which Douglass argued was war-related because it was funded by the Army Corps of Engineers and was connected to war-time manganese production (Douglass to Bunnell, October 9, 1942). Giddings accepted Douglass's argument temporarily and moved to Tucson in November 1942, where he found to his chagrin that the cost of living was almost as high as in Fairbanks. He would not, however, be reconciled to sitting out the war and in June 1943 followed his conscience and joined the navy. He married Ruth Warner of Tucson, on December 3, 1943, and in March 1944 shipped out. In one of the many ironies of war, the navy assigned Giddings, by then a recognized expert on Arctic environments, to an island post in the South Pacific, where he spent the duration of the war. Nevertheless, tree-ring studies did not slip his mind, and before departing he wrote Douglass, "I want to take a borer along just in case my ship anchors in a likely port for sampling conifers" (March 8, 1944). The increment borer went unused.

Giddings earned an honorable discharge from the U.S. Navy on January 1, 1946, and quickly returned to tree-ring studies. Two major projects formed the foci of his immediate postwar research: a 1946 reconnaissance and sampling trip down the MacKenzie River in western Canada (Giddings 1947) and additional excavation and dendrochronological sampling on the Kobuk River in 1947 (Giddings 1948). A trip down the uncharted MacKenzie River had been on his mind since 1943, and a joint husband-wife expedition must have seemed a romantic reunion for the young couple who, like so many others during the war, had spent the first years of their marriage apart. Whatever romance they might have planned quickly vanished, for, unknown to them at the beginning of the voyage, "baby boomer" James Louis Giddings III was

en route, and Ruth Warner Giddings suffered morning sickness throughout the 600-mile journey. To make the situation even more difficult, their
menu consisted of canned sardines and saltine crackers, in addition to
the occasional hunted squirrel and plentiful salmon.

Giddings's return to the Kobuk sites in 1947 had the express purpose
of dating the 350-year, floating chronology constructed from Ekseavik,
Ahteut, and Old Kotzebue specimens in 1942. The situation is remarkably analogous to that of Douglass in the American Southwest in the late
1920s (see Chapter 2). Both had floating archaeological chronologies
based on samples from undated sites, both had well-dated modern and
historic chronologies, and both Douglass in 1928 and Giddings in 1941
already knew, to some reasonable degree, where their chronologies overlapped and therefore dated. Neither one, however, was willing to declare
that the archaeological chronology was actually dated until additional
samples strengthened his understanding of the weak points in his
chronology. Douglass had to wait only two years to bridge the gap with
confidence; Giddings had to wait six. As it turned out, tree-ring samples
from the Intermediate Kotzebue site overlapped the early portion of the
dated chronology, but Giddings needed more samples to strengthen the
chronology and convince himself of the dating. Almost as soon as he
returned to the Intermediate Kotzebue site in 1947, he discovered the
appropriate samples and was able to date Kobuk River archaeological
sites back to A.D. 978 (Giddings 1948, 1954b, 1967).

The 1947 work on the Kobuk sites marked the last published dendroarchaeological field research Giddings undertook, even though his
research design for the Cape Denbigh sites in 1948, 1949, and 1950
included plans for applied tree-ring studies in that area (Giddings
1964). Later work at Cape Krusenstern was also to include dendrochronological analysis, though by then Giddings's research emphasis had shifted to archaeological, and therefore anthropological,
questions. Two of Giddings's students continued archaeological tree-
ring research in Alaska, however. Wendell Oswalt analyzed tree-ring
samples from sites along the Squirrel River, a tributary of the Kobuk,
as part of a special project associated with the 1947 Kobuk excavations (Oswalt 1953). James VanStone conducted additional excavations at the Old Kotzebue and Intermediate Kotzebue sites in 1951,
using Giddings's Kobuk chronology to date eight more houses at these
sites (VanStone 1953). Oswalt (1950, 1951) and VanStone (1958) conducted dendrochronological studies of tree-growth and driftwood patterns as well.

CONCLUSION

The legacy of James Giddings in Arctic anthropology and dendrochronology is strong: he single-handedly produced the first long-term, accurately dated terrestrial paleotemperature record; presented the first good archaeological evidence for interaction between coastal Eskimo and inland Athabaskan populations (Dekin 1973); and excavated several culturally and chronologically important sites: Cape Krusenstern, where he developed horizontal stratigraphic analysis on superimposed beach ridges; Cape Denbigh (Giddings 1964), where he defined the ancient Denbigh Flint Complex; and Onion Portage, where he found a stratigraphic record that has yet to be equaled in the Arctic. More important, Giddings was the first to date successfully prehistoric archaeological sites in the Arctic. In so doing, he verified many of the basic principles of dendrochronology and archaeological tree-ring dating, and did so in an environment radically different from those in which tree-ring dating had been previously applied. He confronted the dendroarchaeologically difficult issues presented by prehistoric driftwood use, the origin of which may only rarely be inferred with any degree of certainty. The most important contribution to archaeological tree-ring dating in Alaska is his Kobuk-Noatak-Selawik River chronology (Giddings 1941, 1942, 1948), which allowed him to address cultural problems in Alaskan prehistory with an unprecedented understanding of regional chronology. In a strong testimonial to his own persistence, Giddings personally established dendroarchaeology and dendroclimatology in Alaska, though the archaeological aspect of his tree-ring research has not been continued since the mid-1950s. Just before his death, Giddings wrote, "The future of dendrochronology seems to be limited only by the enthusiasm of those who have the patience to learn its fascination" (Giddings 1962:130). Unfortunately, few have had the enthusiasm or patience.

It is not entirely clear why archaeological tree-ring dating came to a halt in Alaska in the 1950s, though several factors played a part. First and foremost, Giddings's life became more complicated. The birth of his children in March 1947, March 1949, and May 1951 undoubtedly taxed his time and perhaps brought a degree of parental conservatism to an otherwise adventurous soul: "Fairbanks is rapidly becoming invaded by all sorts of rattletrap cars and crummy people looking for the end of the rainbow" (Giddings to Helge Larsen, May 20, 1947). Giddings was hired as assistant professor of anthropology at the University of Pennsylvania in 1949 and earned his doctorate there in 1951. Increased teaching, administrative, and familial commitments thus chipped away at his days, and though he still conducted summer fieldwork, he did not have the time to devote to dendrochronological research.

The advent of radiocarbon dating had a significant impact on Alaska tree-ring dating as well. The sites to which Giddings turned his attention contained components that were well beyond the range of tree-ring dating, and although his research proposals identified tree-ring analyses, he focused his attention on horizontal stratigraphy at Cape Krusenstern and vertical stratigraphy at Onion Portage to achieve a better understanding of Alaska culture history (Giddings 1954a, 1964, 1967) Giddings's colleague at Pennsylvania, Rainey, was on the original Carbon-14 committee, and Giddings supplied tree-ring-dated wood specimens on which Carbon-14 dating experiments were conducted (Rainey to Giddings, January 11, 1949). Despite the acclaim with which the universally applicable and high-tech radiocarbon dating was received, Giddings refused to relinquish dendrochronology's primacy in archaeological dating: "Some think radiocarbon dating is about to replace the tree-ring method, just as automobiles replaced the horse and buggy. This assumption is doubtful. . . . Even if radiocarbon dating becomes less expensive and more precisely focused, tree-ring dates will still be needed both to verify the general dating and pinpoint the specific" (Giddings 1962:130).

Whatever the causes behind Giddings's departure from tree-ring research, his tone in later publications is almost apologetic. In a 1954 summary article entitled "Tree-Ring Dating in the American Arctic," he wrote: "One may well ask why so much of the dendrochronological work begun or suggested for the far north since the middle 1930's is still unfinished. The answer is . . . the researcher has to explore and collect in many almost inaccessible places, and then to sit endless hours measuring, plotting, and cross-comparing. As a primary discipline, Arctic dendrochronology will progress as students learn the fascination of its precision as a research tool, but it cannot be expected to serve at all if it is not given long hours and proper care" (Giddings 1954b:25). In a critical review of dendrochronology entitled "Development of Tree-Ring Dating as an Archaeological Aid," he added: "An immediate need, it would seem, is for more researchers with the scientific bent of Douglass and [Edmund] Schulman who can continue to observe, induce, and experiment with the almost endless possibilities of climatic and archaeological interpretation. If these students are encouraged as they continue to appear, the future of dendrochronology and of the Tree-Ring

Laboratory is assured for the decades to come" (Giddings 1962:130). Unfortunately, few researchers can match "the scientific bent of Douglass," and once VanStone and Oswalt stopped working on Arctic tree-ring problems by about 1960, archaeologists in Alaska seemed to forget that dendrochronological dating can be applied to selected archaeological problems in the Arctic. Between 1955 and 1995, only 153 archaeological tree-ring specimens from Alaska were submitted to the Laboratory of Tree-Ring Research for analysis.

Dendroclimatic chronology development in Alaska has continued to grow, so it remains for archaeologists working in Alaska to rediscover the possibilities of archaeological tree-ring dating. They must again collect, preserve, and submit tree-ring samples if they want to enjoy the most precise chronometric data available to prehistoric archaeologists (Nash 1995). Unfortunately, as Melzter (1989) pointed out, the rediscovery of a technique does not necessarily lead to its reapplication in analytical contexts. It may well be that until archaeological tree-ring dating finds permanent institutional support in Alaska, Giddings's research will stand alone in testimony to the chronometric possibilities in northwestern North America.

James Louis Giddings, Jr., died in 1964 from injuries sustained in a single-car automobile accident on an expressway near Providence, Rhode Island.

Did Dendrochronology Change North American Archaeology?

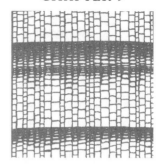

CHAPTER 9

For more than gold was in a ring.

G. K. CHESTERTON

The announcement of common-era calendar dating of southwestern archaeological sites through the analysis of tree rings had an electrifying and immediate impact on archaeologists as well as the general middle-class public, to whom Douglass's (1929) article was primarily addressed. Archaeologists were astonished at how young the classic southwestern sites actually were. Because tree-ring dates compressed, rather than tele-scoped, their age estimates, archaeologists were immediately forced to revise their interpretations of prehistoric occupations of the Southwest. Morris was incredulous; his colleague and friend Kidder was disap-pointed: "[We] have a sneaking sense of disappointment as the pitiless progress of tree-ring dating hauls the Cliff-dwellers, and with them the Basketmakers, farther and farther away from the cherished B.C.'s" (Kidder 1936:143).

The impact of absolute chronology and the compressed timetable on archaeological interpretation is perhaps best conveyed in the words of a witness:

> We found the Southwestern time table sorely in error once tree-time became applicable. As an example, we have the estimates of the mid-1920's for the Basketmakers, the earliest members of what we now call [the] Anasazi, which dated [before tree-ring dating at] some 2000 B.C. This was patently an inferred date based on the assumption that cultural progress in the region was slow. Later, with the applica-tion of tree-time, and as Basketmaker sites were demonstrably shown to have been inhabited during the early centuries of the Christian era, this figure was cut in half. At once, this threw entirely new light on the

rapidity of culture growth, that instead of the slow, measured progress, changes in the Southwest were effected rapidly. The 500-room pueblo of the 12th century assumed to have been the end product of innumerable centuries of tedious groping for better homes, rooted in the individual semi-subterranean house, could now be shown to have developed quickly, in the span of a few centuries. What thus appeared to be true of architecture was therefore also inherent in the growth of arts and crafts. (Haury 1946:3–4)

The general public seems not to have been as surprised as archaeologists about the age of the ruins. Those who wrote to Douglass seemed more interested in applying tree-ring dating to advance their own interests. Businesspeople hoped to better understand perceived cyclicity in their markets; religious fanatics wanted to use tree-ring dates to establish connections between phenomena ranging from the formation of Meteor Crater in Arizona to the construction of the megalithic monuments of Easter Island; and woodworkers, artisans, and pothunters wished to use tree rings to verify the dating of their wares. For the general public, it seems that tree-ring dating of southwestern ruins simply satisfied one aspect of their "back[ward] looking curiosity" (William Camden [1551–1623], quoted in Daniel 1963:20).

More than a dozen archaeology students at the University of Arizona took advantage of local opportunities and enrolled in Douglass's first dendrochronology course in the spring of 1930. In acquiring dendrochronological skills, they differentiated themselves from other archaeologists entering a difficult job market. As a result, many found gainful and full-time archaeological employment during the height of the Great Depression, often at institutions that offered to pay for their continuing graduate study. This situation is nothing short of remarkable and provides additional testimony to the celebrated place of tree-ring dating in North American archaeology during the 1930s. In contrast to these dendrochronological entrepreneurs, established senior archaeologists, with the possible exception of V. Gordon Childe, did not seek training in dendrochronological methods. Most archaeologists working in areas where tree-ring dating had a reasonable chance of success simply chose to submit samples to Douglass or his students to see if tree-ring dates could be derived.

Some institutions structured their research to take advantage of the new dating technique. The Museum of Northern Arizona hired John McGregor and selected sites for excavation based on whether or not burned roof timbers were found in test pits. The Laboratory of

Anthropology hired Sid Stallings and used similar criteria to select sites in the Rio Grande valley. Emil Haury conducted an intensive dendrochronological examination of Canyon Creek Ruin and other cliff dwellings in the Sierra Ancha to supplement the archaeological research being done by Gila Pueblo. Aside from these instances, however, most archaeologists (e.g., Paul Martin, Edgar Lee Hewett, Hattie and Burton Cosgrove) continued to excavate as they always had, collecting tree-ring specimens that they thought, sometimes erroneously, might date.

An examination of site reports before and after 1930 suggests that the presentation of archaeological data did not change in light of dendrochronology—the focus was still on culture history as reflected by variations in architecture, tools, pots, and, to a lesser degree, sherds. Changes visible in the archaeological record were typically attributed to migration, diffusion, and marauding nomads. Archaeologists who were not formally trained in dendrochronology only rarely incorporated tree-ring dates in their analyses of architecture and material culture, and tree-ring date lists were usually relegated to an appendix.

Analytically, tree-ring dates were typically used to establish the upper and lower dates for the occupation of a site, either directly through the dating of samples from that site or indirectly through the crossdating of the recovered ceramic assemblage with nearby tree-ring-dated sites. In other words, absolute, common-era calendar tree-ring dates were often used only to place a site along a relatively dated sequence, such as that provided by the Pecos Classification. If the tree-ring dates and relative classification assignments seemed incongruent, cultural lags were called on to explain any discrepancies. Gladwin chose in such situations to challenge the validity of tree-ring dating.

Haury wrote retrospectively in 1946 that "tree-rings brought a new outlook, a changed form of thinking and a search for new provocative factors which may have lain behind" the variability evident in the archaeological record (Haury 1946:4). Although this assessment may be true, especially in areas where trained dendroarchaeologists could apply their skills, it is far from clear that other archaeologists readily accepted the dendrochronological call to arms, and if they did, the "search for new provocative factors" did not begin immediately.

Once the Central Pueblo and Rio Grande chronologies were in place, archaeologists working in the regions to which those chronologies applied could begin asking increasingly sophisticated human ecological, historical, social, and political questions of their data. They eventually started to make "empirically testable statements," offering interpretations that could for the first time be proved incorrect (Dunnell 1986:29), but again most advances in this vein were made by institutions that employed a dendroarchaeologist. In 1929, Douglass identified and dated the "Great Drought" to A.D. 1276–1299, and archaeologists immediately adopted this event as an explanation for the abandonment of the San Juan region, though their conclusions were fully within the prevailing culture historical, migrationist paradigm prevalent at that time. In the 1930s and 1940s, Colton and McGregor used tree-ring dating to date the eruption of Sunset Crater, thereby initiating an emphasis on the human ecology of the eruption area, a movement that culminated in Colton's (1960) "Black Sand Hypothesis."

With regard to historic questions, Stallings was able to demonstrate conclusively that some sites along the Rio Grande that were said to have been inhabited before the Spanish entrada were instead built and occupied during the historic period, thus forcing a revision of early historic accounts of the area.

Archaeologists across the Southwest could also begin to consider in detail their well-developed ideas regarding population movements, expansions, and cultural diffusions. In moving the estimated date of Basketmaker occupation from estimates as early as 2000 B.C. to tree-ring dates as late as A.D. 200, dendrochronology forced archaeologists to reconsider their hypotheses about site contemporaneity, population density, rates of culture change, and rates of population growth. By 1935, ideas regarding primacy in the manufacture of ceramics had to be revised as the tree-ring chronology was applied to the Hohokam culture via ceramic crossdating. This analysis revealed that ceramics appeared in the southern deserts substantially earlier than in the San Juan region. By the early 1940s, tree-ring dates established ceramics in the Mogollon culture of east-central Arizona and west-central New Mexico by early in the fourth century A.D.

Haury wrote in 1935 that "it may be stated without equivocation that the tree-ring approach has been the single greatest contribution ever made to American archaeology" (Haury 1935a:98). Whether or not tree-ring dating can still claim primacy in this regard is debatable, and certainly a strong case can be made that radiocarbon dating now stands as the "single greatest contribution . . . to American archaeology," at least in terms of sheer applicability to prehistoric archaeological questions. Nevertheless, tree-ring dating provided absolute chronologies for archaeological manifestations in the American Southwest and Alaska, chronologies whose immediate impact was a severely compressed time scale that shocked many archaeologists. Tree-ring dating allowed archaeologists to ask increasingly complex questions of the archaeological record, planting the seeds of change that led to major revolutions in North American archaeological method and theory three decades later.

References

MANUSCRIPT SOURCES
Arizona State Museum Archives, Tucson
Chaco Canyon Archives, National Park Service, University of New Mexico
    Zimmerman Library, Albuquerque
Harold S. Colton Papers, Museum of Northern Arizona, Flagstaff
Department of Anthropology Papers, University of Chicago Regenstein Library
    Special Collections, Chicago
A. E. Douglass Collection, University of Arizona Main Library Special
    Collections, Tucson
Florence Hawley Ellis Archives, Albuquerque
General Correspondence, Southwest Museum, Los Angeles
James Louis Giddings Family Collection of Papers, Laboratory of Tree-Ring
    Research, Tucson
Gila Pueblo Papers, Arizona State Museum, Tucson
Emil W. Haury Papers, Arizona State Museum, Tucson
Neil M. Judd Papers, Pueblo Bonito Correspondence, National Anthropological
    Archives, United States National Museum, Smithsonian Institution,
    Washington, D.C.
Laboratory of Anthropology, Museum of New Mexico, Santa Fe
Laboratory of Tree-Ring Research Archives, University of Arizona, Tucson
John C. McGregor Papers, Museum of Northern Arizona, Flagstaff

SECONDARY SOURCES
Ahlstrom, Richard V. N.
    1985   *The Interpretation of Archaeological Tree-Ring Dates*. Ph.D.
            dissertation, University of Arizona. University Microfilms, Ann
            Arbor.
    1997   Sources of Variation in the Southwestern Tree-ring Record. *The Kiva*
            62(4):321–348.
Ahlstrom, Richard V. N., David A. Breternitz, and Richard L. Warren
    1985   Archival Excavation: New Tree-Ring Dates from Lowry Ruin. *The
            Kiva* 51(1):39–42.
Antevs, Ernst
    1946a   Review of *Tree-Ring Analysis: Methods of Correlation*, by Harold S.
            Gladwin. *American Anthropologist* 48:433–436.
    1946b   Review of *Tree-Ring Analysis: Problems of Dating I: The Medicine
            Valley Sites*, by Harold S. Gladwin. *American Anthropologist*
            48:436–438.
Baillie, M. G. L.
    1995   *A Slice through Time: Dendrochronology and Precision Dating*. B. T.
            Batsford, London.

1982   *Tree-Ring Dating and Archaeology*. University of Chicago Press, Chicago.

Baldwin, Gordon C.
1935   Dates from Kinishba Pueblo. *Tree-Ring Bulletin* 1(4):30.
1938   Basketmaker and Pueblo Sandals. *Southwestern Lore* 4(1):1–6.

Bannister, Bryant
1962   The Interpretation of Tree-Ring Dates. *American Antiquity* 27(4):508–514.
1963   Dendrochronology. In *Science in Archaeology*, edited by D. Brothwell and E. Higgs, pp. 162–176. Thames and Hudson, London.

Bannister, Bryant, Jeffrey S. Dean, and William J. Robinson
1969   *Tree-Ring Dates from Utah S-W: Southern Utah Area*. Laboratory of Tree-Ring Research, Tucson.

Bannister, Bryant, and William J. Robinson
1986   Archaeology and Dendrochronology. In *Emil W. Haury's Prehistory of the American Southwest*, edited by J. Jefferson Reid and David E. Doyel, pp. 49–54. University of Arizona Press, Tucson.

Bell, Robert E.
1951   Dendrochronology at the Kincaid Site. In *Kincaid: A Prehistoric Illinois Metropolis*, edited by Fay-Cooper Cole, pp. 233–292. University of Chicago Press, Chicago.

Blackburn, Fred M., and Roy A. Williamson
1997   *Cowboys and Cave Dwellers: Basketmaker Archaeology in Utah's Grand Gulch*. School of American Research Press, Santa Fe.

Brady, Lionel F.
1932   Geological Activities of the Museum of Northern Arizona, 1931. *Museum Notes* 4(9):1–4.

Brew, Joseph O.
1968   *One Hundred Years of Anthropology*. Harvard University Press, Cambridge.
1978   Neil Merton Judd, 1887–1976. *American Anthropologist* 80(4):352–354.

Browman, David L., and Douglas R. Givens
1996   Stratigraphic Excavation: The First "New Archaeology." *American Anthropologist* 98(1):80–95.

Brown, Peter M., Malcolm K. Hughes, Christopher H. Baisan, Thomas W. Swetnam, and Anthony C. Caprio
1992   Giant Sequoia Ring-Width Chronologies from the Central Sierra Nevada, California. *Tree-Ring Bulletin* 52:1–14.

Carew, Harold D.
1930   Chronicling the Ages from Trees. *Touring Topics* 22(6):32–34, 54–55.

Chazan, Michael
1996   Conceptions of Time and the Development of Paleolithic Chronology. *American Anthropologist* 97(3):457–467.

Chubin, Daryl E., and Ellen W. Chu
1989   Preface. In *Science of the Pedestal: Social Perspectives on Science and Technology*, edited by Daryl E. Chubin and Ellen W. Chu, pp. viii–x. Wadsworth, Belmont, California.

Cole, Fay-Cooper
    1934   *Dendrochronology in the Mississippi Valley.* Committee on State
            Archaeological Surveys, Division of Anthropology and Psychology,
            National Research Council, Circular Series No. 16.
Cole, Fay-Cooper, editor
    1951   *Kincaid: A Prehistoric Illinois Metropolis.* University of Chicago
            Press, Chicago.
Colton, Harold S.
    1932   Sunset Crater: The Effect of a Volcanic Eruption on an Ancient
            Pueblo People. *Geographical Review* 32:582–590.
    1933a   Wupatki: The Tall House. *Museum Notes* 5(11):61–64.
    1933b   The Museum of Northern Arizona. *Museum Notes* 6(2):9–12.
    1934   First Tree-Ring Conference. *American Anthropologist* 34(4):635–636.
    1937   The Museum of Northern Arizona in 1936. *Museum Notes* 9(8):43–46.
    1938   The Museum of Northern Arizona in 1937: Tenth Annual Report of
            Its Director. *Museum Notes* 10(8):25–28.
    1939   *Prehistoric Culture Units and Their Relationships in Northern
            Arizona.* Museum of Northern Arizona Bulletin No. 17, Flagstaff.
    1941   *Winona and Ridge Ruin, Part II: Notes on the Technology and
            Taxonomy of the Pottery.* Museum of Northern Arizona, Flagstaff.
    1945   Sunset Crater. *Plateau* 18(1):7–14.
    1946   *The Sinagua.* Museum of Northern Arizona Bulletin No. 22,
            Flagstaff.
    1960   *Black Sand: Prehistory in Northern Arizona.* University of New
            Mexico Press, Albuquerque.
Colton, Harold S., and Lyndon Lane Hargrave
    1937   *Handbook of Northern Arizona Pottery Wares.* Museum of
            Northern Arizona Bulletin No. 11, Flagstaff.
Cook, Edward R., and Leonardas A. Kairiukstis, editors
    1990   *Methods of Dendrochronology: Applications in the Environmental
            Sciences.* Kluwer Academic, Dordrecht.
Cordell, Linda S.
    1984   *Prehistory of the Southwest.* Academic Press, Orlando.
Cornelius, Oliver Frasier
    1938   Basketmaker Sandals (?). *Southwestern Lore* 3(4):74–78.
Crotty, Helen K.
    1983   *Honoring the Dead: Anasazi Ceramics from the Rainbow
            Bridge–Monument Valley Expedition.* UCLA Monograph Series, No.
            22, Los Angeles.
Cummings, Byron M.
    1940   *Kinishba: A Prehistoric Pueblo of the Great Pueblo Period.*
            Hohokam Museums Association and the University of Arizona,
            Tucson.
    1952   *Indians I Have Known.* Arizona Silhouettes, Tucson.
Daniel, Glyn
    1963   *The Idea of Prehistory.* World, Cleveland.
Dark, K. R.
    1995   *Theoretical Archaeology.* Duckworth, London.

Dean, Jeffrey S.

1969   *Chronological Analysis of Tsegi Phase Sites in Northeastern Arizona.*
         Papers of the Laboratory of Tree-Ring Research, No. 3. University of
         Arizona, Tucson.

1978a   Independent Dating in Archaeological Analysis. In *Advances in
         Archaeological Method and Theory*, vol. 1, edited by M. B. Schiffer,
         pp. 223–255. Academic Press, New York.

1978b   *Tree-Ring Dating in Archaeology.* University of Utah Miscellaneous
         Anthropological Papers, No. 24. University of Utah Press, Salt Lake
         City.

Dean, Jeffrey S., David M. Meko, and Thomas W. Swetnam

1996   *Tree-Rings, Environment, and Humanity: Radiocarbon 1996.*
         Department of Geosciences, University of Arizona, Tucson.

Dean, Jeffrey S., Mark C. Slaughter, and Dennie O. Bowden III

1996   Desert Dendrochronology: Tree-Ring Dating Prehistoric Sites in the
         Tucson Basin. *The Kiva* 62(1):7–26.

Dekin, Albert A., Jr.

1973   The Arctic. In *The Development of North American Archaeology:
         Essays in the History of Regional Traditions*, edited by James E.
         Fitting, pp. 15–48. Anchor Books, Garden City, New York.

Dick, Herbert W., and Albert H. Schroeder

1968   Lyndon Lane Hargrave: A Brief Biography. In *Collected Papers in
         Honor of Lyndon Lane Hargrave*, edited by Albert H. Schroeder, pp.
         1–8. Museum of New Mexico Press, Santa Fe.

Dixon, Roland B.

1913   Some Aspects of North American Archaeology. *American
         Anthropologist* 15(4):549–573.

Douglass, Andrew Ellicott

1909   Weather Cycles in the Growth of Big Trees. *Monthly Weather
         Review* 37(6):225–237.

1914   *A Method for Estimating Rainfall by the Growth of Trees.* Carnegie
         Institution of Washington Publication No. 192:101–121.
         Washington, D.C.

1919   *Climatic Cycles and Tree-Growth: A Study of the Annual Rings
         of Trees in Relation to Climate and Solar Activity.* Carnegie
         Institution of Washington Publication No. 289, vol. 1.
         Washington D.C.

1921   Dating Our Prehistoric Ruins: How Growth Rings in Timbers Aid in
         Establishing the Relative Ages of the Ruined Pueblos of the
         Southwest. *Natural History* 21(2):27–30.

1928   *Climatic Cycles and Tree Growth, vol. 2: A Study of the Annual
         Rings of Trees in Relation to Climate and Solar Activity.* Carnegie
         Institution of Washington Publication No. 289, vol. 2.
         Washington D.C.

1929   The Secret of the Southwest Solved by Talkative Tree-Rings.
         National Geographic 56(6):736–770.

1934a   Editorial. *Tree-Ring Bulletin* 1(1):2–3.

1934b   Accuracy in Dating. *Tree-Ring Bulletin* 1(2):10–11.

1935a   *Dating Pueblo Bonito and Other Ruins of the Southwest*. National Geographic Society Contributed Technical Papers, Pueblo Bonito Series, No. 1. Washington, D.C.

1935b   Accuracy in Dating II. *Tree-Ring Bulletin* 1(3):19–21.

1936   The Central Pueblo Chronology. *Tree-Ring Bulletin* 2(4):29–34.

1937   *Tree-Rings and Chronology*. University of Arizona Bulletin 8(4); Physical Sciences Bulletin 1. Tucson.

1938   Southwestern Dated Ruins: V. *Tree-Ring Bulletin* 5(2):10–13.

1940a   Excavations at Forestdale. *The Kiva* 6(2):5–8.

1940b   New Tree-Ring Dates from the Forestdale Valley, East-Central Arizona. *Tree-Ring Bulletin* 7(2):14–16.

1940c   *Excavations in the Forestdale Valley, East-Central Arizona*. University of Arizona Bulletin 11(4). Tucson.

1941a   Notes on the Technique of Tree-Ring Analysis, II. *Tree-Ring Bulletin* 7(4):28–34.

1941b   Age of Forestdale Ruins Excavated in 1939. *Tree-Ring Bulletin* 8(1):7–8.

1941c   Notes on the Technique of Tree-Ring Analysis, III. *Tree-Ring Bulletin* 8(2):10–16.

1941d   Crossdating in Dendrochronology. *Journal of Forestry* 39(10):825–831.

1942   Checking the Date of Bluff Ruin, Forestdale: A Study in Technique. *Tree-Ring Bulletin* 9(2):2–7.

1944   Tabulation of Dates for Bluff Ruin, Forestdale, Arizona. *Tree-Ring Bulletin* 11(2):10–16.

1946   Researches in Dendrochronology. *Bulletin of the University of Utah, Biological Series* 10(1).

Downum, Christian S.

1988   *One Grand History: A Critical Review of Flagstaff Archaeology, 1951–1988*. Unpublished Ph.D. dissertation, Department of Anthropology, University of Arizona, Tucson.

Dunnell, Robert C.

1986   Five Decades of American Archaeology. In *American Archaeology, Past and Future*, edited by David J. Meltzer, Donald D. Fowler, and Jeremy L. Sabloff, pp. 23–49. Smithsonian Institution Press, Washington, D.C.

Dutton, Bertha P.

1941   Gladwin's Work on Tree-Rings. *El Palacio* 48(4):87–90.

Eighmy, J. L., and R. S. Sternberg

1990   *Archaeomagnetic Dating*. University of Arizona Press, Tucson.

Elliott, Melinda

1987   *Exploring Human Worlds: A History of the School of American Research*. School of American Research Press, Santa Fe.

1995   *Great Excavations: Tales of Early Southwestern Archaeology, 1888–1939*. School of American Research Press, Santa Fe.

El Palacio

1923a   Description of First Beam Expedition. *El Palacio* 15(2):29.

1923b   Description of First Beam Expedition. *El Palacio* 15(4):59.

Fagan, Brian
  1991   *In the Beginning: An Introduction to Archaeology*. Harper Collins,
          New York.
Fagette, Paul
  1996   *Digging for Dollars: American Archaeology and the New Deal*.
          University of New Mexico Press, Albuquerque.
Feathers, James K.
  1997   The Application of Luminescence Dating in American Archaeology.
          Journal of Archaeological Method and Theory 4(1):1–66.
Fewkes, Jesse Walter
  1915   A Sun Temple in Mesa Verde National Park. *Art and Archaeology*
          2:341–346.
Field Trip
  1929   *Museum Notes* 1(10):1.
First Tree-Ring Conference
  1934   *Museum Notes* 7(2):8.
Flora, I. F. "Zeke"
  1940   Durango Tree-Ring Dates. *Sherds and Points* 1(16):1.
Friedman, I., and R. L. Smith
  1960   A New Dating Method Using Obsidian. *American Antiquity* 33:149–
          155.
Frisbie, Theodore R.
  1991   Florence Hawley Ellis, 1906–1991. *The Kiva* 57(1):93–97.
Fritts, Harold C.
  1976   *Tree-Rings and Climate*. Academic Press, New York.
Fritts, Harold C., and Thomas W. Swetnam
  1989   Dendroecology: A Tool for Evaluating Variations in Past and Present
          Forest Environments. *Advances in Ecological Research* 19:111–188.
Getty, Harry T.
  1935a   Tree-Ring Dates from Spruce Tree House, Mesa Verde. *The Kiva*
          1(1):3.
  1935b   New Dates from Mesa Verde. *Tree-Ring Bulletin* 1(3):21–23.
  1935c   New Dates for Spruce Tree House, Mesa Verde. *Tree-Ring Bulletin*
          1(4):28–29.
  1935d   Second Annual Tree-Ring Conference. *Tree-Ring Bulletin* 2(1):4–5.
Giddings, James Louis, Jr.
  1938a   Buried Wood from Fairbanks, Alaska. *Tree-Ring Bulletin* 4(4):3–5.
  1938b   Recent Tree-Ring Work in Alaska. *Tree-Ring Bulletin* 5(2):16.
  1940   The Application of Tree Ring Dates to Arctic Sites. *Tree-Ring
          Bulletin* 7(2):10–14.
  1941   *Dendrochronology of Northern Alaska*. University of Arizona
          Bulletin 7(4), Laboratory of Tree-Ring Research Bulletin No. 1.
  1942   Dated Sites on the Kobuk River, Alaska. *Tree-Ring Bulletin* 9(1):2–8.
  1943   Some Climatic Aspects of Tree Growth in Alaska. *Tree-Ring Bulletin*
          9(4):26–32.
  1947   Mackenzie River Delta Chronology. *Tree-Ring Bulletin* 13:26–29.
  1948   Chronology of the Kobuk-Kotzebue Sites. *Tree-Ring Bulletin*
          14(4):26–32.

1954a Facts and Comments: The Denbigh Flint Complex Is Not Yet Dated. *American Antiquity* 20(4):375–376.

1954b Tree-Ring Dating in the American Arctic. *Tree-Ring Bulletin* 20(3/4):23–25.

1962 Development of Tree-Ring Dating as an Archaeological Aid. In *Tree-Growth*, edited by T. T. Kozlowski, pp. 119–130. Ronald Press, New York.

1964 *The Archaeology of Cape Denbigh*. Brown University Press, Providence, Rhode Island.

1967 *Ancient Men of the Arctic*. Alfred A. Knopf, New York.

Gladwin, Harold S.

1940a *Methods and Instruments for Use in Measuring Tree-Rings.* Medallion Paper No. 27. Gila Pueblo, Globe, Arizona.

1940b *Tree-Ring Analysis: Methods of Correlation.* Medallion Paper No. 28. Gila Pueblo, Globe, Arizona.

1942 *Excavations at Snaketown, III: Revisions.* Medallion Paper No. 30. Gila Pueblo, Globe, Arizona.

1943 *A Review and Analysis of the Flagstaff Culture.* Medallion Paper No. 31. Gila Pueblo, Globe, Arizona.

1944 *Tree-Ring Analysis: Problems of Dating I: The Medicine Valley Sites.* Medallion Paper No. 32. Gila Pueblo, Globe, Arizona.

1945 *The Chaco Branch: Excavations at White Mound in the Red Mesa Valley.* Medallion Paper No. 33. Gila Pueblo, Globe, Arizona.

1946 *Tree-Ring Analysis: Problems of Dating II. The Tusayan Ruin.* Medallion Paper No. 36. Gila Pueblo, Globe, Arizona.

1947 *Tree-Ring Analysis: Tree-Rings and Droughts.* Medallion Paper No. 37. Gila Pueblo, Globe, Arizona.

1948 *Excavations at Snaketown: Reviews and Conclusions.* Medallion Paper No. 38. Gila Pueblo, Globe, Arizona.

1977 A History of Tree-Ring Dating at Gila Pueblo. Ms. on file, Laboratory of Tree-Ring Research, University of Arizona, Tucson.

Gladwin, Winifred, and Harold S. Gladwin

1929a *The Red-on-Buff Culture of the Gila Basin.* Medallion Paper No. 3. Gila Pueblo, Globe, Arizona.

1929b *The Red-on-Buff Culture of the Papagueria.* Medallion Paper No. 4. Gila Pueblo, Globe, Arizona.

1930 *The Western Range of the Red-on-Buff Culture.* Medallion Paper No. 5. Gila Pueblo, Globe, Arizona.

1935 *The Eastern Range of the Red-on-Buff Culture.* Medallion Paper No. 16. Gila Pueblo, Globe, Arizona.

Gladwin, Harold S., Emil W. Haury, E. B. Sayles, and Nora Gladwin

1937 *Excavations at Snaketown: Material Culture.* Medallion Paper No. 25. Gila Pueblo, Globe, Arizona.

Glock, Waldo S.

1933 Tree-Ring Analysis on Douglass System. *Pan-American Geologist* 60:1–14.

1934a Report of the Tree-Ring Conference. *Tree-Ring Bulletin* 1(1):4–6.

1934b The Language of Tree-Rings. *Scientific Monthly* 38:501–510.

1942a   Tree-Growth Rings as Record of Annual Precipitation: A Review. *Pan-American Geologist* 77:273–284.

1942b   Tree-Ring Analysis and Dating in the Mississippi Drainage: A Review. *American Journal of Archaeology* 46:162–164.

Gould, Stephen Jay

1989   *Wonderful Life: The Burgess Shale and the Nature of History.* W. W. Norton, New York.

Haber, Samuel

1991   The Quest for Authority and Honor in American Professions, 1750–1900. University of Chicago Press, Chicago.

Hall, Edward Twitchell, Jr.

1944   *Early Stockaded Settlements in the Governador, New Mexico.* Columbia Studies in Archaeology and Ethnology, vol. 2, part 1. Columbia University Press, New York.

Hargrave, Lyndon L.

1930   Prehistoric Earth Lodges of the San Francisco Mountains. *Museum Notes* 3(5):1–4.

1932   The Museum of Northern Arizona Archaeological Expedition of 1932. *Museum Notes* 5(5):17–24.

1935a   Archaeological Investigations in the Tsegi Canyons of Northeastern Arizona. *Museum Notes* 7(7):25–28.

1935b   Concerning the Names of Southwestern Pottery Types. *Southwestern Lore* 1(3):17–23.

1938   Results of a Study of the Cohonina Branch of the Patayan Culture in 1938. *Museum Notes* 11(6):43–50.

Haury, Emil W.

1930   A Study of Pinyon with Respect to Its Possible Use as a Dating Wood. Ms. on file, Laboratory of Tree-Ring Research, University of Arizona, Tucson.

1934   *The Canyon Creek Ruin and the Cliff Dwellings of the Sierra Ancha.* Medallion Paper No. 14. Gila Pueblo, Globe, Arizona.

1935a   Tree-Rings: The Archaeologist's Time Piece. *American Antiquity* 1(2):98–108.

1935b   Dates from Gila Pueblo. *Tree-Ring Bulletin* 2(1):3–4.

1936   *The Mogollon Culture of Southwestern New Mexico.* Medallion Paper No. 20. Gila Pueblo, Globe, Arizona.

1938   Southwestern Dated Ruins: II. *Tree-Ring Bulletin* 4(3):3–4.

1940a   Excavations at Forestdale. *The Kiva* 6(2):5–8.

1940b   New Tree-Ring Dates from the Forestdale Valley, East-Central Arizona. *Tree-Ring Bulletin* 7(2):14–16.

1940c   *Excavations in the Forestdale Valley, East-Central Arizona.* University of Arizona Bulletin 11(4). Social Science Bulletin 12. University of Arizona, Tucson.

1942   Some Implications of the Bluff Ruin Dates. *Tree-Ring Bulletin* 9(2):7–8.

1946   Tree Rings and Archaeology. Ms. on file, Arizona State Museum Archives, Box 94–120, Tucson.

1962   HH-39: Reflections of a Dramatic Moment in Southwestern Archaeology. *Tree-Ring Bulletin* 74(3–4):11–14.

1985 Reflections: Fifty Years of Southwestern Archaeology. *American Antiquity* 50(2):383–394.

1988 Gila Pueblo Archaeological Foundation: A History and Some Personal Notes. *The Kiva* 54(1):1–77.

1995 Wherefore a Harvard Ph.D.? *Journal of the Southwest* 37(4):710–733.

Haury, Emil W., and I. F. Flora

1937 Basketmaker III Dates from the Vicinity of Durango, Colorado. *Tree-Ring Bulletin* 4(1):7–8.

Haury, Emil W., and Lyndon L. Hargrave

1931 *Recently Dated Pueblo Ruins in Arizona*. Smithsonian Institution Miscellaneous Collections 82(11). Washington, D.C.

Haury, Emil W., and J. Jefferson Reid

1985 Harold Sterling Gladwin, 1883–1983. *The Kiva* 50(4):271–283.

Hawley, Florence M.

1930 Prehistoric Pottery and Culture Relations in the Middle Gila. *American Anthropologist* 32(3):522–526.

1932a Oldest Tree-Ring Record of the Ancient Pueblos. *El Palacio* 32:108–110.

1932b New Dates from Chaco Canyon. *El Palacio* 32:185–186.

1933 Tree-Ring Chronology in Chaco Canyon. *El Palacio* 24(25–6):204–205.

1934a *The Significance of the Dated Prehistory of Chetro Ketl, Chaco Canon, New Mexico*. University of New Mexico Press, Albuquerque.

1934b The Adaptation of Oak and Cedar for Tree-Ring Dating of Prehistoric Mounds in the Mississippi Valley. Ms. on file, Laboratory of Tree-Ring Research, University of Arizona, Tucson.

1938a Southwestern Dated Ruins: IV. *Tree-Ring Bulletin* 5(1):6–7.

1938b Dendrochronology: Can We Fix Prehistoric Dates in the Middle West by Tree Rings? *Indiana History Bulletin* 15(2):118–128.

1938c Report on Research in Dendrochronology of the Mississippi Area, 1937–38. Ms. on file, Florence Hawley Ellis Archives, File Cabinet 1, Drawer 1, Albuquerque.

1941 *Tree-Ring Analysis and Dating in the Mississippi Drainage*. University of Chicago Press, Chicago.

Hawley-Senter, Florence M.

1938 Dendrochronology in the Mississippi Drainage. *Tree-Ring Bulletin* 5(1):3–6.

Haynes, C. Vance

1986 Discovering Early Man in Arizona. In *Emil W. Haury's Prehistory of the American Southwest*, edited by J. Jefferson Reid and David E. Doyel, pp. 75–77. University of Arizona Press, Tucson.

Hewett, Edgar Lee

1930 *Ancient Life in the Southwest*. Bobbs-Merrill, Indianapolis.

Hinsley, Curtis M., Jr.

1976 Amateurs and Professionals in Washington Anthropology, 1879 to 1903. In *American Anthropology: The Early Years*, edited by John V. Murra, pp. 36–68. 1974 Proceedings of the American Ethnological Society, West Publishing, St. Paul.

1985   From Shell-Heaps to Stelae: Early Anthropology at the Peabody
        Museum. In *Objects and Others: Essays on Museums and Material
        Culture*, edited by George W. Stocking, Jr., pp. 49–74. University of
        Wisconsin Press, Madison.

Hughes, Malcolm K., P. M. Kelly, Jon R. Pilcher, and Val C. LaMarche, Jr.,
    editors
1980   *Climate from Tree-Rings*. Cambridge University Press, New York.

Huntington, Ellsworth
1912   The Secret of the Big Trees. *Harper's Monthly* 125:292–302.
1925   *Tree Growth and Climatic Interpretations*. Carnegie Institution of
        Washington Publication No. 352:155–204. Washington, D.C.

Huntington, Ellsworth, and S. S. Visher
1922   The Climate of History. In *Climate Changes: Their Nature and
        Causes*, pp. 64–97. Yale University Press, New Haven.

Hurst, Clarence Thomas
1940   Preliminary Work in Tabeguache Cave, 1939. *Southwestern Lore*
        6(1):4–18.
1941   The Second Season in Tabeguache Cave. *Southwestern Lore* 7(1):4–
        19.

Judd, Neil M.
1930a   Dating Our Prehistoric Pueblo Ruins. In *Explorations and Fieldwork
        of the Smithsonian Institution in 1929*, pp. 167–176. Smithsonian
        Institution, Washington, D.C.
1930b   The Excavation and Repair of Betatakin. *Proceedings of the United
        States National Museum* 77(5):1–77.
1935   Foreword. In *Dating Pueblo Bonito and Other Ruins of the
        Southwest*, by Andrew Ellicott Douglass. National Geographic
        Society Contributed Technical Papers, Pueblo Bonito Series 1:3–5.
        Washington, D.C.
1962   Andrew Ellicott Douglass, 1867–1962. *American Antiquity* 28(1):
        87–89.
1964   *The Architecture of Pueblo Bonito*. Smithsonian Miscellaneous
        Collections 147(1). Washington, D.C.
1968   *Men Met along the Trail: Adventures in Archaeology*. University of
        Oklahoma Press, Norman.

Kidder, Alfred V.
1924   *An Introduction to the Study of Southwestern Archaeology*. Phillips
        Academy, Andover, Massachusetts.
1927a   The Museum's Expedition to Canon de Chelly and Canyon del
        Muerto, Arizona. *Natural History* 27(3):203–209.
1927b   Southwestern Archaeological Conference. *Science* 66(1716):489–491.
1928   Southwestern Archaeological Conference. *American Anthropologist*
        30(1):172.
1932   *The Artifacts at Pecos*. Yale University Press, New Haven.
1936   Speculations on New World Prehistory. In *Essays in Anthropology
        Presented to A. L. Kroeber in Celebration of His Sixtieth Birthday,
        June 11, 1936*, edited by Robert H. Lowie, pp. 143–152. University
        of California Press, Berkeley.

1957   Earl Halstead Morris, 1889–1956. *American Antiquity* 22(4):390–397.

1958   *Pecos, New Mexico: Archaeological Notes.* Papers of the Robert S. Peabody Foundation for Archaeology, No. 5. Andover, Massachusetts.

Kluckhohn, Clyde

1939   The Place of Theory in Anthropological Studies. *Philosophy of Science* 6:328–344.

Kroeber, Alfred

1916   Zuni Culture Sequences. *Proceedings of the National Academy of Sciences* 2:42–45.

1935   History and Science in Anthropology. *American Anthropologist* 37(4):539–569.

Laufer, Berthold

1913   Remarks. *American Anthropologist* 15(4):573–577.

Lange, Frederick W., and Diana Leonard

1985   *Among Ancient Ruins: The Legacy of Earl H. Morris.* University of Colorado Museum. Johnson Press, Boulder.

Libby, Willard F.

1955   *Radiocarbon Dating.* University of Chicago Press, Chicago.

Lister, Florence C., and Robert H. Lister

1968   *Earl Morris and Southwestern Archaeology.* University of New Mexico Press, Albuquerque.

Lutz, Catharine A., and Jane L. Collins

1993   *Reading National Geographic.* University of Chicago Press, Chicago.

Lyon, Edwin

1996   *A New Deal for Southeastern Archaeology.* University of Alabama Press, Tuscaloosa.

McElvaine, Robert S.

1993   *The Great Depression: America, 1929–1941.* Times Books, New York.

McGregor, John C.

1930   Tree-Ring Dating. *Museum Notes* 3(4):1–4.

1932   Additional Prehistoric Dates from Arizona. *Museum Notes* 5(3):13–16.

1934   Dates from Tsegi. *Tree-Ring Bulletin* 1(1):6–8.

1935   *Teocentli* 19:7.

1936   Dating the Eruption of Sunset Crater, Arizona. *American Antiquity* 2:15–26.

1938a   Southwestern Dated Ruins: III. *Tree-Ring Bulletin* 4(4):6.

1938b   *How Some Important Northern Arizona Pottery Types Were Dated.* Museum of Northern Arizona Bulletin No. 18. Flagstaff.

1939   Archaeological Problems. *Southwestern Lore* 5(3):52–56.

1941   *Winona and Ridge Ruin, Part I—Architecture and Material Culture.* Museum of Northern Arizona Bulletin No. 18.

1942   Review of *Tree-Ring Analysis and Dating in the Mississippi Drainage,* by F. M. Hawley. *American Anthropologist* 44(3):482–485.

Mandlebaum, David G.

1948   Clark Wissler, 1870–1947. *Science* 107:338–339.

Martin, Douglas D.
  1960   *The Lamp in the Desert: The Story of the University of Arizona.*
          University of Arizona Press, Tucson.
Martin, Paul S.
  1936   *Lowry Ruin in Southwestern Colorado.* Field Museum of Natural
          History Anthropological Series 23(1). Chicago.
  1941a   *The SU site: Excavations of a Mogollon Village, Western New
          Mexico, Second Season, 1941.* Field Museum of Natural History
          Anthropological Series 32(2). Chicago.
  1941b   Review of *Kinishba: A Prehistoric Pueblo of the Great Pueblo Period,*
          by Byron Cummings. *American Anthropologist* 43(4):653–654.
Mellars, Paul A., M. J. Aitken, and C. B. Stringer
  1993   Outlining the Problem. In *The Origin of Modern Humans and the
          Impact of Chronometric Dating,* edited by M. J. Aitken, C. B.
          Stringer, and P. A. Mellars, pp. 3–11. Princeton University Press,
          Princeton.
Meltzer, David J.
  1985   North American Archaeology and Archaeologists, 1879–1934.
          American Antiquity 50(2):241–260.
  1989   A Question of Relevance. In *Tracing Archaeology's Past: The
          Historiography of Archaeology,* edited by Andrew L. Christenson,
          pp. 5–19. Southern Illinois University Press, Carbondale.
Michael, Henry N.
  1971   Climates, Tree-Rings, and Archaeology. In *Dating Techniques for the
          Archaeologist,* edited by Henry N. Michael and Elizabeth K. Ralph,
          pp. 49–56. MIT Press, Cambridge.
Michels, Joseph W.
  1973   *Dating Methods in Archaeology.* Seminar Press, New York.
Miller, Carl F.
  1934   Report of Dates on the Allantown, Arizona, Ruins. *Tree-Ring
          Bulletin* 1(2):15–16.
  1935   Additional Dates on the Allantown, Arizona, Ruins. *Tree-Ring
          Bulletin* 1(4):31.
Moorehead, Warren K.
  1890   *Fort Ancient: The Great Prehistoric Earthwork of Warren County,
          Ohio.* R. Clarke, Cincinnati.
  1934   A Forgotten Tree-Ring Record. *Science* 80(2062):16–17.
Morris, Earl
  1927   *Teocentli* 4:8.
  1929   *Teocentli* 8:11.
  1936   Archaeological Background of Dates in Early Arizona Chronology.
          Tree-Ring Bulletin 2(4):34–36.
  1939   *Archaeological Studies in the La Plata District, Southwestern
          Colorado and Northwestern New Mexico.* Carnegie Institution of
          Washington Publication No. 519. Washington, D.C.
Murdock, George P.
  1948   Clark Wissler, 1870–1948. *American Anthropologist* 50(3):516–524.
  1937   Museum of Northern Arizona in 1936. *Museum Notes* 9(8):43–46.

Nash, Stephen E.

1995 The "Rediscovery" of Alaska Archaeological Tree-Ring Dating. *Alaska Anthropological Association Newsletter* 20(1):4–5.

1997a *A History of Archaeological Tree-Ring Dating, 1914–1945.* Ph.D. dissertation, University of Arizona, Tucson. University Microfilms, Ann Arbor.

1997b Archaeological Cutting Date Estimation and the Interpretation of Estimated Tree-Ring Dates. *American Antiquity* 62(2):260–272.

1998 Time for Collaboration: A. E. Douglass, Archaeologists, and the Establishment of Tree-Ring Dating in the American Southwest. *Journal of the Southwest* (Fall).

Nelson, Nels C.

1914 *Pueblo Ruins of the Galisteo Basin, New Mexico.* Anthropological Papers of the American Museum of Natural History, vol. 15. New York.

1916 Chronology of the Tano Ruins, New Mexico. *American Anthropologist* 18(2):159–180.

1917 Excavation of Aztec Ruin. *American Museum Journal* 17(2):85–99.

1918 Chronology in Florida. *Anthropological Papers of the American Museum of Natural History* 22(pt. 2):75–103.

1948 Clark Wissler, 1870–1947. *American Antiquity* 8(3):244–247.

Nesbitt, Paul H.

1931 *The Ancient Mimbrenos.* Logan Museum Publications in Anthropology, Bulletin No. 4. Beloit, Wisconsin.

1938 *Starkweather Ruin: A Mogollon-Pueblo Site in the Upper Gila of New Mexico, and Affiliative Aspects of the Mogollon Culture.* Logan Museum Publications in Anthropology, Bulletin No. 6. Beloit, Wisconsin.

1931 1930 at the Museum. *Museum Notes* 3(7):1–4.

1931 1931 at the Museum. *Museum Notes* 4(8):1–4.

1934 1933 at the Museum. *Museum Notes* 6(8):39–42.

Oswalt, Wendell

1950 Spruce Borings from the Lower Yukon River, Alaska. *Tree-Ring Bulletin* 16(4):26–30.

1951 The Origin of Driftwood at Hooper Bay, Alaska. *Tree-Ring Bulletin* 18(1):6–8.

1953 Dated Houses on the Squirrel River, Alaska. *Tree-Ring Bulletin* 16(1):7–8.

Parezo, Nancy J.

1993 Anthropology: The Welcoming Science. In *Hidden Scholars: Women Anthropologists and the Native American Southwest,* edited by Nancy J. Parezo, pp. 3–37. University of New Mexico Press, Albuquerque.

Rainey, Froelich

1965 J. Louis Giddings (1909–1964). *American Anthropologist* 67(6):1503–1508.

Renaud, Etienne

1928 Evolution of Population and Dwellings in the Indian Southwest. *El Palacio* 26(5):75–86.

Renfrew, Colin
  1973   *Before Civilization: The Radiocarbon Revolution and Prehistoric Europe.* Alfred A. Knopf, New York.
Restivo, Sal
  1994   *Science, Society, and Value: Toward a Sociology of Objectivity.* LeHigh University Press, Bethlehem, Pennsylvania.
Roberts, Frank H. H.
  1935   A Summary of Southwestern Archaeology. *American Anthropologist* 37(1):1–35.
  1937   Archaeology in the Southwest. *American Antiquity* 3(1):3–33.
Robinson, William J.
  1976   Tree-Ring Dating and Archaeology in the American Southwest. *Tree-Ring Bulletin* 36(1):9–20.
Schweingruber, Fritz H.
  1988   *Tree-Rings: Basics and Applications of Dendrochronology.* D. Reidel, Dordrecht.
Scott, Stuart D.
  1966   *Dendrochronology in Mexico.* Papers of the Laboratory of Tree-Ring Research, No. 2. University of Arizona Press, Tucson.
Shanks, Michael, and Christopher Tilley
  1987   *Social Theory and Archaeology.* University of New Mexico Press, Albuquerque.
Shapin, Steven
  1989   The Invisible Technician. *American Scientist* 77(6):554–563.
Smiley, Terah L.
  1955   The Geochronological Approach. In *Geochronology*, edited by T. L. Smiley, pp. 15–28. University of Arizona Physical Science Bulletin No. 2. Tucson.
Smiley, Terah L., Stanley A. Stubbs, and Bryant Bannister
  1953   *A Foundation for the Dating of Some Late Archaeological Sites in the Rio Grande Area, New Mexico.* Laboratory of Tree-Ring Research Bulletin No. 6. Tucson.
Smith, Watson
  1987   Emil W. Haury's Southwest: A Pisgah View. *Journal of the Southwest* 29(1):107–120.
Spicer, E. H.
  1934   Some Pueblo I Structures of the San Francisco Mountains, Arizona. *Museum Notes* 7(5):17–20.
Spier, Leslie
  1917a   Zuni Chronology. *Proceedings of the National Academy of Sciences* 3:280–283.
  1917b   *An Outline for a Chronology of Zuni Ruins.* Anthropological Papers of the American Museum of Natural History 18(3):207–331.
  1931   N. C. Nelson's Stratigraphic Technique in the Reconstruction of Prehistoric Sequences in Southwestern America. In *Methods in Social Science: A Case Book*, edited by Stuart A. Rice, pp. 275–283. University of Chicago Press, Chicago.

Stahle, David

1979   Tree-Ring Dating of Historic Buildings in Arkansas. *Tree-Ring Bulletin* 39:1–28.

Stahle, David, Edward R. Cook, James W. C. White

1985   Tree-Ring Dating of Baldcypress and the Potential for Millennia-Long Chronologies in the Southeast. *American Antiquity* 50(4):796–802.

Stahle, David, and D. Wolfman

1985   The Potential for Archaeological Tree-Ring Dating in Eastern North America. In *Advances in Archaeological Method and Theory*, vol. 8, edited by M. B. Schiffer, pp. 279–302. Academic Press, New York.

Stallings, W. Sidney, Jr.

1932   The Development of Dendrology. *The Masterkey* 6(3):89–90.

1933   A Tree-Ring Chronology for the Rio Grande Drainage in Northern New Mexico. *Proceedings of the National Academy of Sciences* 19(9):803–806.

1937   Southwestern Dated Ruins: I. *Tree-Ring Bulletin* 4(2):3–5.

1939   *Dating Prehistoric Ruins by Tree-Rings*. General Series Bulletin No. 8, Laboratory of Anthropology. Santa Fe.

1940   Using Heartwood to Estimate Sapwood. Ms. on file, Laboratory of Tree-Ring Research, University of Arizona, Tucson.

1941   A Basketmaker II Date from Cave Du Pont, Utah. *Tree-Ring Bulletin* 8(1):3–6.

Steibing, William H., Jr.

1993   *Uncovering the Past: A History of Archaeology*. Oxford University Press, Oxford.

Steward, Julian

1937   Ecological Aspects of Southwestern Society. *Anthropos* 32:87–104.

Stocking, George W., Jr.

1982   The Santa Fe Style in American Anthropology: Regional Interest, Academic Initiative, and Philanthropic Policy in the First Two Decades of the Laboratory of Anthropology, Inc. *Journal of the History of the Behavioral Sciences* 18(1):3–19.

Stokes, Marvin A., and Terah L. Smiley

1968   *An Introduction to Tree-Ring Dating*. University of Chicago Press, Chicago.

Studhalter, R. A.

1955   Tree Growth: Some Historical Chapters. *Botanical Review* 21(1):1–72.

Taylor, R. E.

1985   The Beginnings of Radiocarbon Dating in *American Antiquity*: An Historical Perspective. *American Antiquity* 50:309–325.

1987   *Radiocarbon Dating: An Archaeological Perspective*. Academic Press, San Diego.

Taylor, Walter W., and Robert C. Euler

1980   Lyndon Lane Hargrave, 1896–1978. *American Antiquity* 45(3):477–482.

Thomas, David Hurst
    1979   *Archaeology*. Holt, Rinehart, and Winston, New York.

Thompson, Raymond H.
    1995   Emil W. Haury and the Definition of Southwestern Archaeology. *American Antiquity* 60(4):640–661.

Trigger, Bruce G.
    1989   *A History of Archaeological Thought*. Cambridge University Press, Cambridge.

VanStone, James
    1953   Notes on Kotzebue Dating. *Tree-Ring Dating* 20(1):6–8.
    1958   The Origin of Driftwood on Nunivak Island, Alaska. *Tree-Ring Bulletin* 22(1–4):12–15.

Webb, George S.
    1978   A Dedication to the Memory of A. E. Douglass, 1867–1962. *Arizona and the West* 20(2):103–106.
    1983   *Tree-Rings and Telescopes: The Scientific Career of A. E. Douglass*. University of Arizona Press, Tucson.

Wedel, Waldo
    1978   Neil Merton Judd, 1887–1976. *American Antiquity* 43(3):399–404.

Willey, Gordon R.
    1937   Notes on Central Georgia Dendrochronology. *Tree-Ring Bulletin* 4(2):6–8.

Willey, Gordon R., and Jeremy A. Sabloff
    1980   *A History of American Archaeology*. 2d ed. W. H. Freeman, San Francisco.

Williams, Stephen
    1991   *Fantastic Archaeology: The Wild Side of North American Prehistory*. University of Pennsylvania Press, Philadelphia.

Wissler, Clark
    1919   *The Archer M. Huntington Survey of the Southwest, Zuni District*. Anthropological Papers of the American Museum of Natural History 18:i-ix. New York.
    1921   Dating Our Prehistoric Ruins. *Natural History* 21(1):13–26.

Woodbury, Richard B.
    1993   *Sixty Years of Southwestern Archaeology: A History of the Pecos Conference*. University of New Mexico Press, Albuquerque.

Wroth, William
    1982   *Christian Images in Hispanic New Mexico: The Taylor Museum Collection of Santos*. Taylor Museum of the Colorado Fine Arts Center, Colorado Springs.

Zeuner, Frederick Eberhard
    1951   *Dating the Past: An Introduction to Geochronology*. Longman's, Green, New York.

Acknowledgments

Many scholars contributed to the successful completion of this work. Bryant Bannister, emeritus professor of dendrochronology and director of the Laboratory of Tree-Ring Research, guided me on several occasions in which I was doomed to err. Our informal morning discussions remain one of the fondest memories of my graduate experience. Jeffrey S. Dean, professor of dendrochronology at the Laboratory of Tree-Ring Research, served as chair of my dissertation committee. In that capacity, he allowed me to pursue my own research agenda while reining in various flights of fancy. He has helped me in numerous ways over the years, and I am grateful for his considered endorsements. Nancy J. Parezo, curator of ethnology at the Arizona State Museum, directed my successful attempts to obtain funding for this research. In so doing, she encouraged me to push my research and analysis a step further than I might have otherwise done; the end product is much improved as a result of her admonishments. Raymond H. Thompson, emeritus director of the Arizona State Museum, reminded me to consider the nondendrochronological aspects of the history of North American archaeology. Each of these scholars will recognize his or her influence on this book; I alone remain responsible for errors of fact or interpretation.

The bulk of the data considered in this study were gathered during detailed analysis of more than 3500 documents archived at nine institutions. The Andrew Ellicott Douglass Collection at the University of Arizona Main Library, Special Collections Division, is a remarkably complete and extremely well organized collection spanning seven decades of Douglass's professional career. Relevant documents from this collection serve as the baseline against which data from all other archives were compared.

Data presented in Chapters 2, 3, and 8 come from the Douglass Collection and appropriate archives at the Laboratory of Tree-Ring Research, University of Arizona, Tucson. Chapter 2 benefited from analysis of the Neil M. Judd Papers at the Smithsonian Institution, Washington, D.C., as well. The bulk of the documents considered in Chapter 4 can be found in the Emil W. Haury Papers and the Gila Pueblo Archaeological Foundation Papers at the Arizona State Museum in Tucson. Documents analyzed for Chapter 5 can be found in the John

C. McGregor Papers and Harold S. Colton Papers at the Museum of Northern Arizona in Flagstaff. Archives for Chapter 6 can be found at the Laboratory of Anthropology in Santa Fe, New Mexico, and the National Park Service's Chaco Canyon Archives at the University of New Mexico in Albuquerque. Documents considered for Chapter 7 are housed at the Department of Anthropology Archives in the Joseph Regenstein Library at the University of Chicago and the Florence Hawley Ellis Archives in Albuquerque, New Mexico. Additional supporting documents were found in the general correspondence files at The Southwest Museum, Highland Park, California.

Detailed references to the analyzed documents encumber the text and are offered in this volume only when letters or manuscripts are quoted directly. Interested readers may find complete, detailed citations in my dissertation (Nash 1997a).

Additional scholars commented on various parts of this work. Thanks are due especially to James VanStone, Wendell Oswalt, Richard Woodbury, Andrew Christenson, and Jeff Grathwohl. Many colleagues at the Laboratory of Tree-Ring Research deserve mention as well, but Rex Adams and Gregg Garfin are especially worthy of note for lending an ear to the history of dendrochronology. Jonathan Haas, MacArthur Curator of North American Archaeology at the Field Museum of Natural History, facilitated completion of this book and offered valuable insights.

A number of archivists and librarians assisted my data collection efforts. Thanks are due especially to Alan Ferg, Mary Graham, and Madelyn Cook of the Arizona State Museum (Tucson); Barbara Thurber of the Museum of Northern Arizona (Flagstaff); Andrea Ellis of the Florence Hawley Ellis Archives (Albuquerque); Willow Powers of the Laboratory of Anthropology, Museum of New Mexico (Santa Fe); and Suzy Taraba of the University of Chicago Regenstein Library. In addition, unnamed staff members at the Southwest Museum (Los Angeles) and the National Anthropological Archives at the United States National Museum (Washington, D.C.) provided much-needed assistance.

A National Science Foundation Anthropology Program Dissertation Improvement Grant (SBR 9528790) and the Southwest Foundation of Tucson, Arizona, funded the research presented here. The Arizona Chapter of the Sigma Xi and the Graduate College of the University of Arizona funded travel to scholarly meetings, at which preliminary results were presented. The Arizona Archaeological and Historical Society and the William Shirley Fulton and Emil W. Haury Funds of the Department of Anthropology at the University of Arizona also provided monetary assistance at some point during my graduate career. To each of these agencies, I am grateful and appreciative.

Thanks are also due to my wife, Carmen Carrasco, my mother-in-law, Mary Carrasco, and my parents, Edward G. Nash and Katie Appleby Nash, who supported this endeavor in ways that only family members can.

Index